Unpacking the Death Penalty in ASEAN

Sriprapha Petcharamesree · Mark P. Capaldi ·
Alan Collins
Editors

Unpacking the Death Penalty in ASEAN

Springer

Editors
Sriprapha Petcharamesree
Institute of Human Rights and Peace Studies
Mahidol University
Nakornpathom, Thailand

Mark P. Capaldi
Institute of Human Rights and Peace Studies
Mahidol University
Nakornpathom, Thailand

Alan Collins
Politics, Philosophy, and International Relations, Faculty of Humanities and Social Sciences
Swansea University
Swansea, UK

ISBN 978-981-19-8842-4 ISBN 978-981-19-8840-0 (eBook)
https://doi.org/10.1007/978-981-19-8840-0

This Springer imprint is published by the registered company Springer Nature Singapore Pte Ltd.
The registered company address is: 152 Beach Road, #21-01/04 Gateway East, Singapore 189721, Singapore

"The inhumane and cruel punishment of death undermines the basic right to life that should be cherished. In a region that is witnessing the resurgence in its use, our thoughts and prayers are with those, and their families, blighted by this state-induced brutality".

Foreword

The completion and launch of this volume gives me much delight, personally and academically. It provides multi-angled perspectives on the death penalty, its use and policies in the ten countries of the Association of Southeast Asian Nations (ASEAN), and the interaction and direction of ASEAN and the punishment.

In the landmark year of 2015, the ten leaders of the ASEAN proclaimed ASEAN as a Community that was politically cohesive, economically integrated, and socially responsible. It would also be a people-oriented, people-centred Community. The Charter of ASEAN, adopted in 2008, also includes human rights as one of its foundational principles. Reiterating the Universal Declaration of Human Rights, the ASEAN Intergovernmental Commission on Human Rights (AICHR) enshrines the inherent right to life in its ASEAN Human Rights Declaration. With these clear pronouncements of mandate and vision, what has ASEAN done to safeguard human rights and the right to life in particular? More pertinently, how can we reconcile human centrality and rights with the fact that in the majority of ASEAN Member States, termination of life is endorsed and practiced as a legal punishment?

The study of right to life and its legal termination can be as complex as life itself. In 2016, when serving as the Representative of Thailand to the AICHR, I proposed three studies under the theme of 'access to justice', envisaging a regional contribution to the Global Goals, particularly Goal 16. The first of these, the AICHR thematic studies on legal aid, was successfully launched in 2018. The second study focuses on children in conflict of the law or juvenile justice, which is awaiting final review. The third study focuses on the right to life. Since ASEAN relies on consensus and views diverged on the focus of the third volume, it was decided that abolition of the death penalty would not be part of the study. The emphasis was instead placed on the treatment of those on death row. During the course of their research, the research team took the view that the study of right to life without the reference to the death penalty would be incomplete. The negotiation on their draft study submitted in 2020 did not achieve a common ground and pursuant to the AICHR's arrangement, it would have been shelved internally. However, the research team took the initiative to expand their draft and publish it as their own work. This volume is therefore the culmination of the AICHR program and the team's academic originality. Whilst it is not published as an AICHR paper, the study shines a light on a subject matter that is hitherto studied on a country basis. The regional approach fills the gap and paves the way for further advocacy and action by stakeholders at the national and ASEAN levels.

As regards the death penalty, there are shades of a spectrum between the polarity of abolitionist and retentionist. Many of these are represented among the ten Member States of ASEAN. From my observation, the policy direction is highly dynamic and reversible, on the whole towards the use of capital punishment. Critically, those that have edged towards de facto abolition have restarted the death penalty. After a nine-year absence, Thailand carried out in 2018 execution by lethal injection of a man guilty of robbery resulting in death. Following the 2021 coup in Myanmar, death sentences have been handed down on political activists and the military government has announced that execution is a required action, despite a three-decade moratorium. Perhaps a notable exception is the case of Malaysia which has initiated a reform program to abolish the mandatory death penalty. Most alarmingly, prior to the general election in 2022, there were plans in the Philippines to reintroduce the death penalty which has already been repealed.

The AICHR study of the death penalty is not per se a call for its abolition, although that is the ultimate goal. Whilst the merit of 'a life for a life' approach debate continues, there are incidental issues that must also be examined. I exemplify a few: The minimum age of criminal liability; the types of crimes on which it is imposed and availability of legal representation or legal aid for the accused; the possibility of clemency or pardon; the duration between the sentence and the execution—it is not uncommon for incarceration to be more than a decade; the treatment of those awaiting execution, especially women and prisoners with disabilities; the execution methods; and the availability, timeliness and comprehensiveness of disaggregated data. Thus despite the existence of the death penalty in law, an exchange of views and data and further in-depth studies of related topics will be imperative for a better understanding of the cost that it incurs in addition to the termination of life.

This volume is the first regional reference on the issue of the death penalty in ASEAN. I hope that it will serve as a benchmark and an inspiration for other relevant topics that will help promote the protection of the right to life of the ASEAN peoples.

Bangkok, Thailand

Dr. Seree Nonthasoot
Member of the UN Committee on
Economic, Social and Cultural Rights,
Representative of Thailand to
the AICHR (2013–2018)

Preface

The issue of the death penalty has always been a contentious one. Those in favour of retaining it—retentionists—maintain that the retributive effect of the death penalty is necessary for closure for the victim's family, and that the death penalty is needed for crime control, particularly heinous crimes. Whilst those that argue against the death penalty—abolitionists—highlight the possibility of a wrongful conviction, the lack of empirical data to show its deterrent effect, and the permanence of the punishment. Regardless of politics, moral values, economic indicators and the presence or absence of data (which have been used by both sides to support their arguments), international human rights law places strict constraints on the conditions under which an exception to the right to life may be permissible. This book argues that taking away a person's life, even via legal means, diminishes society and humanity into a state of brutality, transgressing human decency and restraint. That a commitment to maintaining the death penalty and recognising the right to life is incongruous.

The right to life is universally recognised as a fundamental human right, and is often described as a supreme human right, upon which all other human rights depend. Article 3 of the Universal Declaration of Human Rights (UDHR) states 'everyone has the right to life, liberty, and security of person' and Article 5 acknowledges that 'no one shall be subjected to torture or to cruel, inhuman or degrading treatment or punishment'. In addition, Article 7 and 8 of the UDHR guarantees that 'all are equal before the law and are entitled without any discrimination to equal protection of the law and everyone has the right to an effective remedy by the competent national tribunals for acts violating the fundamental rights granted him by the constitution or by law'. Moreover, the right to life is also recognised by international legal instruments such as the International Covenant on Civil and Political Rights (ICCPR), the Convention on the Rights of the Child (CRC), to name but a few. However, it is also true that—as yet—there is no general prohibition against the death sentence in international law, yet the death penalty is arguably anathema (of the most irreversible kind) to that which has time and again been called the most fundamental human right; the inherent right to life.

Most of countries in ASEAN enshrine the right to life in their respective constitutions. Yet, laws in 8 out of 10 ASEAN states still allow capital punishment. Although reform and abolition, as well as de facto non-execution, are the current global trend, the death penalty situation in the eight ASEAN Member States remains unmoved; at the start of 2020, at least 2,189 people were believed to be awaiting execution in the region. Looking at each country's situation, the record on which crimes invoke the death penalty and how many executions have taken place, reveals a very mixed reality, reflecting the absence of any shared policy on the death penalty among ASEAN members other than the proviso 'in accordance with law'. One thing is clear though, many ASEAN Member States seem to be expanding the crimes to which the death penalty shall be considered a 'most serious crime'.

It is this dichotomy of a global trend towards the abolition of the death penalty and its resistance in the ASEAN region that this book examines, with each chapter grounded in theoretical and empirical perspectives of each issue under study. Is the region simply a decade or two behind other parts of the world or are there a policy or value-based 'particularities' within the ASEAN region that mean capital punishment is likely to persist? We add to our understanding of the utilisation of the death penalty by arguing there is a threefold explanation for the retentionist disposition: The 'Asian Values' argument; the power of authoritarian governments in Southeast Asia; the limitations of AICHR. Specifically, the book examines: why the death penalty is considered necessary in the fight against certain crimes in ASEAN, the evidence to support these claims, the issues and contexts that have widened the range of offences for which the death penalty is applicable, and how the international human rights mechanisms have specifically called for ASEAN Member States to refrain from extending the application of the death penalty and to limit it to the 'most serious crimes'; how public opinion shapes state policies towards the death penalty and how it varies according to different offences and different states; how states can defend the rights of victims and punish criminals whilst respecting fundamental human rights in the context of these different crimes; if religion(s) shape the decision for abolition or retention of the death penalty in ASEAN, and if so, how; the history and trajectory of the only two countries in ASEAN (Cambodia and the Philippines) where the death penalty has been abolished; and finally, the book updates the literature and data available on the use of the death penalty in ASEAN. Written by scholars based in Southeast Asia, the chapters provide insights not only from the perspective of academics that have conducted studies on the death penalty in the region but who have also been advocating for legal reforms.

The death penalty is perceived as politically sensitive within ASEAN, and a number of the chapters touch upon the different justifications for the use of capital punishment in the region and expose the secrecy, sensitivities, and dilemmas that mask violations of international human rights laws. For example, the 'Asian Values' argument has long been used as putting the interests of the community over and above that of the individual in the pro-death penalty rhetoric. The apparent reasoning is that Asian societies have a different conceptualisation of the right to life whereby potential victims' right to life trumps those that deprive others of this right. Most chapters add new perspectives which have been overlooked in the traditional discourse surrounding the use of the death penalty, such as around crimes that do not meet the threshold of 'most serious'; the dignity of death row inmates and their families;

and contradictions within religion and capital punishment. What is apparent is the way in which growing authoritarianism and the media are adversely influencing the public's perception and support for capital punishment in the region. Clearly, the number and power of authoritarian governments within ASEAN is a major reason for the persistent number of retentionist states found in the region. What remains to be seen is whether continuing economic growth and social change can influence authoritarian governance and whether shifts towards or away from democracy will impact current execution policy. Certainly, the inability of a regional organisation in ASEAN to look at issues such as the death penalty and other concerns related to human rights limitations and state power is apparent. The major obstacle for the ASEAN Intergovernmental Commission on Human Rights (AICHR) is the individual governments unwillingness to subject themselves to international standards under the guise of 'non-interference' and state sovereignty.

This book has its origins in a thematic study on the right to life focusing on the death penalty, commissioned by AICHR in late 2017. Taking over two years to finalise, the AICHR thematic report was never published as some country representatives argued that the researchers went beyond the original terms of reference for the study and that the report leaned towards calling for the abolition of the death penalty within the region. Spurred on by this lack of progress regionally, some of the original researchers invited others to join, and this book evolved as part of a project funded by the High Education Council for Wales (HEFCW) Global Challenges Research Fund under Grant W20/16HE. Whilst being abolitionists at heart, the authors of this book have factually and objectively analysed the human rights implications of the use of the death penalty in ASEAN. It is our hope that the new learning and increased attention given to the issue of capital punishment through this book can help agitate for positive change in this region.

As editors, we are grateful to all the authors for contributing conceptually, theoretically and morally to a deeper understanding of the distinctive Asian perceptions of punishment, justice and human rights.

Nakornpathom, Thailand — Sriprapha Petcharamesree
Nakornpathom, Thailand — Mark P. Capaldi
Swansea, UK — Alan Collins

Authors Note

Information contained in these chapters were finalized in early 2022 before the Philippine national election and the reported resumption of the use of capital punishment in Myanmar.

Contents

Editors and Contributors

About the Editors

Sriprapha Petcharamesree Ph.D., is a senior advisor at the Institute of Human Rights and Peace Studies, Mahidol University in Thailand. She received her Ph.D. (Doctorat) in international politics from the University of Paris-X Nanterre, France. Sriprapha was awarded, in 2017, an Honorary Doctor by the University of Oslo, Norway for her contribution to human rights. From 2009-2012, she has served as the Representative of Thailand to the ASEAN Intergovernmental Commission on Human Rights (AICHR).

Her recent works focus, among others, on issues of citizenship, migration, refugees and asylum seekers as well as statelessness, human rights in international relations, and human rights education. She was entrusted by the AICHR (ASEAN Intergovernmental Commission on Human Rights) to synthesise the country reports on right to life focusing death penalty in ASEAN. She continues her research on the issues and advocates for the abolition of death penalty in the region.

Mark P. Capaldi Ph.D., is a lecturer at the Institute of Human Rights and Peace Studies at Mahidol University. Much of Mark P. Capaldi's work has been in South and East Asia, where he has lived for 30 years when he worked with the International NGOs Concern Worldwide, PACT Inc., Save the Children UK and ECPAT International. As Deputy Director of ECPAT International (2001-2011), he worked to end the commercial sexual exploitation and trafficking of children, supporting a wide range of programming and advocacy in all regions of the world. From 2011 to 2018, he took on the role of ECPAT's global Head of Research and Policy.

Mark P. Capaldi has a doctorate degree with the Institute of Human Rights and Peace Studies at Mahidol University, Bangkok, where he currently works as a lecturer. The research topic of his dissertation was children's agency within independent child migration in Thailand. Other recent research areas have included a 10 countries study on the death penalty in ASEAN and also the issue of religions and its impact on sexuality within Southeast Asia.

Alan Collins Ph.D., is a Professor of International Relations at the Department of Political and Cultural Studies, Swansea University, United Kingdom. Prior to this he was a British Academy Post-Doctoral Fellow at the University of Wales, Aberystwyth, where he also completed his Ph.D. He has held visiting fellow positions at the S. Rajaratnam School of International Studies in Singapore. He works in the field of international security, with a specialist interest in Southeast Asian security, and the Association of South East Asian Nations (ASEAN). He is the author of four single authored books, and is the editor of Contemporary Security Studies (Oxford University Press), a leading global textbook in international Security.

Contributors

Raine Boonlong Freelance, Huai Khwang, Thailand

Danthong Breen Union for Civil Liberty, Huai Khwang, Thailand

Mark P. Capaldi Institute of Human Rights and Peace Studies, Mahidol University, Salaya, Thailand

Ma. Ngina Teresa V. Chan-Gonzaga School of Law, Ateneo de Manila University, Makati City, Philippines

Sriprapha Petcharamesree Institute of Human Rights and Peace Studies, Mahidol University, Nakornpathom, Thailand

Khemthong Tonsakulrungruang Faculty of Political Science, Chulalongkorn University, Bangkok, Thailand

Patricia Rinwigati Waagstein Faculty of Law, Universitas Indonesia, Depok City, Indonesia

The Death Penalty in ASEAN: Steadfastly Retentionist?

Mark P. Capaldi

Abstract This chapter provides an overview and recent data on the use of capital punishment within the ASEAN region—such as is available—and notes the effect that the COVID-19 pandemic has had on the use of capital punishment in the region. The legal and judiciary systems of the ASEAN Member States (AMS) are introduced examining the right to life and where the death penalty is stipulated. Whilst acknowledging that the death penalty is not explicitly banned by international human rights law, the chapter highlights the global trend towards abolition and contrasts this with AMS preference for retention. It examines why the death penalty remains popular/acceptable in the region and exposes trends that indicate its use is declining (e.g. moratoriums, reducing the extent of "most serious" crimes, decreasing criminal acts that carry a mandatory death sentence). The chapter also highlights examples of criminal injustices related to the death penalty in ASEAN retentionist states and concludes that although regional changes indicate less reliance on the death penalty, retention is still prominent. It questions whether the convenient politics of growing authoritarianism in the region and the wish to be seen as 'tough on crime' is thus bucking the inclination towards abolition in ASEAN.

Keywords Death penalty · ASEAN · Practice · Human rights

1 Introduction

On the 16th December 2020, 123 nations voted on a United Nations General Assembly (UNGA) resolution calling for a moratorium on the use of the death penalty, reinforcing the global trend to abolish capital punishment (UNGA, 2020).

Sadly, of the 10 member states of the Association of Southeast Asian Nations (ASEAN), only three voted in favour (Cambodia, Malaysia and the Philippines) whilst Brunei and Singapore voted against. The remaining five ASEAN retentionist countries abstained.

M. P. Capaldi (✉)
Institute of Human Rights and Peace Studies, Mahidol University, Salaya, Thailand
e-mail: mark.cap@mahidol.edu

S. Petcharamesree et al. (eds.), *Unpacking the Death Penalty in ASEAN*,
https://doi.org/10.1007/978-981-19-8840-0_1

The UNGA has held such a resolution every two years since 2007 and has seen the list of supporting nations steadily grow from the original 104 affirmative votes. Over the last two years, the number increased from 121 of those in favour of the resolution. Yet while the UN vote indicates a growing consensus against the use of the death penalty, eight out of the 10 ASEAN member states still retain capital punishment within their legislature (the two abolitionist countries are Cambodia and the Philippines).

One of the most ardent advocates of the death penalty is Singapore, once referred to as the 'world execution capital' (Johnson & Zimring, 2009). Whilst over the last two decades its' per capita rates of executions have fallen significantly (as much as 90% from 1996 to 2007), the decline has not brought differential impact on homicide levels or drug crimes, questioning the effectiveness of capital punishment as a deterrent. Although Indonesia abstained from the vote, in 2019 it reportedly handed down 80 death sentences, up from 48 the previous year. Two other abstaining nations, Vietnam and Laos, hold data on the use of the death penalty as a state secret. Whilst Laos is said not to have carried out an execution for more than 30 years, Vietnam reportedly executed 429 people between 2013 and 2016, suggesting it could average 147 executions per year (Hutt, 2017). Ironically, Malaysia, whose 2018 elected reformist government vowed to ban capital punishment and who seemed a newly converted ally at the UNGA, still has 1,324 people on death row and more recently watered down their earlier pledge to merely eliminating the mandatory use of the death penalty. Even the Philippines, a bastion of abolitionism in the region has recently been threatening to reintroduce it (especially for drug-related crimes) under President Rodrigo Duterte.

Similar to the global estimates, the number of executions in the region has dropped from 2019 to 2020, most likely in part due to COVID-19 and related pandemic restrictions within the justice system. However, as Indonesia and Singapore turned to digital courtroom hearings, prisoners have been condemned to die over Zoom, WhatsApp and other video applications drawing international outcries of defendants being deprived of their rights to dignity and a fair trial (Harm Reduction, 2021). Although no executions were officially recorded in ASEAN in 2020, the death penalty was still metered out in the region for crimes that do not meet the threshold stated under international law of 'most serious crimes'.

This chapter, therefore, aims to explore ASEAN's obstinacy in holding on to the death penalty. The following section examines the region's motives and mentality that sustain its seeming popularity. Looking at the region's situation, the record reveals a very mixed reality, reflecting the absence of any shared policy on the death penalty among ASEAN members other than the proviso "in accordance with law". The robustness and irregularities of the legal frameworks around the death penalty are unpacked in the next section where contrasts exist as most countries in ASEAN enshrine the right to life in their respective constitution. The chapter then moves on to look at the dichotomies between the international and regional human rights obligations to ensure the effective protection of the right to life in ASEAN. Whilst retentionist countries in the region often seek to justify the use of capital punishment on grounds of punishment theories that focus on drawing a distinction between an infliction of just punishment from arbitrary and unjust violence, the chapter also identifies violations of the international human rights regime in relation to the use of capital punishment. The concluding section identifies important research gaps and propositions that growing authoritarianism and an obduracy to foreign criticism may in part be contributing to the region's slow progress towards full abolition of the death penalty.

2 The Social Context of the Death Penalty in ASEAN

As stated, no executions were reportedly carried out in 2020 in ASEAN although not all member states provide information on their use of the death penalty. This is a decrease from four in 2019 (all carried out by Singapore) although countries in the region have still sentenced people to death amidst the epidemic. Table 1 presents data on the death penalty as collated by Amnesty International for 2020 in ASEAN:

Whilst collating data and making comparisons across the retentionist countries in ASEAN is not easy, from a compilation of sources, the following executions seemingly took place over the last 13 years which at least illustrates trends (Table 2):

These historical trends demonstrate the dominant theories of punishment within ASEAN of wanting to be seen to be 'tough on crime' as per the correctional goals of retribution, incapacitation and deterrence. The 'Asian Values' argument (a political ideology first articulated in the 1990s) further posits a preference for community interests rather than individual interests, social order, discipline and paternalistic state. To achieve these aims, criminal law within retentionist states imposes capital punishment for certain criminal offenders. For those that commit a death-eligible offence, a harsh penalty is seen as 'just' ('an eye for an eye and a tooth for a tooth') and meant to persuade other individuals from committing such a crime.

Whilst evidence for the death penalty acting as an effective deterrence is lacking, within ASEAN it appears that doubts about the robustness of deterrence data do

Table 1 Record of death sentences and executions in 2020 in ASEAN countries

Country	2020 recorded executions	2020 recorded death sentences
Brunei Darussalam	0	0
Indonesia	0	117 +
Lao PDR	0	9 +
Malaysia	0	22 +
Myanmar	0	1
Singapore	0	8
Thailand	0	35
Vietnam	+	54 +

Source Amnesty International (2021)

Table 2 Number of executions in the last 13 years in ASEAN countries

	Brunei Darussalam	Indonesia	Lao PDR	Malaysia	Myanmar	Singapore	Thailand	Vietnam
2020	0	0	0	0	0	0	0	N/A
2019	0	0	0	0	0	4	0	N/A
2018	0	0	0	N/A	0	N/A	1	N/A
2017	0	0	0	12	0	8	0	N/A
2016	0	4	0	9	0	4	0	N/A
2015	0	14	0	1	0	4	0	N/A
2014	0	0	0	6	0	2	0	N/A
2013	0	5	0	3	0	0	0	N/A
2007–2012	0	N/A	0	3	0	18	0	N/A

N/A = Not Available. *Source* Compilation based on Country Reports from the AICHR study on the Right to Life and Amnesty International

not stand in the way of executions if it is believed that there is the possibility of saving more lives of innocent victims as discussed in Chapter 2. Indonesia's primary justification for the use of the death penalty is deterrence against drug trafficking despite the fact that the WHO has repeatedly said that punitive policies the world over have little impact on the prevalence of drug use (Degenhardt et al., 2008). Furthermore, Singapore's increased use of the death penalty and higher prevalence of drug trafficking further illustrates that it is not an effective deterrent (Leechainan & Longmire, 2013). Even more revealing is data for Singapore covering the period 2003–2015 published by the UN Office on Drugs and Crime which also showed there was no apparent correlation between execution trends and murder rates (UNODC, 2020).

Some religious doctrine also supports the use of capital punishment and has significant influence over the hearts and minds of the 600 million plus people living in ASEAN (see Chapter 6). Islam recognises the death penalty and so in the majority Muslim countries in the region such as Indonesia, Malaysia and Brunei, the death penalty is not viewed as unconstitutional. However, there was international outrage when in 2019, Brunei adopted its Sharia Penal Code which included the punishment of death by stoning for offences such as sodomy and adultery—which was later walked back by the Sultan (BBC, 2019).[1] Despite the concept of capital punishment not being found in Buddhist moral law and 'refraining from killing' being one of the 5 precepts of Buddhism, Buddhist countries in the region consider that the law is not a religious instrument (which is an individual practice) and that law is the legal instrument to facilitate social justice. The Old Testament of the Bible has a number of verses that appear to support the death penalty, although leaders of the Christian church have long preached otherwise, as validated by the recent concern by religious leaders in the Philippines towards recent political rhetoric in favour of the death penalty (CNN

[1] As international criticism escalated, the Sultan of Brunei eventually extended a moratorium on the death penalty for adultery and same-sex activities.

Philippines, 2019). In reality, interpretations both for and against the death penalty can be found in the religious doctrines of Islam, Buddhism and Christianity leaving it to followers to decide which they wish to believe as the correct reading. As such, religious influence shapes the public—and thus policymakers—position on the death penalty.

Indeed, public support for the death penalty in ASEAN is high and politicians feed into this. The Indonesian President in his 'war against drugs' has frequently cited data saying that as many as 50 die a day in Indonesia due to drug-related crimes, fueling the public support for the death penalty at 84.6% in a poll carried out in 2017 (Straits Times, 2017). The Singaporean Foreign Minister in 2016 endorsed capital punishment saying it was "keeping Singapore drug free and keeping Singapore safe" even though Singapore actually has one of the highest drug problems in the region (Balakrishnan, 2016). In the Philippines there is a proposed re-imposition of the death penalty with President Rodrigo Duterte regularly stating his support for the re-imposition of death penalty. In July 2020, during his fifth State of the Nation Address he said "I reiterate the swift passage of a law reviving the death penalty by lethal injection for crimes specified under the Comprehensive Dangerous Drugs Act of 2002. This law will not only help us deter criminality, but also save our children from the dangers posed by the illegal and dangerous drugs" (Limpot, 2020). Another prominent proponent of the reintroduction of the death penalty is world famous boxer Manny Pacquiao who recently announced his intention to run for the Philippine Presidency in 2022. Pacquiao (notably also a pastor) has said the death penalty was "moral and lawful" and that "God allows governments to use capital punishment. Even Jesus Christ was sentenced to death" (Elemia, 2017). Politicians feed into (and off) the wave of public opinion as illustrated by a study in 2019 of registered voters in Maramag, a municipality in the Philippines which reported 81.3% agreeing with its re-instatement in light of it incapacitating criminals from committing heinous crimes (Odchigue & Sobradil, 2019). Regardless of the fact that public opinion polls are notoriously unscientific, where the general public and politicians seemingly believe that the death penalty is a deterrent then wanting to be 'tough on crime' stalls meaningful debates otherwise.

The waning in recourse to executions in 2020 may seem an opportunity to consider the law and practices central to the use of capital punishment across ASEAN. However, the recorded number of death sentences given out in the year appeared to increase by 32 (to a total of 246) despite pandemic restrictions to judicial proceedings (Amnesty International, 2021). In fact, against the backdrop of COVID-19, officials suspended prison visits (of both families and legal representatives) and in-person court proceedings adding to concerns of the cruelty of capital punishment and a likely reduction in fair trial guarantees. Whilst the world moved forward towards global abolition, within ASEAN, progress remains slow with some changes in legislation (e.g. the mandatory use of the death penalty) offset by threats in the Philippines to reintroduce capital punishment. Furthermore, without greater support for abolition from the ASEAN public then retentionist politicians will claim they are only following the people's will.

3 International Human Rights, the Right to Life and Legislation on the Death Penalty in ASEAN

At international and certain regional levels—at least in ASEAN—it is also true that there is no general prohibition against the death sentence, although the death penalty is arguably anathema (of the most irreversible kind) to that which has time and again been called the most fundamental human right, i.e. the inherent right to life.

Article 3 of the Universal Declaration of Human Rights (UDHR) provides that "everyone has the right to life, liberty and security of person." This universal recognition is by no means an isolated pronouncement. Article 6 of the International Covenant on Civil and Political Rights (ICCPR) reiterated this reverence by stating that "every human being has the inherent right to life." Article 6 went further by expressly mandating legal protection for this right and underscoring the fact that no one should be arbitrarily deprived of life. As already stated, there is no general prohibition against death sentence in international law but it can only be used for the most serious crimes.[2]

The basis for the legal framework protecting the right to life, therefore, comprises the pertinent provisions of the Universal Declaration of Human Rights (UDHR) and the International Covenant on Civil and Political Rights (interpreted within the context of other United Nations instruments). The right to life is also recognised by Article 6 of the CRC[3] the Convention on the Rights of Persons with Disabilities in Article 10.[4] It is evident that whatever stage and conditions of life, the right to life is recognised by international human rights instruments. It is worth noting that all ASEAN Member States (AMS) have ratified the CRC and CRPD whilst only 6 countries have ratified the ICCPR.[5]

The general recognition of the right to life is also manifested in regional mechanisms in various areas of the world. In the American system, Article 1 of the American Declaration of the Rights and Duties of Man (also known as the Bogota Declaration)—an instrument that actually predates the UDHR by a few months—has almost identical language as that of Article 3 of the latter: "Every human being has the right to life, liberty and the security of his person."[6] The Convention on Human Rights (also known as the Pact of San Jose) that came later is interesting in that it joined the general recognition of the right together with pronouncements regarding capital

[2] There is no clear definition of what constitutes 'the most serious crimes' in international law.

[3] Convention on the Rights of the Child, Article 6. which stipulates that "1. States Parties recognise that every child has the inherent right to life; and 2. States Parties shall ensure to the maximum extent possible the survival and development of the child".

[4] The Convention on the Rights of Persons with Disabilities, Article 10. States Parties reaffirm that every human being has the inherent right to life and shall take all necessary measures to ensure its effective enjoyment by persons with disabilities on an equal basis with others.

[5] 6 AMS include Cambodia, Indonesia, Lao PDR, the Philippines, Thailand and Vietnam.

[6] American Declaration of the Rights and Duties of Man (adopted April 1948; entry into force 1948).

punishment.[7] Other notable Inter-American instruments include the Inter-American Convention to Prevent and Punish Torture,[8] and the Protocol to the American Convention on Human Rights to Abolish the Death Penalty[9] which has resulted in the Latin American region now being almost free of capital punishment (with the exception of Cuba and Guatemala).

The other long-standing regional instrument on human rights can be found within the European system. Anchoring what is considered the most advanced regional mechanism on human rights protection, the European Convention for the Protection of Human Rights and Fundamental Freedoms (ECHR), entered into force in 1953 also enshrining the right to life.[10] An additional protocol to the ECHR (Protocol No. 13) which entered into force in 2003 abolished capital punishment in all circumstances, including for crimes committed in times of war or imminent threat of war,[11] allowing for no derogation or reservation.

---

[7] American Convention on Human Rights (adopted 1969; entry into force 1978).
Article 4. Right to Life:

1. Every person has the right to have his life respected. This right shall be protected by law and, in general, from the moment of conception. No one shall be arbitrarily deprived of his life.
2. In countries that have not abolished the death penalty, it may be imposed only for the most serious crimes and pursuant to a final judgment rendered by a competent court and in accordance with a law establishing such punishment, enacted prior to the commission of the crime. The application of such punishment shall not be extended to crimes to which it does not presently apply.
3. The death penalty shall not be re-established in states that have abolished it.
4. In no case shall capital punishment be inflicted for political offenses or related common crimes.
5. Capital punishment shall not be imposed upon persons who, at the time the crime was committed, were under 18 years of age or over 70 years of age; nor shall it be applied to pregnant women.
6. Every person condemned to death shall have the right to apply for amnesty, pardon, or commutation of sentence, which may be granted in all cases. Capital punishment shall not be imposed while such a petition is pending decision by the competent authority.

[8] Inter-American Convention to Prevent and Punish Torture (adopted 1985; entry into force 1987); Article 13: [...] Extradition shall not be granted nor shall the person sought be returned when there are grounds to believe that his life is in danger, that he will be subjected to torture or to cruel, inhuman or degrading treatment, or that he will be tried by special or ad hoc courts in the requesting State.

[9] Protocol to the American Convention on Human Rights to Abolish the Death Penalty (entry into force 1990); Article 1: The States Parties to this Protocol shall not apply the death penalty in their territory to any person subject to their jurisdiction.

[10] European Convention for the Protection of Human Rights and Fundamental Freedoms (adopted 1950; entry into force 1953).

[11] The earlier Protocol No. 6 (1985) mandated the abolition of the death penalty and was very categorical in that "no one shall be condemned to such penalty or executed". It allowed a State to make provision for capital punishment in time of war or imminent threat of war, but such penalty could only be applied in instances provided by the State's laws. Article 1 of Protocol No. 13 states: Abolition of the death penalty: The death penalty shall be abolished. No one shall be condemned to such penalty or executed.

As far as existing regional ASEAN human rights mechanisms are concerned, the system within Southeast Asia can be considered as being the "youngest" arrangement in place. The preamble of the ASEAN Charter[12] states that ASEAN adheres "to the principles of democracy, rule of law and good governance, respect for and protection of human rights and fundamental freedoms". In 2009, ASEAN created the ASEAN Inter-governmental Commission on Human Rights (AICHR) whose main purpose includes the "[promotion] and [protection] of human rights and fundamental freedoms of the peoples of ASEAN" (AICHR, 2009). At the 21st ASEAN Summit in 2012, the ASEAN Human Rights Declaration (AHRD) was adopted. The AHRD begins with the ASEAN Heads of State/Government reaffirming once again their commitment to all the civil and political rights contained in the UDHR; in fact, Article 11 of the AHRD expressly asserts that: "Every person has an inherent right to life which shall be protected by law. No person shall be deprived of life save in accordance with law." A more recent development was when in 2017, AICHR identified the right to life as one of its thematic studies; specifically in relation to existing national legal frameworks regarding the right to life and the death penalty as well as to identify 'good practice' when it comes to the treatment of convicted persons on death row. An independent team of academics and researchers were tasked with carrying out national-level research and the writings of a regional synthesis. Unfortunately, significant editing of the researchers' draft report saw much of the rights-based analysis and any critical findings removed. Although the more descriptive version was eventually approved by AICHR in early 2021, the report has yet to be published. The obstacle is some ASEAN member states' resistance to pushing for more transnational standards in light of the regional body's rigid adherence to the non-interference principle.

As state compliance with international and regional obligations, particularly in ASEAN, leaves much to be desired, it is, therefore, an imperative to entrench human rights in domestic law, preferably constitutional law. Most of the constitutions found in ASEAN have specific provisions recognising the "right to life" which many would argue should discourage the use of the death penalty. However, where capital punishment is applied within AMS, phrases such as "No person shall be deprived of his life or personal liberty save in accordance with law" (AICHR, 2020a); "Nothing shall, except in accord with existing laws, be detrimental to the life and personal freedom of any person" (AICHR, 2020b); "No person shall be deprived of his life or personal liberty save in accordance with law" (AICHR, 2020c) are found in the provisions of their Constitutions.

In 'accordance with the law' relates to where the death penalty is stipulated in other organic laws, especially criminal codes as well as other national laws. Under the Criminal Procedure Code (Chapter 7) of Brunei Darussalam, the right to life may only be taken away upon a finding of guilty after trial in relation to certain

[12] ASEAN Charter (adopted 2007, entry into force in December 2008). Article 2.1 reiterates that ASEAN and its Member States "reaffirm and adhere to fundamental principles contained in the declarations, agreements, conventions, concords, treaties and other instruments of ASEAN". Article 2.2(i) in fact identifies "respect for fundamental freedoms, the promotion and protection of human rights, and the promotion of social justice" as a key principle.

offences (unless the defendant has offered a plea of guilty). Indonesia's criminal code, chapter II article 10 states that capital punishment is part of the main criminal sentence. Additionally, capital punishment is also imposed in other laws such as Law No.22 Year 1997 (later amended with the Law No.35 2009) on Drugs which states that those who have processed, produced, procure, export, give or channel drugs are defined as "category 1". In Lao PDR, Articles 82, 88, 89, 90 and 92 of the Penal Law prescribe that any person causing another person's death intentionally, negligently or inadvertently shall be punished by house arrest, deprivation of liberty, death penalty or/and shall be fined (AICHR, 2020d). In Malaysia, mandatory death penalty was stated in the Penal Code on various grounds ranging from offences against the King to terrorist acts that result in death and murder. Other laws provide for discretionary death penalty in relation to a range of other crimes.

In Myanmar, punishment by death was prescribed by the Penal Code for offences such as high treason, acts causing death, murder, drugs, etc. Capital punishment has been an integral part of Singapore's criminal justice system and there are thirty-two offences on the statute books that attract the death penalty, with some of them being mandatory sanctions upon conviction. In Thailand, the death penalty is provided for by the Penal Code and the Military Code for 63 different crimes, the largest number in the region. In Vietnam, their Penal Code also includes a number of crimes grouped in various categories on which capital punishment is imposed.

Therefore, far from the retentionist countries in the region retaining the death penalty for heinous crimes (such as homicide), it can be observed that the death penalty is given for a large variety of crimes within ASEAN as can be seen in Table 3. Offences can include blasphemy, adultery, corruption, apostasy, homosexual acts and most common of all within ASEAN, drug-related offences.

All eight of the retentionist states in ASEAN enact the death sentence for drug related crimes and it is by far the most frequent application of the death penalty. In 2019, 61% of prisoners on death row in Indonesia were because of drug offences, in Malaysia 70%, and in Thailand 64% (Sader et al., 2020). The UN Commission on Human Rights in a 2005 resolution clarified 'most serious crimes' as those intentional crimes of violence with an immediate life-threatening effect. Non-violent crimes—such as drug-related offences, financial crimes, sexual relations between consenting adults or unclear internal and external security offences should not be included. Of note is that most retentionist States in ASEAN applying capital punishment are slowly reducing the number of crimes eligible for the death penalty; an exception being Thailand where over the last five years the number of crimes subject to the death penalty has increased from 55 to 63 (AICHR, 2020e). There is also a decrease in the number of offences regionally that warrant the mandatory death penalty.

Only in two countries of ASEAN is capital punishment prohibited. The Cambodian Constitution states that "capital punishment is prohibited" (AICHR, 2020f). Section 19, Art. III, 1987 Constitution of the Philippines stipulates that "Excessive fines shall not be imposed, nor cruel, degrading or inhuman punishment inflicted. Neither shall death penalty be imposed, unless, for compelling reasons involving heinous crimes, the Congress hereafter provides for it. Any death penalty already imposed shall be reduced to reclusion perpetua." (AICHR, 2020g). This means that all

Table 3 Types of crimes eligible for the death penalty in ASEAN countries*

	Brunei Darussalam	Indonesia	Lao PDR	Malaysia	Myanmar	Singapore	Thailand	Vietnam
Drug offences	√	√	√	√	√	√	√	√
Treason, National Security, Military Crimes, War Crimes, Genocide, Crimes against humanity, Offences against the State	√	√	√	√	√	√	√	√
Murder	√	√	√	√	√	√	√	√
Firearms crimes/explosive (plus may result in death)	√	√	√	√		√	√	
Kidnapping & trafficking in persons	√		√	√	√	√	√	
Corruption & bribery, robbery of state assets		√	√				√	√
Arson							√	
Rape of children/use of children			√				√	
Chemical weapons, against a nuclear facility, terrorism, acts against public places etc	√	√	√	√		√	√	√
Certain offences against Syariah Law	√							

*Compiled for a regional synthesis report ('Thematic Study on Right to Life: Protection of the Rights of Persons Convicted of the Death Penalty') produced in 2018–2019 and finalised by AICHR in April 2021 but yet unpublished capital punishment was abolished and that all death penalties would be commutated to life sentences. Although as mentioned earlier, President Duterte of the Philippines is currently advocating for the re-introduction of the death penalty as part of his 'war on drugs' policy; as of 2020, a total of 23 bills seeking its reimposition were filed in both the House of Representatives and the Senate (BBC, 2020).

From the section above it is clear that although the right to life is recognised by laws across the region, including the highest law of the land (i.e. the Constitution), capital punishment remains. At international and regional levels, at least in ASEAN, it is also true that—as yet—there is no general prohibition against the death sentence in international law. However, it bears pointing out that even where relevant constitutional guarantees are present, appropriate mechanisms need to be established to ensure that robust safeguarding of the right to life and protection from criminal injustice is in fact provided.

4 The ASEAN Way: A Tool for Justice or a Brutal Method of Punishment?

Practices on how the death penalty is implemented vary across the region. Retentionist countries in ASEAN will draw attention to what they see as 'good practices' in their jurisdictions although in relation to the death penalty, this is arguable an oxymoron. The supposed 'Asian Values', which place a greater emphasis on social harmony and the good of the community, are seen as prioritising justice and retribution.

The right to legal aid is found in the constitutions, laws or judicial practices across ASEAN although differences in how it can be accessed exist. Whilst in Brunei and Indonesia legal aid is mandatory for all offenders (national or foreign), Singapore only offers legal aid to its citizens. For other countries, eligibility for access to legal aid depends upon the financial position of the defendant or whether they are from particular vulnerable groups. Regardless, the quality of legal aid provided in the region can vary and instances of ineffective legal representation are easily found. For example, in Vietnam foreign prisoners have been assigned attorneys who couldn't speak English and death row inmates have reported facing obstacles when trying to meet with their clients (Pascoe, 2017). In Indonesia, officials are believed to have prevented Pakistani Zufiqar Ali from contacting the consulate or seeing a lawyer (Amnesty International, 2012).

All AMS afford convicted persons the right to appeal against their death penalty sentence. However, while a death sentence may be reduced to a life sentence on appeal, a life sentence may also be enhanced to a death sentence. Even where an appeal is not pursued, based on available data, Thailand, Vietnam and the Lao PDR adopt such an automatic review procedure for all capital sentences. There is very little data on the rates of success of appeals on the death penalty in AMS, but success rates mean little in practice. A high rate of appeal could imply that judges are constantly having their judgments overturned, which in turn would be a cause for concern, whilst in Vietnam, for example, up to 99.93% of criminal appeals (not limited to death penalty cases) fail (Pascoe, 2017). The Singapore government's approach to criminal justice emphasises crime control and the need to "prioritise successful convictions over procedural rights" (Chen, 2014, p. 264).

While at first glance the Head of State, whether in the form of a President or Monarch, in each AMS appears to have full authority to grant clemency to death convicts, in practice and often in law the discretion to do so is to varying degrees limited by the recommendations or advice given by another authority. The Indonesian President has strong discretion in deciding whether or not to grant clemency whilst the Singaporean Head of State's role is essentially that of rubber-stamping. Clemency rates vary from AMS to AMS. From 1991 to 2016, Thailand reportedly gave clemency to 95% of those on death row (after exhausting judicial appeals) yet the figure for Singapore is apparently less than 1% (Pascoe, 2019). In Vietnam, clemency is granted largely based on utility, such as building good relations with foreign governments concerning foreign convicts; rewarding death convicts for providing intel on accomplices; or retrospectively applying the reduction of death penalty offences (Pascoe, 2017).

The suspension of executions (i.e. a moratorium) in a retentionist country is considered to be important progress in the abolition of the death penalty. Specifically, a 10-year halt in executions is considered a major turning point in the protection of the right to life and the eventual abolition of the death penalty by a state. The use of the death penalty is becoming increasingly restrained in some retentionist countries within ASEAN. The last known executions in Lao PDR and Myanmar were in 1988. Other countries could be in a good position to move towards a moratorium (e.g. Indonesia) and the new government elected in Malaysia in 2018 had stated plans to abolish the death penalty for all crimes and halt the 1,200 pending executions (Aljazeera, 2018). One ASEAN country recently re-started using the death penalty after having previously suspended the practice for a long period; Thailand was in its ninth year of a de facto moratorium and nearing the goal of abolition until June 2018 with the execution of 26-year-old Teerasak Longji (Agerholme, 2018). Following his death, public opinion polls in Thailand showed an approval rating for capital punishment of 90% for 'cruel murders' (FIDH, 2018).

As stated, 'limitation to the most serious crimes' is an established principle of international law in relation to the death penalty and the death penalty should not be given for economic crimes, drug-related offences, victimless offences and actions relating to moral values. Yet as shown, some ASEAN retentionist states have a long litany of capital crimes with only the Lao PDR and Vietnam in recent years reducing the categories that can be given the death penalty (although the death penalty for drug trafficking still remains in all countries).

Mandatory death sentence is another manifestation of criminal injustice in relation to the death penalty as it fails to take into consideration mitigating circumstances and allows a judge the option to give a sentence other than death. This point is made clear by the Human Rights Council in relation to the First Optional Protocol to the ICCPR. Mandatory death sentence is still imposed in Brunei, Malaysia,

Myanmar, Thailand and Singapore, for certain types of drug trafficking; murder (Malaysia, Myanmar, Singapore); terrorism-related offences (Malaysia, Singapore); robbery, burglary, treason, kidnapping (Malaysia); military offences, war crimes, crimes against humanity and genocide, piracy (Singapore).[13] Fortunately, there has recently been certain progress in eliminating mandatory death sentences in ASEAN. For example, Malaysia—the ASEAN country with the highest number of crimes that are punished with a mandatory death sentence—is in the process of re-considering the use of the death penalty, initially with the abolition of the mandatory death penalty (Death Penalty News Blogspot, 2021).

Article 6. Para 5 of the ICCPR states that the "Sentence of death shall not be imposed for crimes committed by persons below eighteen years of age and shall not be carried out on pregnant women." In 2012, the UN GA released a report that further clarified that capital punishment should also not be given to persons with mental disabilities. All AMS have legislated against capital punishment for those with mental disabilities, pregnant women and also for juveniles and persons who are under the age of 18 years at the time of the offence (Brunei Darussalam,[14] Indonesia,[15] Laos,[16] Malaysia,[17] Singapore,[18] Thailand[19] and Vietnam[20]). For crimes committed by children that are normally punishable by the death penalty, they are generally replaced by lengthy prison sentences of 10 years or more. However, as birth registration rates are low in ASEAN some offenders may be unable to prove their age then it seems possible that children could face execution in ASEAN. For example, in Indonesia, a National Economic Survey suggested 14% of children under 18 do not have a birth certificate (Wandasari et al., 2021). In 2017 a young convict was given the death penalty but later said that police and members of the justice system forced him to lie about his age. When age determination from a dental examination confirmed he was only 15 years of age, he was reportedly later beaten by the police (Belarminus, 2017). Unfortunately, such criminal injustices related to death penalty cases are clearly present in ASEAN with confessions having been extracted through

[13] See: Cornell Center on the Death Penalty Worldwide, https://www.deathpenaltyworldwide.org/about-us/.

[14] Brunei Darussalam Criminal Procedure Code (Chapter 7) and Syariah Courts Criminal Procedure Code Order 2018 and Children and young Persons Act (Chapter 219).

[15] Indonesia Juvenile Court Law, art. 26, Law No. 3 of 1997, cited in U.N. Human Rights Committee, Consideration of reports submitted by States parties under article 40 of the Covenant: Initial reports of States parties: Indonesia (Advance Version), para. 342, U.N. Doc. CCPR/C/IDN/1, Jan. 19, 2012. Indonesian Working Group on the Advocacy Against Torture (WGAT), Shadow Report, p. 39.

[16] Lao People's Democratic Republic, Penal Law, art. 32, Law No. 12/NA, Nov. 9, 2005.

[17] Penal Code of Malaysia, art. 82, 1936, as amended by Act 574 of 2006.

[18] Criminal Procedure Code of Singapore, sec. 213, Cap. 68, 1985 Rev. Ed., amended by 51 of 2007.

[19] Whilst Thailand had not executed any juveniles since 1990, it was only in 2012 that the law was changed when Thailand withdrew its interpretive declarations to Article 6(5) of the International Covenant on Civil and Political Rights regarding the abolition of the death penalty for persons below the age of 18 at the time of the crime.

[20] Vietnam Penal Code, art. 74(1), Law No. 15/1999/QH10, Dec. 21, 1999, as amended through to Jun. 19, 2009.

torture or other ill-treatment. Similarly, torture has also been reported in Malaysia and Singapore (ADPAN, 2011). In Indonesia, between July 2014 and May 2015, the Commission on the Disappeared and Victims of Violence (KontraS) recorded 84 cases of torture including those involving the death penalty (Cornell Center on the Death Penalty Worldwide, 2018). With respect to Vietnam, the UN Committee Against Torture (UN-CAT) in 2018 raised concerns about "reports of the physical and psychological suffering of persons sentenced to the death penalty as a result of the particularly harsh conditions of their detention that may amount to torture or ill-treatment, including solitary confinement in unventilated cells; inadequate provision of food and drink; being shackled round-the-clock; being subjected to physical abuse; such persons often commit suicide and develop psychological disorders as a result" (CAT, 2018). From elsewhere in the region, other forms of physical and psychological abuse have been reported including sexual abuse, being confined in dark rooms or staying near to the gallows where it was possible to hear executions taking place (see Chapter 4).

The treatment of convicts has multiple implications for their human dignity and the time spent on death row clearly impacts how humane and forbidding the experience is. Whilst some prisoners in ASEAN can languish on death row for up to 10 years or more, the time period between execution order and execution time can vary from just a few hours in Thailand to 72 h in Indonesia, adding mental stress to the prisoners and their families, leaving barely time for final family visits. To avoid unwanted publicity, details and timelines of impending executions are thus kept short and confidential from the public.

ASEAN's more punitive approach to its criminal justice system is interrelated to dimensions of authoritarianism that hold strong in the region. In fact, the 'Asian Values' that leaders in the region still speak of may actually be more of a legacy of past authoritarian rule. Authoritarians expect a high degree of uncritical obedience to authority and its institutionalised laws. Whilst limited research exists on the role of authoritarianism as a root cause of death penalty support, covariates such as religious fundamentalism and political conservatism are found (Stack, 2003). Dimensions of authoritarianism run deep and within penal history, the communal impact of capital punishment served a political function to not only punish but to instill obedience into the public. In Vietnam, the death penalty is openly prized for maintaining social and political stability and order (Luyen, 2019). The death penalty is thus the ultimate expression of State power and authoritarian governments are dominant across ASEAN such as Brunei, Laos, Myanmar, Philippines, Thailand, Vietnam not to mention Cambodia where extrajudicial killings arguably negate the need for legally sanctioned executions. Even Indonesia, Malaysia and Singapore struggle with conservatism and/or maintaining secularism. Notably, whilst capital punishment and other aspects of criminal justice in AMS law exist as a historical colonial import, this has not encouraged governments to throw off the shackles of the past. In fact, the imperial past is still a part of contemporary politics as western countries pressure AMS with threats to trade relations and foreign aid if countries do not give up the death penalty. In what is viewed by AMS as a form of 'neo-colonialism' retaining the death penalty can be perceived as a country's struggle to fight off 'foreign interference' (Simandjuntak, 2015). In Indonesia, the perception of foreign pressure surrounding planned executions of non-nationals led to a Presidential statement on "the sovereignty of our law" and in an attempt to show Indonesia's political strength to Indonesians, for the Home Affairs Minister to state that the UN and foreign governments would not be able to stop the executions (Emont, 2015). What remains to be seen is whether these regimes' positions will soften with time and international pressure, or fuel the resistance of authoritarian governments to limits on their power to punish?

This section has shown that justice and injustice are two sides of the same coin. Notwithstanding one's position over the justness or not of the death penalty as a deprivation of the right to life, in countries where the justice system is flawed, criminal injustice is related to the irreparable aspect of the death penalty and the risk of executing an innocent person. Capital punishment is an important policy for many authoritarian regimes as state interests are accorded higher value than individual interests and rights. Nevertheless, the downward trend of mandatory death sentences, the continuing application of moratoriums in some retentionist countries, and legal reform that reduces the number of crimes eligible for the death penalty could be potential opportunities for promoting abolishment of the death penalty and in reducing injustice in the application of capital punishment in ASEAN in particular.

5 Conclusion

Over the last 60 years, the world has been moving away from a pro-execution mindset, but with limited success in ASEAN. Favouring a retributive approach to its criminal justice in the region and the belief that capital punishment deters crime, it clearly exposes opportunities for future research. For example, could not Life Without Parole (LWP) be a more effective deterrent than a singular effect of execution? To what extent could drug-related crimes be better addressed through improved policing and more intensive law enforcement and sentencing of drug traffickers to disrupt drug sellers? Why is public opinion in overwhelming support for the death penalty despite the lack of evidence of its effectiveness in fighting crime? Politicians assert they listen to the voice of the people and are happy to curry political favour in order to be seen as 'tough on crime'. More in-depth research on public opinion, as seen by more recent surveys undertaken in Malaysia, Thailand, Singapore and the Philippines (Girelli, 2019), would expose the nuanced misunderstandings and myths that exist due to the public's lack of knowledge of capital punishment beyond the superficial media headlines around crime and statements from politicians. Under the guise of 'public order' and 'national stability', AMS take a very broad view of what counts as 'most serious crimes' meriting the death penalty. Research to establish whether capital punishment actually contributes towards the reduction of these criminal acts is only starting to gain momentum in the region (Purba et al., 2020). The relationship between religious belief and support for the death penalty also requires further study as religion is a significant factor that influences people's acceptance or rejection of the death penalty. Rather than being an 'Asian Value', the death penalty is actually anathema to the philosophical and religious doctrine in the region.

With no executions recorded across ASEAN during the COVID pandemic in 2020 and bearing in mind that at least half of the eight AMS allowing capital punishment have been continuing to practice de facto moratoriums, abolitionists may optimistically argue that these curbs are a step in the right direction. However, whilst a country like Indonesia has not executed anyone since 2016, increasing numbers of people have been steadily given the death sentence—in 2019 up by 67% from the year before (Strangio, 2020). Conspicuously, extensive media coverage has led some to believe that the issue of the death penalty is more about fighting off 'foreign pressure' and boosting the government's popularity whilst distracting from other issues (Simandjuntak, 2015). Authoritarianism imbedded in many countries in the Asia region has sustained "the belief that common people can be made to obey the law only through fear instilled by harsh punishment" (Justice Project Pakistan, 2019). Showing political strength is becoming a popular strategy to demonstrate state power. Governments in Southeast Asia thus build their own constructions of the 'most serious crimes' leading to a large array of crimes punishable by the death penalty. 'Legal sovereignty' is an image important to many AMS who want to shake off the colonial shackles of the past and show that they are their own masters with their own values. Yet not bending to the global trend as a rejection of neo-colonialism is ironic in light of the colonial history that introduced the laws in the first place.

Finally, such an entrenched approach to the use of capital punishment in ASEAN should not detract from the real concerns over the quality of the judicial systems found in the region that make use of this ultimate punishment. It, therefore, remains critical to ensure that over the coming years, the small steps of progress towards a reduction in the use of the death penalty seen over recent years are not undone.

References

ADPAN. (2011). When justice fails: Thousands executed in Asia after unfair trials. Amnesty International. https://www.amnesty.org/en/documents/asa01/023/2011/en/. Accessed 26 December 2021.

Agerholme, H. (2018). Thailand uses lethal injection to execute first prisoner in nearly a decade. *The Independent*. https://www.independent.co.uk/news/world/asia/thailand-execution-death-penalty-lethal-injection-amnesty-international-a8405711.html. Accessed 15 September 2021.

AICHR. (2009). 2009 ASEAN Intergovernmental Commission on Human Rights (Terms of reference). https://aichr.org/wp-content/uploads/2020/02/TOR-of-AICHR.pdf. Accessed 4 October 2021.

AICHR. (2020a). Thematic study on the right to life: Protection of the rights of personas convicted of the death penalty, Malaysia country report [Unpublished].

AICHR. (2020b). Thematic study on the right to life: Protection of the rights of personas convicted of the death penalty, Myanmar country report [Unpublished].

AICHR. (2020c). Thematic study on the right to life: Protection of the rights of personas convicted of the death penalty, Singapore country report [Unpublished].

AICHR. (2020d). Thematic study on the right to life: Protection of the rights of personas convicted of the death penalty, Lao PDR country report [Unpublished].
AICHR. (2020e). Thematic study on the right to life: Protection of the rights of personas convicted of the death penalty, Thailand country report [Unpublished].
AICHR. (2020f). Thematic study on the right to life: Protection of the rights of personas convicted of the death penalty. Cambodia country report [Unpublished].
AICHR. (2020g). Thematic study on the right to life: Protection of the rights of personas convicted of the death penalty, The Philippines country report [Unpublished].
Aljazeera. (2018, October 11). Malaysia to abolish the death penalty. https://www.aljazeera.com/news/2018/10/malaysia-abolish-death-penalty-181011083607761.html. Accessed 26 December 2021.
Amnesty International. (2012, October 10). Indonesia: ADPAN case on Zulfiqar. https://www.amnesty.org/en/documents/ASA21/024/2012/en/. Accessed 26 December 2021.
Amnesty International. (2021). Amnesty international global report: Death, sentences and executions 2020. www.amnesty.org.au/death-penalty-report-2020/. Accessed 26 December 2021.
Balakrishnan, V. (2016). Intervention at the high-level side event at the UN General Assembly, "Moving away from the death penalty: victims and the death penalty." Ministry of Foreign Affairs, Singapore. https://www.mfa.gov.sg/Newsroom/Press-Statements-Transcripts-and-Photos/2016/09/MFA-Press-Release-Transcript-of-Minister-Vivian-Balakrishnans-Intervention-at-the-HighLevel-Side-Eve. Accessed 26 December 2021.
BBC. (2019, April 12). Brunei says controversial Sharia law aimed at 'prevention'. https://www.bbc.com/news/world-asia-47906070. Accessed 15 September 2021.
BBC. (2020). Philippines Death Penalty: A fight to stop the return of capital punishment, news report dated 16 August 2020. https://www.bbc.com/news/world-asia-53762570. Accessed 17 January 2023.
Belarminus, R. (2017, August 23). Kisah Yusman, Mantan Terpidana di Bwah Umur yang mengaku kena rekayasa. *Kompas*. https://nasional.kompas.com/read/2017/08/23/12060601/kisah-yusman-mantan-terpidana-mati-di-bawah-umur-yang-mengaku-kena-rekayasa?page=all. Accessed 26 December 2021.
CAT. (2018). Concluding observations: Vietnam, CAT/C/VNM/CO/1. https://atlas-of-torture.org/en/document/urrka70n92?page=1. Accessed 26 December 2021.
Chen, S. (2014). Case note: Singapore's new discretionary death penalty for drug couriers: Public Prosecutor v Chum Tat Suan. *The International Journal of Evidence and Proof, 18*(3), 260–266. https://doi.org/10.1350/ijep.2014.18.3.456
CNN Philippines. (2019). Catholic church vs. reimposition of death penalty: Solons should work for the people, not Duterte. http://cnnphilippines.com/news/2019/7/24/Death-penalty-drugs-plunder.html. Accessed 4 October 2021.
Cornell Center on the Death Penalty Worldwide. (2018). Justice denied: A global study of wrongful death row convictions. https://files.deathpenaltyinfo.org/legacy/files/pdf/innocence_clinic_report_2018_R4_final.pdf. Accessed 26 December 2021.
Death Penalty News Blogspot. (2021, June 13). Malaysia | Mandatory death penalty still being meted out for drug offences. https://deathpenaltynews.blogspot.com/2021/06/malaysia-mandatory-death-penalty-still.html. Accessed 26 December 2021.
Degenhardt, L., Chiu, W., Sampson, N., Kessler, R. C., Anthony, J. C., Angermeyer, M., de Bruffaerts, R., Girolamo, G., Gureje, O., Huang, Y., Karam, A., Kostyuchenko, S., Lepine, J. P., Mora, M. E. M., Neumark, Y., Ornell, J. H., Pinto-Meza, A., Posada-Villa, J., Stein, D. J., & Wells, J. E. (2008). Towards a global view of alcohol, tobacco, cannabis and cocaine use: Findings from the WHO world mental health surveys. *PLoS Medicine, 5*(7), 1053–1067. https://doi.org/10.1371/journal.pmed.0050141
Elemia, C. (2017). Pacquiao defends death penalty: Even Jesus was sentenced to death. *Rappler*. https://www.rappler.com/nation/manny-pacquiao-death-penalty-jesus-christ. Accessed 26 December 2021.

Emont, J. (2015, May 1). Welcome to Indonesia, death penalty for drug traffickers!. *The New Republic*. https://newrepublic.com/article/121692/indonesia-executes-bali-nine-duo-despite-australian-outcry. Accessed 26 December 2021.

FIDH. (2018, October 10). Thailand: Still dragging fee on death penalty. https://www.fidh.org/en/issues/death-penalty/thailand-suffered-a-massive-setback-on-the-road-to-the-abolition-of. Accessed 26 December 2021.

Girelli, G. (2019, October 17). The death penalty for drugs: What public opinion surveys in Asia teach us. *FILTER*. https://filtermag.org/death-penalty-drugs-public-opinion-asia/. Accessed 26 December 2021.

Harm Reduction International. (2021). The death penalty for drug offences: Global overview 2020. http://files.idpc.net/library/HRI_Global_Overview_2020_web_final.pdf. Accessed 5 October 2021.

Hutt, D. (2017, April 20). Beware Vietnam's death machine. The Diplomat. https://thediplomat.com/2017/04/beware-vietnams-death-machine/. Accessed 26 December 2021.

Johnson, D., & Zimring, F. (2009). *The next frontier: National development, political change, and the death penalty in Asia*. Oxford University Press.

Justice Project Pakistan. (2019). The death penalty law exploited by the British for oppression is still being used in Pakistan. Scroll.in. https://scroll.in/article/930053/the-death-penalty-law-exploited-by-the-british-for-oppression-is-still-being-used-in-pakistan#:~:text=The%20primary%20justification%20of%20the%20death%20penalty%20itself,law%20only%20through%20fear%20instilled%20by%20harsh%20punishment%E2%80%9D. Accessed 26 December 2021.

Leechainan, Y., & Longmire, D. (2013). The use of the death penalty for drug trafficking in the United States, Singapore, Malaysia, Indonesia and Thailand: A Comparative Legal Analysis. *Laws*, *2*(2), 115–149. https://doi.org/10.3390/laws2020115

Limpot, K (2020), 'Duterte calls for revival of death penalty by lethal injection for drug-related crimes' CNN Philippines. http://cnnphilippines.com/news/2020/7/27/Duterte-death-penalty-revival-fifth-SONA.html. Accessed 15 September 2021.

Luyen, T. V. (2019). Capital punishment in Vietnam, a study from the perspective of traditional and modern values. *The Journal of Middle East and North Africa Sciences*, *5*(6). https://www.jomenas.org/2019--vol5-06-.html. Accessed 15 September 2021.

Odchigue, B., & Sobradil, M. (2019, August 28–29). Perceptions of the registered voters on the re-imposition of death penalty in the Philippines [Conference Proceedings]. The 9th International Conference on Public Organisation, Asia Pacific Society for Public Affairs (APSA), Khon Kaen, Thailand.

Pascoe, D. (2017). The functions of death penalty clemency in Southeast Asia: Comparative lessons for Vietnam. ALC Briefing Paper 7.

Pascoe, D. (2019). Last chance for life: Clemency in Southeast Asia death penalty cases. *Oxford Scholarship Online*. https://doi.org/10.1093/oso/9780198809715.001.0001

Purba, N., Tanjung, A., Sulistyawati, S., Pramono, R., & Purwanto, A. (2020). Death penalty and human rights in Indonesia. *International Journal of Criminology and Sociology*, *9*, 1356–1362.

Sader, G., Girelli G., & Fenandez, A. C. (2020). The death penalty for drug offences: Global overview 2019. Harm Reduction International.

Simandjuntak, D. (2015). Spectacle of the scaffold? The politics of death penalty in Indonesia. Perspective. ISEAS Yusof Ishak Institute. https://www.iseas.edu.sg/images/pdf/ISEAS_Perspective_2015_46.pdf. Accessed 26 December 2021.

Stack, S. (2003). Authoritarianism and support for the death penalty: A multivariate analysis. *Sociological Facus*, *36*(4), 333–352.

Straits Times. (2017, March 28). Indonesia's president Joko Widodo says open to death penalty review. *The Straits Times*. https://www.straitstimes.com/asia/se-asia/indonesias-presdent-joko-widodo-says-open-to-death-penalty-review. Accessed 26 December 2021.

Strangio, S. (2020, November 20). Explaining Southeast Asia's addiction to the death penalty. The Diplomat. https://thediplomat.com/2020/11/explaining-southeast-asias-addiction-to-the-death-penalty/. Accessed 26 December 2021.

UNGA. (2020). UN General Assembly Resolution 75/183. *Moratorium on the use of the death penalty,* A/RES/75/183 (16 December 2020). https://undocs.org/en/A/RES/75/183. Accessed 15 September 2021.

UNODC. (2020). Intentional murder data retrieved from the UNODC statistical database. https://data.unodc.org/#ste:0. Accessed 26 December 2021.

Wandasari W., Kusumaningrum, S., & Sari W. (2021, April 21). The unregistered: The fragile foundations of civil registration in Indonesia. The Conversation. https://theconversation.com/the-unregistered-the-fragile-foundations-of-civil-registration-in-indonesia-158434. Accessed 26 December 2021.

Mark P. Capaldi PhD, is a lecturer at the Institute of Human Rights and Peace Studies at Mahidol University. Much of Mark P. Capaldi's work has been in South and East Asia, where he has lived for 30 years when he worked with the International NGOs Concern Worldwide, PACT Inc., Save the Children UK and ECPAT International. As Deputy Director of ECPAT International (2001–2011), he worked to end the commercial sexual exploitation and trafficking of children, supporting a wide range of programming and advocacy in all regions of the world. From 2011 to 2018, he took on the role of ECPAT's global Head of Research and Policy.

Mark P. Capaldi has a doctorate degree with the Institute of Human Rights and Peace Studies at Mahidol University, Bangkok; the research topic of his dissertation was children's agency within independent child migration in Thailand. Other recent research areas have included a 10 countries study on the death penalty in ASEAN and also the issue of religions and its impact on sexuality within Southeast Asia.

Fact or Fiction? Deconstructing the Death Penalty as a Deterrent to Crime in ASEAN

Mark P. Capaldi

Abstract A review of the global literature and research on the effectiveness of the death penalty as a deterrent show that both sides of the argument can come to varying conclusions. Within ASEAN, research and data on the use of the death penalty are especially problematic resulting in politicians being influenced more by perceptions and public opinion rather than evidence-based fact. Based upon an in-depth literature review of secondary data, this paper, therefore, looks at the various theories of deterrence for capital crimes and deconstructs them within the context of ASEAN. It argues that the theories and assumptions popular in the region in support of capital punishment are on shaky ground and that the crime rates in ASEAN retentionist countries for a number of offences suggest a much weaker prospect for effective deterrence. The paper concludes with a philosophical argument: given the lack of any evidence and the extreme severity of the punishment, then the issue of it being a deterrent should be removed from any discussion of the death penalty in ASEAN.

1 Introduction

There is no shortage of research that claims both sides of the argument on whether the death penalty is an effective deterrent to serious crime. However, these studies are predominantly carried out in the United States, are primarily examining only the capital crime of homicide and virtually all can be critiqued or undermined due to technical and conceptual interpretations. For ASEAN, there is very little published research or empirical studies on the death penalty as a deterrent. The design of scientific research is made particularly difficult due to the wide spectrum of death-eligible offences in the region and the challenges in identifying and collecting reliable measures and crime statistics.

M. P. Capaldi (✉)
Institute of Human Rights and Peace Studies, Mahidol University, Phutthamonthon, Thailand
e-mail: mark.cap@mahidol.edu

S. Petcharamesree et al. (eds.), *Unpacking the Death Penalty in ASEAN*,
https://doi.org/10.1007/978-981-19-8840-0_2

In ASEAN (where eight out of 10 Member States retain the death penalty), deterrence[1] is one of the fundamental justifications for its use. In Indonesia, for example, deterrence is the central explanation for the death penalty for offences such as intentional murder, terrorism, drug trafficking and firearm offences amongst others (Fagan, 2019). Even under Article 1 of Law No. 21 (1959), the threat and fear of the death penalty for economic crimes was aimed at 'deterrence of corruption and other economic crimes' (ICJR, 2017). States also view capital punishment as retribution for crimes that cause specific harms or as a measure to incapacitate serious offenders (Fagan, 2019). In certain countries in the region such as Vietnam, the value of the death sentence is seen as helping to maintain social order and a stable political structure (Luyen, 2019).

Public belief in capital punishment in ASEAN is presumed to be high and politicians look to this to support its continued use. For example, in 2016, Singapore's Foreign Minister V. Balakrishnan stated that "there is very high levels of support on the part of our people for the death penalty to remain on our books" (Balakrishnan, 2016). Being seen to be tough on crime is used as a strong deterrent argument where societies wish to deter heinous or serious crimes and in the Philippines, this is currently being touted by certain politicians to bring back the death penalty (De Ungria & Jose, 2019). In Thailand, Malaysia and Singapore, polls have consistently shown that these retentionist countries have some of the highest public approval rates for the use of the death penalty globally (Chan et al., 2018; Hood, 2013; Likhitpreechakul, 2013). The issues then are: (i) is there a clear justification for the use of the death penalty? (ii) what is the evidence that the death penalty actually deters crimes? and (iii) is the death penalty as a deterrent more effective than other forms of punishment?

As with any controversial subject, there are two sides to the coin of whether the death penalty leads to a crime deterrent effect. The majority of retentionists *for* capital punishment believe that the basic fear of death generally deters people from committing serious crimes and that the best line of defence against these grave offences is the harshest of punishments. The Singapore Foreign Minister referenced above also went on to say in 2016 "In our view, capital punishment for drug-related offences and for murder has been a key element in keeping Singapore drug free and keeping Singapore safe" (Balakrishnan, 2016). In 2019, Senator Ronald 'Bato' dela Rosa of the Philippines went further by proposing that criminals guilty of drug trafficking should be executed in public as a deterrent (Ariate, 2019). In other words, those that commit a death-eligible offence deserve harsh penalties and thus would themselves decide to refrain from committing such a crime (Odchigue & Sobradil, 2019). Whilst proponents of the death penalty can cite key research that supports these claims, they may equally also argue that doubts about robustness of deterrence evidence should not stand in the way of executions if there is the possibility of saving more lives of innocent victims (Kirchgässner, 2011a, 2011b). Life imprisonment is

[1] The two countries that have abolished the death penalty are Cambodia and the Philippines (although in the latter, some politicians are calling for its return).

expensive they contend and the money could be better spent on helping victims' families.

The obvious argument *against* the deterrent effect is that many capital crimes are carried out in the heat of the moment with no rational thinking. Furthermore, the death penalty for political crimes and terrorism could also have the opposite effect by creating martyrs leading to further upheaval. Dr. Ahmad Sofian from Bina Nusantara University in Indonesia argues that there are those who want to be put to death because of the ideologies they embrace (Henschke & Nurdin, 2020; Rusito & Suwardi, 2019).[2] Interestingly, religious arguments can be used to justify or argue against capital punishment; Islam allows the death penalty—although Islamic law is said to prioritise repentance and forgiveness (Arifin, 2015) whilst Christianity and Buddhism have mixed doctrines in relation to the death penalty.[3]

To accurately assess the deterrent effects of the death penalty (as well as comparatively with other punishments) different data sets using various statistical models, across different institutions need to be generated. This information is lacking across Southeast Asia and so skepticism of the assumptions and data around the use of the death penalty in ASEAN is growing. In 2015, Indonesian academics and criminologists voiced concerns that unreliable data was being used to legitimise capital punishment (Simandjuntak, 2015). A study commissioned by the Singapore government in October 2016 indicated 80% support for the retention of the death penalty whilst in a December 2016 study carried out by the National University of Singapore, support for the death penalty ranged from between 56–32% for different crimes (Chan et al., 2018). As such, public opinion on the death penalty is often based on an incomplete understanding of the facts, simplistic poll questions or can be influenced by media headlines of sensational crimes. It has been shown however that the more people know about the full range of facts surrounding the use of the death penalty, the less strong is their support for it (Chan et al., 2018; The Council of Europe, 2010).

Within ASEAN, the deterrence issue remains a topic of sensitive and polarizing debate. This chapter, therefore, aims to ascertain if there is sufficient evidence-base and logic as to whether or not the death penalty is an effective deterrent. A detailed review of the literature and secondary data has been undertaken (including scholarly articles, International Organisations and INGO reports and media stories from the region) where relevant information can be found. Unfortunately, specific information related to the death penalty is not widely available across all countries in ASEAN that

[2] This BBC World Service article by Henschke and Nurdin (2020) describes the meeting (in prison) between a terrorist who killed several people in 2004 near the Australian embassy in Jakarta and family members of one of the victims of the terrorist attack whereby the defendant waved his fist after the guilty verdict was announced, declaiming, "*I am thankful for being sentenced to death... because I will die a martyr*!".

[3] In Christianity, the Old Testament in the book of Exodus, chapter 21, verses 23–36 states "But if there is any further injury, then you shall appoint as a penalty life for life, eye for eye, tooth for tooth, hand for hand, foot for foot, burn for burn, wound for wound, bruise for bruise." Whilst Buddhism is founded on a principle of 'non-violence' some Buddhist scholars have found textual justification for the death penalty in the Buddhist Cannon. Others argue that in the teachings of the Buddha, the death penalty is rejected more explicitly than in other major world religions.

retain the death penalty; some countries feature more prominently due to the higher rates of execution (e.g. Singapore, Indonesia, Malaysia) whereas others have de facto moratoriums (e.g. Brunei, Lao PDR, Myanmar). Nevertheless, as detailed in the following section of this paper, for an array of reasons, the evidence to irrefutably back up either side of the deterrent argument is clearly lacking. Regardless, acknowledging the extent of unsubstantiated research on both sides of the argument is not going to influence ASEAN policymakers in making more informed decisions about the deterrent effects of capital sanctions, so the third and fourth sections of the chapter go on to examine the theories around deterrence for capital crimes. The chapter then deconstructs these various theoretical models and concludes with a clear philosophical argument: if there is no evidence of deterrence, then the issue of deterrence should not be used in arguments to justify the death penalty given the lack of reliable evidence.

2 The Technical and Conceptual Errors Plaguing the Statistical Research

With 106 countries around the world having already abolished the death penalty by the end of 2019 (Amnesty International, 2020), it might be reasonably assumed that data exists to assess the effect of any deterrent by comparing with retentionist countries. However, the effectiveness of the death penalty as a deterrent to serious crime, despite decades of empirical studies, remains inconclusive. There are plenty of academic papers that claim some degree of deterrent effects[4] whilst an equal number fail to provide such evidence and assert capital punishment does not work as a deterrent[5]; others claim a mixture of findings depending upon the frequency of execution and the concerned crimes (Shepherd, 2005).

The occurrence of disparate results for these studies is actually not surprising. One of the more informative reviews of panel data literature on the issue was undertaken by Durlauf et al. (2011, p. 487) and they stated:

> Social scientists have long understood that the data 'do not speak for themselves' and so empirical analyses that involve substantive social science questions such as the measurement of deterrence, can only do so conditional on the choice of a statistical model.

Here lays the first problem. Incongruent research on the death penalty as a deterrent is the norm, as studies, when critiqued, have often been found to have used

[4] See studies such as Zimmerman (2004, 2009), Gius (2015), Battiston and Vidal (n.d.), and Dezhbakhsh et al. (n.d.) to reference pro-deterrence research.

[5] See studies such as Donohue and Wolfers (2010), Abdorrahman Boroumand Center (2018), Muramatsu et al. (2018), Brandt and Kovandzic (2015), National Research Council. (2012), Chalfin et al. (2013), Nagin (2014), Kirchgässner (2011a, 2011b), Gerritzen and Kirchgässner (2016) to reference against deterrence or stressing the inconclusive nature of most research. Most of these studies say that existing research is inconclusive. The key message is: *results ought not to be used to influence policy decisions regarding the appropriateness of the death penalty and the deterrence argument can no longer be used to defend the use of the death penalty.*

incomplete or even implausible data models and statistical analyses. Understanding criminal behaviour is complex as deterrents to various crimes cannot be assessed using unitary measures; relevant additional factors may include police effectiveness but also social, economic, or political aspects that are outside the criminal justice system. For example, if studying the deterrent effects of the death penalty on drug crimes, then data collection and analysis need to be on various levels such as individual indicators (e.g. drug use, drug types, drug selling, links to other crimes) and on aggregate effects of the death penalty, e.g. on drug use, drug types, drug trafficking and other crimes (Fagan, 2019). Furthermore, the death penalty cannot be the only factor in decreasing a particular crime as there can be others as issues such as policing and the efficacy of the criminal justice system also have an impact.[6] Similarly, the existing studies do not factor in the effects of noncapital punishments that could be used as alternatives, i.e. there is a difficulty in isolating deterrent effects of a single component of any sanction regime. The choice of variables or coefficients that a study measures (or an analyst assumes as relevant), plays a fundamental role in determining whether deterrence effects are concluded as positive or negative.

Here rests the second challenge. The multiple baseline datasets required for deterrence analysis simply do not exist (or are not accurate) in many countries, including in ASEAN (UNODC, 2019). They may be maintained by different institutions, not centralised or are simply not collected accurately. Furthermore, in many countries in the region, there is a lack of official, transparent and public data. In some ASEAN Member States (AMS), the exact number of death sentences remains a state secret (Vietnam) whilst in others, the information is not readily or publicly made available, such as in Malaysia and Singapore. In the Lao PDR, due to tight government control, information of people on death row is not released.

One regional study that tried to ascertain any deterrent effect of capital punishment that deserves special mention is that of Zimring et al. In 2010 they compared homicide levels in two comparable cities: Hong Kong which abolished the death penalty in 1993 (although the last execution had been in 1966) and Singapore whose execution rates up till that time were considered high (Zimring et al., 2010). Both jurisdictions have similarities in demography, culture, history, economics as well as population growth and density. The study tried to overcome the difficulties in accessing data on executions from the Singapore government by using responses the state had given to refute figures claimed by Amnesty International. The researchers justified and examined estimated data versus actual executions which were felt to well reflect trends of actual state executions. By conducting a series of regression analyses, homicide levels were shown to be remarkably similar in both cities over a 35-year

[6] See problems related to statistics in *Deterrence and the Death Penalty* by National Research Council (2012). The study identifies three major shortcomings summarised in the brief by the National Academies (2012, pp. 2–3): (i) The studies do not factor in the effects of noncapital punishments that may also be imposed; (ii) The studies use incomplete or implausible models of potential murderers' perceptions of and response to the use of capital punishment; (iii) Estimates of the effect of capital punishment are based on statistical models that make assumptions that are not credible.

period.[7] Furthermore, neither the surge in Singapore executions (around 1995) nor the later reduction in execution rates appeared to produce any differential impact.

To conclude, it is clear that existing scientific studies support both sides of the debate and many explanations can be used to conclude whether the death penalty does or does not deter certain crimes. Depending upon your stance, it is possible to select from the research one way or another and counter-arguments over which position is right are masked by complex statistical models that few can understand. As such, having considered the arguments for and against the death penalty as a deterrent and the statistical and data difficulties in measuring its effectiveness, it seems unlikely that the existing research will sway policymakers either way. At best, the statistical research is inconclusive and within ASEAN has hardly been attempted.[8] It is therefore necessary to turn the debate to the deterrent concepts and theories around the use of the death penalty.

3 The Theoretical Models of Deterrence for Capital Crimes

The dominant, historical notion has always been that the fear of a certain punishment can reduce or eliminate unacceptable behaviour.[9] The deterrence or preventative theory of punishment can be traced back to the early works of classical philosophers such as Thomas Hobbes (1588–1678), Cesare Beccaria (1738–1794), and Jeremy Bentham (1748–1832). The theory of deterrence that has developed from these philosophers is built on the premise that for a deterrent to crime to work, the punishment must be administered with 'severity, certainty and celerity'. The death penalty is perceived as a 'general deterrent', i.e. designed to prevent crime in the general population by targeting those who have yet to commit criminal acts by making them fearful of the consequences of their action.[10] The more severe and fearful the punishment, the more likely that people will desist from criminal acts; too mild and it will not deter. If pain and suffering are what most people fear and if human life is what they value the most, then execution can be presumed as a terrifying option. Historically, to drive the deterrent message home, executions in many

[7] The study noted that they did not use a theoretical model to predict the nonpenal social and economic determinants of variations in homicide as it was considered too complex and implausible.

[8] Although at the time of writing this paper, The Death Penalty Project (DPP) with the support of global experts on the capital punishment (Professor Carolyn Hoyle of the University of Oxford and Professor Jeffrey Fagan of Columbia University) and in partnership with academic partners in Indonesia, is carrying out research into the deterrent effects of the death penalty in Indonesia. See: Fagan (2019).

[9] Note that from the wider theories of justice and punishment (i.e. retribution, deterrence, incapacitation, rehabilitation), for the purposes of this paper, the issue of deterrence is the sole focus.

[10] A 'specific deterrent' is designed to stop criminals re-committing a crime. Clearly this is not valid in the case of the death penalty but is the theory behind other sanctions such as corporal punishment.

places around the world were often held in public so that people were clearly able to see what happens to those who carried out certain crimes.[11]

Theorists concerned with deterrence believe that if a punishment is seen to be certain, severe and swift, then a rational person will weigh up the gains against the risks before choosing whether to violate the law. This links deterrence and rational choice theories which in the context of lawbreaking presume criminals to be rational actors who consciously weigh up their decisions. However, many critics argue that in death penalty crimes committed 'in the heat of the moment', crimes of passion or those committed under the influence of substances, offenders are not thinking rationally and their actions are not influenced by a coherent risk–benefit analysis. As imperfect as the use of rational choice theories may be in certain contexts, it still makes up the bedrock of criminal justice systems the world over.

When examining criminal justice systems, the theory of crime, therefore, becomes pertinent as support for capital punishment in this context is based largely on the reasons why crimes are being committed. The noted French sociologist Emile Durkheim (1858–1917), theorised that crime was 'normal' and even necessary in order for society to function well, as criminal activities helped "reinforce social stability by clarifying social norms and uniting conventional society against deviants who are punished" (Durkheim, 1933, p. 104). This thinking stems from conflict theory used by Karl Marx which positions the criminal justice system as reflecting the values or interest of a more powerful group in society over others (Barkan, 1997). It could be argued that within Southeast Asia, this doctrine is additionally solidified through the 'Asian Values' discourse[12] which forms the foundation of certain political approaches of countries in the region. The traditions, culture and values of paternalism and Confucianism found in Southeast Asia strongly emphasise respect for authority and the expectation that citizens should adhere to the laws. Conversely, the people assume their governments to set rules and maintain the stability and prosperity of the nation, including the administration of appropriately tough punishments to deter crimes. This justice model is meant to ensure that the 'punishment fits the crime' and satisfies the public's expectation that the criminal is fittingly punished. Although the concept of *Lex Talionis* or 'an eye for an eye' has retributive aspects to it, the principle also suggests that those who go forward to commit a death-eligible offence should expect the harshest of penalties. By understanding that it is 'just' means it becomes a rational deterrent as would-be offenders could thus decide to refrain from committing the worst of crimes.

Applications within ASEAN for the use of capital punishment for various crimes such as drug trafficking or corruption have led to certain economic theories of deterrence. The theory is that offenders weigh up the economic benefits of say drug use or trafficking which are valued against the risks and punishments associated with

[11] Public executions are still carried out in some parts of the world (Amnesty International has cited Iran, N. Korea and Saudi Arabia, not to mention public executions carried out by non-state actors such as ISIS).

[12] A set of values, promoted by some regional leaders in the latter part of the twentieth century which prioritised discipline, hard work, deference to authority and balancing individual and societal needs.

the criminal act and the likelihood of being caught. In these cases, deterrence is a component to be managed within a context of net cost and economic gain. Fagan propositions that there is potential for a deeper analysis of the 'perceived net costs' in light of the health costs, risks to offender's employment and family lives and eventual legal costs that come with say drug use and trafficking but this has yet to be reflected in existing deterrence studies (Fagan, 2019).

Whatever deterrence theory is preferred, to varying degrees they remain the foundation for criminal law and criminal justice systems within Southeast Asia. The belief that sanctions deter criminals continues to influence the popularity of capital punishment in the region, despite the lack of empirical evidence. However, the merits of the philosophical ideas of the deterrence doctrine soon unravel once the realities of its application within the ASEAN region are analysed in more depth.

4 Theories and Arguments that De-construct the Deterrence Position

As mentioned in the introductory section of this chapter, within a number of political regimes found in Southeast Asia, whatever the crime, e.g. murder, drug trafficking or terrorism, the belief in capital punishments' deterrence is steadfast. Yet not all supporters of the death penalty within the general public are equally enamored with the deterrent effect. In a study in Singapore in 2002, '40% of death penalty supporters did not think that the death penalty prevents future crimes' (Ng Thiam Tuan, 2002). A 2013 survey in Malaysia suggested there was minimal opposition to abolishing at least the *mandatory* death penalty and that overall, support for the death penalty for murder was lower than previously presumed.[13]

Fagan (2019) states that from a detailed examination of the empirical research on deterrence, there are three preconditions of prior decision-making for criminal activities that are necessary for a deterrent to be real: (i) knowledge of punishments and their implications; (ii) rationality in choosing to commit a crime or not; and (iii) perceived net cost of the benefit versus the likelihood of being caught, convicted and the severity and certainty of the sentence (Fagan, 2019). In the following section these will be examined in the context of ASEAN along with further ways of assessing the theoretical justifications for capital punishment as an effective deterrent.

From the onset, the strength of the reasoning of deterrence theories across some of the retentionist countries in ASEAN is already on shaky ground. In light of the concepts of severity, certainty and celerity, long-standing moratoriums on the use of capital punishment in Laos, Myanmar and Brunei cannot meaningfully contribute to the claims that the death penalty deters.[14] Thailand had refrained from carrying out

---

[13] See: the Death Penalty Project (2013).

[14] Lao PDR and Myanmar have had moratoriums on the use of the death penalty for more than 30 years. The last execution in Brunei was reportedly in 1957.

any executions for nine years until 2018 when there was an unexpected execution.[15] This is relevant because a compelling argument for the deterrent effect of the death penalty is that it is less about the severity but more about the certainty and promptness of the punishment which reduces crime.[16] Of the remaining countries in ASEAN, Singapore is perhaps the better fit to test the theory of deterrence as there is greater certainty of punishment and speed of administration; homicide trials are disposed of quite quickly and death penalty appeal processes generally completed within 18 months of conviction (Zimring et al., 2010). However, as already mentioned in the introductory section, a 2010 study of Singapore does not confirm a deterrent effect. Furthermore, different data collected by the UN Office on Drugs and Crime for Singapore between the period 2003–2015 also showed no apparent correlation between execution trends and murder rates (UNODC, n.d.).

4.1 Knowledge and Understanding of Implications of the Law

A key assumption of deterrence theories is that the offender knows and understands the implications of the law. Studies on deterrence have paid little attention to where, how and to what extent criminals acquire and process such information. Suggesting that newspaper stories or media reports of executions are influential presumes a level of literacy that is not certain amongst the more socio-economically disadvantaged inmates who end up on death row.

In 2017, Amnesty International studied the socio-economic backgrounds of those individuals in Singapore sentenced to death finding that most were either unemployed or unskilled workers. They generally cited having financial problems and required state-appointed counsel for all or parts of their criminal proceedings (Amnesty International, 2017). In other cases, offenders (particularly in the case of women) often claimed that even if they had known they were couriering packages, they had not checked or been aware of the contents. In Malaysia, foreign nationals on death row have been found to exhibit similar factors, for example; socio-economic difficulties, they don't speak the language of the country or are not fluent, and they are not clear on the laws and procedures in place (CND, 2019). In these cases, the presumption of knowledge is under dispute suggesting that those from marginalised and disadvantaged socio-economic contexts are at higher risk of receiving the death penalty but less likely to be influenced by general deterrence approaches.

Some studies have any way suggested that publicising information about executions does not deter crimes or, if they do, it is only in the very short term.[17] An

[15] Theerasak Longji (26 years old) was executed in 2018. See: Human Rights Watch (2018).

[16] This was the key argument of the nineteenth century philosopher Cesare Beccaria. See Beccaria (1819) cited in Likhitpreechakul (2013).

[17] See: Chan and Oxley (2004, p. 9) and Hjalmarsson (2009) on public awareness. This is also mentioned by Fagan to disprove the validity of this argument in relation to the Bali 9 case (ABC News, 2015).

illustrative example is given when in 2014, a warden at the Nusakambangan Prison in Indonesia was detained for a narcotic crime despite only months earlier executions having taken place (ICJR, 2017). In Thailand, the execution of Theerasak Longji occurred in June 2018 after a long period of non–executions and was largely publicised (Agerholm, 2018). However, it does not seem to have deterred criminals as in the months afterwards numerous arrests for drug-related offences continued to be made (AAITF, 2018; THE NATION, 2018; Thongtub, 2018).

4.2 The Rational Choices Between Illegal and Legal Behaviour (Challenges to the Rational Choice Theory in the Context of Deterrence)

The most commonly used criticism of deterrence theories in the context of homicide is that it is not a homogenous criminal behaviour. Rational choice theory in the context of deterrence does not adequately cater for unplanned murders or crimes of passion/jealousy. Studies have repeatedly shown that homicide events are generally unintended products of complex social interactions (Fagan, 2005) and that additionally, the presence of firearms, rage or the use of drugs or alcohol compromises reasoning. Within ASEAN countries, there are multiple examples of people sentenced to death for crimes of jealousy (particularly femicide) or whilst under the influence of alcohol or drugs.[18] Furthermore, as seen in the US, half of the capital-eligible homicides committed between 1976 and 2016 were felony murders (robbery homicides) where struggles with weapons or fear of identification instinctively escalated the crime to a death penalty offence (Pierce et al., 2017). Whilst similar statistics in ASEAN countries do not exist, there are cases of people sentenced to death while being involved in robbery that then turned into homicide (NST, 2019a, 2019b). It should also be noted that the UN Special Rapporteur on extrajudicial, summary or arbitrary executions has also stated that the term "most serious crimes" must be restricted to cases of *intentional killing* (Penal Reform International, 2017) whilst in ASEAN countries, capital-eligible crimes include those that are committed without the intent to kill.

In short, the rationality test expects offenders, presuming they're already aware of the risks of detection and punishment, to make a sound decision at the critical moment of a crime. However, the shortcomings in rationality illustrated above suggest a weaker prospect for effective deterrence due to a heightened risk of cognitive errors that dominate the assessment of a crime.

[18] See examples: (a) Indonesia on a case with drunk (Agence France-Presse, 2016); (b) Singapore on cases with jealousy (Lum, 2019; Stevens, 2020; Yang, 2016), and a case with drug user (Amnesty International, 2004, p. 7); (c) Malaysia on a case with jealousy (Hilmy, 2019); (d) Thailand on a case with drunk (Factsanddetails.com, 2014) and cases with jealousy (Ibbetson, 2019; Morris & Nguyen, 2020). In Thailand they are even proposing death penalty for a man who committed murder while driving (Online Reporters, 2019).

4.3 Perceived Net-Cost

Even with knowledge and rationality, does the offender still make a sound choice based on deterrence theory? Robinson and Darley refer to a 'perceived net cost hurdle' that leads to irrational decisions due to an immediate desire framed by circumstances of the moment (Robinson & Darley, 2004) as criminal offenders frequently inflate emotional rewards and underestimate risks (Yokoyama & Takahashi, 2013). Drug-related crimes are examples where the perception of quick and significant gains is inflated and the negative costs are pushed more to the background. Rationality in drug-related crimes is weighted towards the context of business dealings concerning the quality, marketing and selling of the drugs to maximise profit and the perceived probability of getting caught and punished (Fagan, 2006). This is particularly the case for drug-related crimes in ASEAN countries where even with the record number of seizures recorded, the low market price for drugs suggests the presence of much larger undetected clandestine manufacturing facilities (Robinson, 2008; The ASEAN Post Team, 2019). This point was further illustrated in a study of executions in Singapore and Indonesia between 1999 and 2005 (Fagan, 2007). Despite much higher execution numbers in Singapore (notwithstanding Indonesia's much greater population), wholesale drug prices in Singapore were cheaper and drugs were more prevalent than in Indonesia. This potentially indicated that drug trafficking was not being especially deterred as a result of Singapore's higher levels of executions. Furthermore, Malaysia has one of the highest rates of drug addiction in the world and reports a continued rise in trafficking arrests, despite death sentences remaining. In fact, in 2018 for example there were 190 new death penalty sentences, including 132 sentences for drug-related offences (Lee, 2019). In Thailand, more than half of death row inmates were convicted of drug-related offences; in Indonesia, 115 people were sentenced to death for drug crimes from October 2019 to October 2020 (which was a 62% increase from the year before); and in Vietnam, reports indicate that at least 79 death sentences were given for drug transportation and trafficking in 2020; all despite a rise in drug use in each of the countries (Larasati & Girelli, 2021). Clearly, drug trafficking is very high across the ASEAN region yet the fear of execution to the traffickers and drug syndicates seems very low and is not acting as a deterrent (Skylar, 2019). Indeed, the United Nations has found the world over that punitive policies have minimal influence on drug use (United Nations, 2015, p. 93).

> Evidence suggests that executions do not appear to have a deterrent effect in these countries or the surrounding regions. Instead, there has been a steady increase in drug seizures over the past decade, a sign of increased availability and trafficking, even in the face of executions in the countries that are nearest to the producing areas and supply routes. Data from the 2012 U.N. World Drug Report showed that in the regions where drug executions are most frequent, availability (as indicated by drug seizures) has either remained stable or increased compared to the previous reporting period.

Lastly, in relation to homicide, in the US, gun crime studies amongst young men have repeatedly shown that lethal violence was instrumental in providing an intrinsic emotion or valued behaviour that trumped the concern of detection or punishment by law enforcement (United Nations, 2015). Within the criminal networks of drug lords and gangs in the US, the greater risk is said to be retaliation or the threat of violence from within their own communities rather than retribution from the State. Organised crime groups within Southeast Asia are said to be similarly complex and use tactical violence to control illicit markets, enforce contracts and govern trafficking routes (Broadhurst, 2016). The risks and costs of legal punishments, therefore, appear to become secondary.

4.4 The 'Brutalisation Effect' and the Political Function of the Death Penalty

A further counter-argument against the deterrent effect of capital punishment is the 'brutalisation theory' which suggests that state-sanctioned executions stimulate rather than inhibit violence. In essence, it is argued to be condoning killing as vengeance (Cochran & Chamlin, 2000). The 18th century philosopher Cesare Beccaria also commented on this saying: "the death penalty cannot be useful because of the example of barbarity it gives men…." (Waldo, n.d.).

More contemporary examples of state-sanctioned violence and brutality is perhaps the controversial 2003 'war on drugs' in Thailand and more recently, the Philippine President Rodrigo Duterte's campaign against drug pushers. Both have been accused of resorting to extrajudicial police killings, undermining the rule of law and have failed to bring those controlling the drug syndicates to justice (Broadhurst, 2016). In the case of the death penalty such force is intended to create terror in the hearts of drug traffickers and deter them from this illicit crime. For example, posters with graphic images of a hangman's noose and the words "Dadah means Death" have been used in Malaysia in previous decades (Sanello, 1988). Messaging like this is meant to promote the State (and the police) as supreme protectors and the ultimate guardians. These measures are appealing to politicians as a way to be seen to be tough on crime, yet Beccaria also warned about allowing the state such power to kill (Beccaria cited in Likhitpreechakul, 2013, p. 8):

> The punishment of death is pernicious to society, from the example of barbarity it affords. If the passions, or the necessity of war, have taught men to shed the blood of their fellow creatures, the laws, which are intended to moderate the ferocity of mankind, should not increase it by examples of barbarity…..Is it not absurd, that the laws, which detest and punish homicide, should, on order to prevent murder, publicly commit murder themselves?

A Bangkok Post article of 2019 on Thailand describes well other potential brutalisation effects of the death penalty suggesting the death penalty could lead to rapists killing their victims in order to silence them. In other cases, the report suggested suspects could end up as scapegoats for others' crimes or be forced to confess through torture (Bangkok Post, 2019). Similarly, in the case of drug trafficking, more often than not the recipients of the brutalisation effect are not the big traffickers but those more vulnerable such as women. The introduction of the death penalty for drug-related offences has most likely induced big syndicates to use women as drug couriers or as intermediaries for human trafficking meaning that women suffer most in the war on drugs due to their vulnerabilities (LBHM, 2018). Generally speaking, when a crime is punished with higher sentences, it is not the core criminals who are usually those paying the highest price.

4.5 Other Possible Deterrents/Alternatives

Life Without Parole sentences (LWOP) certainly have the same incapacitative result as execution and in the US, there have been recorded cases of some multiple murderers who have said that death was preferable to life in prison (Fagan, 2005). In 2013 in Vietnam, lawmaker Nguyen Van Hien said as prisoners have been waiting to be executed for five to six years, some have been begging to be executed; this following the suicide of one death row convict (TN News, 2013). Similarly, in 2012, a British grandmother arrested, convicted and sentenced to death for carrying drugs in her suitcase when arriving in Bali, Indonesia, said that she'd rather be executed than face years in prison with endless appeal cases (Parry, 2019). This raises the question: could LWOP be a stronger deterrent than execution? Radelet and Borg (2000) pointed out that research had failed to provide additional information as regards to the impact on crime of long-term imprisonment as a comparison and this has still not been studied or factored into existing research on the deterrent effect of the death penalty. Yet for those members of the public who support the death penalty, this is still not an attractive alternative. A 2002 study in Singapore found that 49% opposed LWOP, primarily due to concerns over the high cost to taxpayers of life imprisonment (Ng Thiam Tuan, 2002). Nevertheless, studies from around the world have consistently shown that appeal processes can in many cases be higher in cost.[19] The cost differential reflects the longer time period for completion of capital trials (i.e. appeals, retrials or reversals).

To conclude, many criminals do not commit crimes based on prior rational reasoning of risks nor do they rate highly the likelihood of getting caught. The masterminds and ring leaders behind crimes such as drug trafficking are rarely convicted and so it is the socio-economically disadvantaged and vulnerable who pay the price. Furthermore, there is no robust and truly scientific evidence that the death penalty deters crime more than say a life prison sentence. Therefore, if deterrence has been one of the major beliefs fueling support for the death penalty in ASEAN, the question is whether the considerations given in this section could influence this view? Some research testing this hypothesis has been attempted. A study in Malaysia in 2013 undertook a public opinion survey on the death penalty asking if people would still favour its use if it was shown not to be a better deterrent than alternative sentences.

---

[19] In 2005, it was reported that the average costs for incarceration and execution in the US as between US$2.5 and US$5 million compared to less than US1 million for convicts given life without parole. See Fagan (2005).

The proportion of those in support of the death penalty dropped from 91 to 57% for murder, 75% to 42% for drug trafficking and from 83 to 40% for firearm offences (Hood, 2013). A similar 2018 study in Singapore found that even though most people polled supported the death penalty, a sizeable proportion of between 35.5% to 47.2% would oppose the death penalty if it were clearly no longer an effective deterrent (Chan et al., 2018).

5 Conclusion: In the Absence of Evidence

Globally, the death penalty is in decline, but within ASEAN, capital punishment remains firmly entrenched with eight of ten member states being retentionist countries. Two core perceptions appear to contribute towards this: that the death penalty is an effective deterrent and that the wider public support its use. Yet these assumptions have yet to be scientifically tested or proved within any ASEAN member state. Even globally, where studies are confounded by statistical inconsistencies, the most evidence-based studies cannot agree on whether capital punishment deters serious crime. Public opinion polls, whilst often indicating support for the death penalty, are usually based on a superficial framing of questions that disguise the intricacies and nuances of actual real-life cases and scenarios. Retentionist governments within the region stand tough on the assertion that the death penalty is not a human rights issue but is essential to curb crime and keep its citizens safe—despite the fact that capital punishment related crimes remain high or are growing in these countries.

So, if the evidence of a deterrent effect is inconclusive, then what is the penological justification for such a severe form of punishment? This paper has examined the theoretical arguments and philosophies around the deterrent effects of using capital punishment. By challenging the core elements of the various deterrence theories, it has attempted to de-construct the beliefs of retentionists, stripping away the foundation that supports the argument that the death penalty is an effective deterrent to crime. With the absence of empirical evidence, a neutral person should conclude that the hypothesis that the death penalty deters serious crime cannot be factually supported and should not be used as the justification to retain the death penalty.

A clear imperative is to assess the extent that more humane penalties, such as life sentences without parole can be as much, if not a more effective deterrent. The financial costs of capital punishment are in fact very high and this money could be better spent on policing in order to more successfully prevent and reduce crime. After all, criminologists have long asserted that the best deterrents are those that raise the certainty of detection, arrest and conviction, not the threat of punishment per se (Human Rights in ASEAN, 2018). As an urgent interim step, retentionist ASEAN Member States should at least re-evaluate which crimes better warrant the punishment of life imprisonment as opposed to the death penalty.

This suggests pressing areas where further research could better inform ASEAN policy makers and public opinion. As mentioned above, one aspect requiring further examination is the potential of life imprisonment as an alternative deterrent. The impact of mass media on the publics' opinions concerning the death penalty—and thus ultimately political preferences—is another possible area of research. Closely linked to this within ASEAN is to better understand the relationship between religious beliefs and support for the death penalty as religions are known to have significant influence on individuals' acceptance or rejection of the death penalty which then plays out at the political level. This is particularly relevant because where the empirical evidence for the effectiveness of the death penalty as a deterrent is weak, then justification often shifts to moral and religious values. Likewise, future studies on the deterrent effect of the death penalty in ASEAN cannot ignore the political and economic agenda prevailing in a country. The deterrent debate within the region is strongly influenced by underlying variables such as political will which impacts on public perception and vice-versa.

In conclusion, if studies surrounding the use of the death penalty as a deterrent are inconclusive, then data claiming it is, should not be used to shape public opinion and inform policy in countries within ASEAN. In light of the ultimate severity of the punishment, the deterrence argument cannot be justifiably used to defend the use of the death penalty. The spectre of death row and execution as a state-sanctioned punishment is highly questionable when it cannot be vindicated for the very purpose, it is said to support. Being seen to favour strict criminal penalties may be politically popular or even laudable but as has been argued in this paper, the death penalty in fact does not solve serious crimes. Public opinion is not based on factual information and many are unaware that the death penalty is not contributing towards making their communities safer. If in the region public support for the death penalty as an effective deterrent was less strong (as some of the more scientific and in-depth polling suggests) then it is presumably possible that governments that use it to be seen to be strong on crime may be willing to look at alternatives. The death penalty is the toughest of punishments with brutal consequences but it is not tough on crime nor tough on the causes of crime. To return to the philosophical debates that form a foundation for this paper, it is worth reflecting on one of the many quotes from Friedrich Nietzsche's book 'Beyond Good and Evil': "He who fights with monsters should look to it that he himself does not become a monster…." (Nietzshe, n.d.).

Acknowledgements The author would like to thank Ms. Alessia Altamura for her support and assistance in researching this paper.

References

AAITF. (2018). AAITF Thailand team arrested the West African syndicate with drug bound for New Zealand. *ASEAN Airport Interdiction Task Force—AAITF*. https://aseannarco.oncb.go.th/ewt_news.php?nid=406&filename=index___EN. Accessed 4 January 2022.

ABC News. (2015, May 4). Fact check: No proof the death penalty prevents crime. *ABC News*. https://www.abc.net.au/news/2015-02-26/fact-check3a-does-the-death-penalty-deter3f/6116030?nw=0. Accessed 2 May 2020.

Abdorrahman Boroumand Center. (2018, December 13). *What happens to murder rates when the death penalty is scrapped? A look at eleven countries might surprise you.* https://www.iranrights.org/library/document/3501. Accessed 11 January 2022.

Agence France-Presse. (2016, May 26). Indonesia introduces death penalty and chemical castration for paedophiles. *The Guardian.* https://www.theguardian.com/world/2016/may/26/indonesia-introduces-death-penalty-and-chemical-castration-for-paedophiles. Accessed 2 May 2020.

Agerholm, H. (2018). Thailand uses lethal injection to execute first prisoner in nearly a decade. *The Independent.* https://www.independent.co.uk/news/world/asia/thailand-execution-death-penalty-lethal-injection-amnesty-international-a8405711.html. Accessed 4 January 2022.

Amnesty International. (2004, February 24). *Singapore: Medical action. The death penalty: A hidden toll of executions.* https://www.amnesty.org/en/wp-content/uploads/2021/09/asa360052004en.pdf. Accessed 2 May 2020.

Amnesty International. (2017). *Cooperate or die: Singapore's flawed reforms to the mandatory death penalty.* Amnesty International.

Amnesty International. (2020). *Death penalty in 2019: Facts and figures.* https://www.amnesty.org/en/latest/news/2020/04/death-penalty-in-2019-facts-and-figures/. Accessed 4 January 2022.

Ariate, J. (2019). How we kill: Notes on the death penalty in the Philippines. *ResearchGate.* https://doi.org/10.13140/RG.2.2.12609.71523. Accessed 11 January 2022.

Arifin, T. (2015). Misunderstanding of the Indonesian human rights activists on the application of the death penalty. *Asy-Syari'ah, 17*(2), 185–198. https://journal.uinsgd.ac.id/index.php/asy-syariah/article/view/7607. Accessed 11 January 2022.

Balakrishnan, V. (2016). Moving away from the death penalty: Victims and the death penalty. *Intervention at the high-level side event at the UN General Assembly.* https://www.mfa.gov.sg/content/mfa/media_centre/press_room/pr/2016/201609/press_20160922.hml. Accessed 11 January 2022.

Bangkok Post. (2019). *Death penalty is no answer.* https://www.bangkokpost.com/opinion/opinion/1686044/death-penalty-is-no-answer. Accessed 11 January 2022.

Barkan, S. (1997). *Criminology: A Sociological understanding.* Upper Saddle River.

Battiston, D., & Vidal, J. B. (n.d.). *The local effect of executions on serious crime.* http://personal.lse.ac.uk/BATTISTO/webtempl_files/Executions-Draft2.pdf. Accessed 11 January 2022.

Brandt, P. T., & Kovandzic, T. V. (2015). Messing up Texas?: A Re-analysis of the effects of executions on homicides. *PLoS ONE, 10*(9). https://doi.org/10.1371/journal.pone.0138143

Broadhurst, R. (2016). Asia is in the grip of a transnational crime crisis. *The Diplomat.* https://thediplomat.com/2016/12/asia-is-in-the-grip-of-a-transnational-crime-crisis/. Accessed 11 January 2022.

Chalfin, A., Haviland, A. M., & Raphael, S. (2013). What do panel studies tell us about a deterrent effect of capital punishment? A critique of the literature. *Journal of Quantitative Criminology, 29*, 5–43 (2013). https://doi.org/10.1007/s10940-012-9168-8

Chan, J., & Oxley, D. (2004, October). *Deterrent effect of capital punishment: A review of the research evidence.* New South Wales Bureau of Crime Statistics and Research. https://www.bocsar.nsw.gov.au/Documents/CJB/cjb84.pdf. Accessed 2 May 2020.

Chan, W., Tan, E., Lee, J., & Mathi, B. (2018). *How strong is public support for the death penalty in Singapore?* NUS Working Paper 2018/002. National University of Singapore. https://www.researchgate.net/publication/323142951_Public_Opinion_On_The_Death_Penalty_In_Singapore_Survey_Findings. Accessed 11 January 2022.

CND. (2019). Side event: The death penalty for drug-related offences: The impact on women and vulnerable groups. *CND Blog.* http://cndblog.org/2019/03/side-event-the-death-penalty-for-drug-related-offences-the-impact-on-women-and-vulnerable-groups/. Accessed 4 January 2022.

Cochran, J., & Chamlin, M. (2000). Deterrence and brutalization: The dual effects of executions. *Justice Quarterly, 17*(4), 685–706. https://doi.org/10.1080/07418820000094721

De Ungria, M., & Jose, J. (2019). The war on drugs, forensic science and the death penalty in the Philippines. *Forensic Science International: Synergy, 2*, 32–34.

Dezhbakhsh, H., Rubin, P. H., & Shepherd, J. M. (n.d.). *Does capital punishment have a deterrent effect? New evidence from post-moratorium panel data*. https://cjlf.org/deathpenalty/DezRubShepDeterFinal.pdf. Accessed 11 January 2022.

Donohue, J. J., & Wolfers, J. (2010). Use and abuses of empirical evidence in the death penalty debate. *Stanford Law Review, 58*(3), 791–846.

Durkheim, E. (1933). *The division of labour in society*. Free Press.

Durlauf, S., Fu, C., & Navarro, S. (2011). *Capital punishment and deterrence: Understanding disparate results*. https://www.ssc.wisc.edu/~cfu/capitalJQC.pdf. Accessed 11 January 2022.

Factsanddetails.com. (2014, May). *Crime and foreigners in Thailand: Scams, murdered tourists and crimes by foreigners*. https://factsanddetails.com/southeast-asia/Thailand/sub5_8f/entry-3281.html. Accessed 2 May 2020.

Fagan, J. (2005, July 14). *Public policy choices on deterrence and the death penalty: A critical review of new evidence, testimony before the Joint Committee on the Judiciary of the Massachusetts Legislature on House Bill 3834*. https://files.deathpenaltyinfo.org/legacy/files/pdf/MassTestimonyFagan.pdf. Accessed on 24 April 2020.

Fagan, J. (2006). Death and deterrence redux: Science, law and causal reasoning on capital punishment, Walter C. Reckless Memorial Lecture. *Ohio State Journal of Criminal Law, 4*, 255–320.

Fagan, J. (2007, May 2). *Deterrence and the death penalty: Expert opinion and testimony to the MKRI 19*.

Fagan, J. (2019). *The feasibility of systematic research on the deterrent effects of the death penalty in Indonesia*. The Death Penalty Project and LBH Masyarakat, Indonesia.

Gerritzen, B., & Kirchgässner, G. (2016). Facts or ideology: What determines the results of econometric estimates of the deterrent effect of the death penalty? A meta-analysis. *Open Journal of Social Sciences, 4*(6), 178–202. https://doi.org/10.4236/jss.2016.46020

Gius, M. (2015). The impact of the death penalty and executions on state-level murder rates: 1980–2011. *Journal of Applied Economics, 23*(3), 199–201. https://doi.org/10.1080/13504851.2015.1064074

Henschke, R., & Nurdin, E. (2020, February 17). What would you say to the men who killed your mum? *BBC World Service, Jakarta*. https://www.bbc.com/news/stories-51502032. Accessed 11 January 2022.

Hilmy, I. (2019, December 18). Jealousy a possible motive for murder. *The Star*. https://www.thestar.com.my/news/nation/2019/12/18/jealousy-a-possible-motive-for-murder?itm_source=parsely-api. Accessed 2 May 2020.

Hjalmarsson, R. (2009). Does capital punishment have a "local" deterrent effect on homicides? *American Law and Economics Review, 11*(2), 310–334. https://doi.org/10.1093/aler/ahn004

Hood, R. (2013). *The death penalty in Malaysia: Public opinion on the mandatory death penalty for drug trafficking, murder and firearms offenses*. The Death Penalty Project.

Human Rights in ASEAN. (2018). *Malaysian's abolition of death penalty and the argument against it being a deterrence to crime*. https://humanrightsinasean.info/news/malaysians-abolition-of-death-penalty-and-the-argument-against-it-being-a-deterrence-to-crime/. Accessed 11 January 2022.

Human Rights Watch. (2018, June 21). *Thailand: Resuming death penalty a major setback*. https://www.hrw.org/news/2018/06/21/thailand-resuming-death-penalty-major-setback. Accessed 2 May 2020.

Ibbetson, R. (2019, May 31). *Brother-in-law who paid two hitmen to kill British expat and his wife is sentenced to death in Thailand*. Mail Online. https://www.dailymail.co.uk/news/article-7090493/Brother-law-paid-two-hitmen-kill-British-expat-wife-sentenced-death-Thailand.html. Accessed 2 May 2020.

ICJR. (2017). *Death penalty policy in Indonesia*. Jakarta: Institute for Criminal Justice Reform.

Kirchgässner, G. (2011a). *Econometric estimates of deterrence of the death penalty: Facts or ideology*. Discussion Paper no. 2011–15. University of St. Gallen. https://core.ac.uk/download/pdf/6387467.pdf. Accessed 11 January 2022.

Kirchgässner, G. (2011b, April). *Econometric estimates of deterrence of the death penalty: Facts or ideology*. Discussion Paper no. 2011–15. CORE Metadata. https://core.ac.uk/download/pdf/6387467.pdf. Accessed 11 January 2022.

Larasati, A., & Girelli, G. (2021). *The death penalty for drug offences: Global overview 2020*. Harm Reduction International. https://idpc.net/publications/2021/04/death-penalty-for-drug-offences-global-overview-2020. Accessed 11 January 2022.

LBHM. (2018). *The forgotten vulnerability of female drug couriers*. https://lbhmasyarakat.org/en/the-forgotten-vulnerability-of-female-drug-couriers/. Accessed on 11 January 2022.

Lee, A. (2019). Drug-trafficking the reason for bulk of death row inmates. *Malaysiakini*. https://www.malaysiakini.com/news/495243. Accessed 11 January 2022.

Likhitpreechakul, P. (2013). *Death penalty in "Buddhist" Thailand*. https://www.academia.edu/25073007/Death_Penalty_in_Buddhist_Thailand. Accessed 11 January 2022.

Lum, S. (2019, September 18). Circuit Road murder trial: Accused tried to have sex with nurse's corpse after strangling her. *The Straits Times*. https://www.straitstimes.com/singapore/courts-crime/murder-of-nurse-in-circuit-road-accused-tried-to-have-sex-with-corpse-after. Accessed 2 May 2020.

Luyen, T. V. (2019). Capital punishment in Vietnam, a study from the perspective of traditional and modern values. *The Journal of Middle East and North Africa Sciences, 5*(6), 30–33. https://oaji.net/articles/2019/2705-1558883315.pdf. Accessed 11 January 2022.

Morris, J., & Nguyen, S. (2020, February 3). Senior police officer murdered and sexually mutilated by jealous husband in Kalasin province. *Thai Examiner.com*. https://www.thaiexaminer.com/thai-news-foreigners/2020/02/03/police-officer-kalasin-murdered-sexual-organs-affair-suspect-husband-woman/. Accessed 2 May 2020.

Muramatsu, K., Johnson, D. T., & Yano, K. (2018). The death penalty and homicide deterrence in Japan. *Punishment & Society, 20*(4), 432–457. https://doi.org/10.1177/1462474517706369

Nagin, D. (2014). Deterrence and the death penalty: Why the statistics should be ignored. *Significance, 11*(2), 9–13. https://doi.org/10.1111/j.1740-9713.2014.00733.x

National Research Council. (2012). *Deterrence and the death penalty*. The National Academies Press. https://doi.org/10.17226/13363.

New Straits Times. https://www.nst.com.my/news/nation/2019/03/471832/despite-appeals-malaysian-michael-garing-executed-singapore. Accessed 4 January 2022.

Ng Thiam Tuan, T. (2002). *A cross-sectional analysis of death penalty views* [Unpublished master thesis, University of Singapore]. ScholarBank@NUS Repository. https://scholarbank.nus.edu.sg/handle/10635/13794. Accessed 11 January 2022.

Nietzshe, F. (n.d.). *Beyond good and evil*. https://resources.saylor.org/wwwresources/archived/site/wp-content/uploads/2011/09/PHIL101-5.3.3.pdf. quote 146. Accessed 11 January 2022.

NST. (2019a). Singapore urged to stay execution of Michael Anak Garing. *New Straits Times*. https://www.nst.com.my/news/crime-courts/2019a/03/471306/singapore-urged-stay-execution-michael-anak-garing. Accessed 4 January 2022.

NST. (2019b). *Despite appeals, Malaysian Michael Garing executed in Singapore*.

Odchigue, B., & Sobradil, M. (2019). *Perceptions of the registered voters on the re-imposition of death penalty in the Philippines*. http://dx.doi.org/10.2139/ssrn.3530631. Accessed 4 January 2022.

Online Reporters. (2019, April 12). Drunk driver kills policeman, wife. *Bangkok Post*. https://www.bangkokpost.com/thailand/general/1660776/drunk-driver-kills-policeman-wife. Accessed 2 May 2020.

Parry, S. (2019). British grandmother Lindsay Sandiford's life on Bali's death row: 'If you want to shoot me, shoot me'. *Post Magazine*. https://www.scmp.com/magazines/post-magazine/article/2188013/british-grandmother-lindsay-sandifords-life-balis-death-row. Accessed 11 January 2022.

Penal Reform International. (2017). *Death penalty information pack*. https://cdn.penalreform.org/wp-content/uploads/2014/11/PRI-Death-penalty-info-pack_2017-3rd-edition_WEB.pdf. Accessed 4 January 2022.

Pierce, G., Radelet, M., & Sharp, S. (2017). Race and death sentencing for Oklahoma homicides committed between 1990 and 2012. *Journal of Criminal Law & Criminology, 107*(4), 733–756. https://scholarlycommons.law.northwestern.edu/jclc/vol107/iss4/5. Accessed 4 January 2022.

Radelet, M., & Borg, M. (2000). The changing nature of death penalty debates. *Annual Review of Sociology, 26*, 43–61. https://doi.org/10.1146/annurev.soc.26.1.43

Robinson, P. H. (2008). Distributive principles of criminal law: Who should be punished how much? *Oxford University Press*. https://doi.org/10.1093/acprof:oso/9780195365757.001.0001

Robinson, P., & Darley, J. (2004). Does criminal law deter? A behavioural science investigation. *Oxford Journal of Legal Studies, 24*(2), 173–205.

Rusito, R., & Suwardi, K. (2019). Development of death penalty in Indonesia in human rights perspective. *Ganesha Law Review, 1*(2), 38–54. https://ejournal2.undiksha.ac.id/index.php/GLR/article/view/53. Accessed 4 January 2022.

Sanelo, F. (1988). Despite the mother's struggle, 'Dadah is Death' to her son. *The Chicago Tribune*. https://www.chicagotribune.com/news/ct-xpm-1988-10-28-8802110316-story.html. Accessed 11 January 2022.

Shepherd, J. M. (2005). Deterrence versus brutalization: Capital punishment's differing impacts among states. *Michigan Law Review, 104*(2), 203–255. https://repository.law.umich.edu/mlr/vol104/iss2/13. Accessed 11 January 2022.

Simandjuntak, D. (2015). *Spectacle of the scaffold? The politics of death penalty in Indonesia*. Yuof Ishak Institute, Issue 2015, No. 46. https://www.iseas.edu.sg/images/pdf/ISEAS_Perspective_2015_46.pdf. Accessed 11 January 2022.

Skylar, L. (2019). ASEAN's drug trade rakes in profits despite strict laws. *ASEAN Today*. https://www.aseantoday.com/2019/08/aseans-drug-trade-rakes-in-profits-despite-strict-laws/. Accessed 11 January 2022.

Stevens, K. (2020, January 7). Australian podiatrist, 48, shows no emotion as he is charged with murdering his wife, 43, at their Singapore condo—And if found guilty he could face the death penalty. *Mail Online*. https://www.dailymail.co.uk/news/article-7859567/Australian-podiatrist-faces-death-penalty-charged-wifes-murder-Singapore.html. Accessed 2 May 2020.

The ASEAN Post Team. (2019). The shocking methamphetamine trade in ASEAN. *The ASEAN Post*. https://theaseanpost.com/article/shocking-methamphetamine-trade-asean. Accessed 4 January 2022.

The Council of Europe. (2010). *Death is not justice. Directorate general of human rights and legal affairs, Council of Europe*.

The Death Penalty Project. (2013, July 8). *DPP launches report on the public opinion survey on the mandatory death penalty in Malaysia*. https://www.deathpenaltyproject.org/dpp-launches-report-on-the-public-opinion-survey-on-the-mandatory-death-penalty-in-malaysia/. Accessed 11 January 2022.

THE NATION. (2018). *Police arrest 261 on drugs charges after six-year operation*. https://www.nationthailand.com/news/30351749. Accessed 4 January 2022.

The National Academies. (2012, April). The deterrence and the death penalty. *Report brief*. https://files.deathpenaltyinfo.org/legacy/documents/NatResCouncil-Deterr.pdf. Accessed 11 January 2022.

Thongtub, E. (2018). Police bust Phuket toy car drug gang. *The Phuket Times*. https://www.thephuketnews.com/police-bust-phuket-toy-car-drug-gang-68809.php. Accessed 4 January 2022.

TN News. (2013). *Vietnam's death row inmates enduring a wait worse than death*. http://www.thanhniennews.com/society/vietnams-death-row-inmates-enduring-a-wait-worse-than-death-1953.html. Accessed 11 January 2022.

United Nations. (2015). *Moving away from the death penalty: Arguments, trends and perspectives*. https://www.ohchr.org/EN/newyork/Documents/Moving-Away-from-the-Death-Penalty-2015-web.pdf. Accessed 11 January 2022.

UNODC. (2019). *Transnational organised crime in Southeast Asia: Evolution, growth and impact*. United Nations Office on Drugs and Crime. https://www.unodc.org/documents/southeastasiaandpacific/Publications/2019/SEA_TOCTA_2019_web.pdf. Accessed 11 January 2022.

UNODC. (n.d.). *Intentional murder data. UNODC statistical database*. https://data.unodc.org/#state:0. Accessed 11 January 2022.
Waldo, G. P. (n.d.). *Why the death penalty should be abolished: Examining the evidence*. https://tcadp.net/why-the-death-penalty-should-be-abolished/. Accessed 11 January 2022.
Yang, C. (2016, May 14). Guilty as charged: Dance hostess Mimi Wong murdered her Japanese lover's wife. *The Straits Times*. https://www.straitstimes.com/singapore/courts-crime/guilty-as-charged-dance-hostess-mimi-wong-murdered-her-japanese-lovers-wife. Accessed 2 May 2020.
Yokoyama, T., & Takahashi, T. (2013). Mathematical neurolaw of crime and punishment: The q-exponential punishment function. *Applied Mathematics, 4*, 1371–1375. https://doi.org/10.4236/am.2013.410185
Zimmermann, P. R. (2004). State executions, deterrence, and the incidence of murder. *Journal of Applied Economics, 7*(1), 163–193. https://doi.org/10.1080/15140326.2004.12040607
Zimmermann, P. R. (2009). Statistical variability and the deterrent effect of the death penalty. *American Law and Economics Review, 11*(2), 370–398. https://doi.org/10.1093/aler/ahp003
Zimring, F., Fagan, J., & Johnson, D. (2010). Executions, deterrence and homicide: A tale of two cities. *Journal of Empirical Legal Studies, 7*(1), 1–29.

Mark P. Capaldi, PhD, is a lecturer at the Institute of Human Rights and Peace Studies at Mahidol University. Much of Mark P. Capaldi's work has been in South and East Asia, where he has lived for 30 years when he worked with the International NGOs Concern Worldwide, PACT Inc., Save the Children UK and ECPAT International. As Deputy Director of ECPAT International (2001–2011), he worked to end the commercial sexual exploitation and trafficking of children, supporting a wide range of programming and advocacy in all regions of the world. From 2011 to 2018, he took on the role of ECPAT's global Head of Research and Policy.

Mark P. Capaldi has a doctorate degree with the Institute of Human Rights and Peace Studies at Mahidol University, Bangkok; the research topic of his dissertation was children's agency within inde-pendent child migration in Thailand. Other recent research areas have included a 10 countries study on the death penalty in ASEAN and also the issue of religions and its impact on sexuality within Southeast Asia.

'Most Serious Crimes': Searching for a Common Interpretation in ASEAN

Sripapha Petcharamesree

Abstract In all ASEAN countries, capital punishment is widely applied except in Cambodia and the Philippines where the death penalty was abolished. International human rights law does not prohibit capital punishment deeming 'it may be imposed' whilst making it clear it should only apply to 'the most serious crimes' (ICCPR, Article 6(2)). However, the concept of 'most serious crimes' is itself ambivalent and subject to different interpretations by different countries. In the ASEAN region and its ASEAN Member States (AMS), capital punishment is prescribed to an extensive array of crimes, in most cases exceeding the guidelines laid down by international law. Despite this, governments in ASEAN continue to construct their own interpretation of the 'most serious crimes'. This paper examines several interpretations of 'most serious crimes' and the underlying concepts espoused by different AMS and analyses how these became the norm in the region. It also attempts to unpack regional trends and deconstruct existing discourses in order to elicit guidelines for the establishment of a potential common regional interpretation of 'most serious crimes' that meet the international standard.

1 Introduction

In all ASEAN countries, capital punishment is widely applied except in Cambodia and the Philippines where the death penalty was abolished. International human rights law does not prohibit capital punishment deeming that '**it may be imposed**' whilst making it clear it should only be applied to '**the most serious crimes**' (ICCPR, Article 6 (2)). However, the concept of 'most serious crimes' itself is ambivalent and subject to different interpretations by different countries. As a result, divergence remains as to which crimes constitute this category. In the ASEAN region, capital punishment is prescribed for an extensive array of crimes, in most cases exceeding the parameters laid down by international law. Under the guidelines formulated by the UN, 'most serious crimes' are limited to crimes depicting an intention to

S. Petcharamesree (✉)
Institute of Human Rights and Peace Studies, Mahidol University, Nakornpathom, Thailand
e-mail: sripraphapet@gmail.com

S. Petcharamesree et al. (eds.), *Unpacking the Death Penalty in ASEAN*,
https://doi.org/10.1007/978-981-19-8840-0_3

kill where a resulting loss of life can be demonstrated (OHCHR, 2016). However, governments in the region routinely construct their own interpretation of the concept by including crimes wherein an intent to kill is absent and loss of life does not occur, such as corruption. As a result, many ASEAN Member States (AMS), including the Philippines, where a draft bill has been introduced to re-impose the death penalty and which uses the phrase, 'certain serious crimes', appear now to hold the view that any crimes legislators deem serious may be subject to the death penalty.

Thus, there is a real need to examine different interpretations of 'most serious crimes' and the concepts behind them as used by AMS to understand how these have become the norm in the region. This paper attempts to unpack regional trends and deconstruct existing discourses in order to search for a potential common regional interpretation of 'most serious crimes' that meets the international standard set out by the authoritative UN agencies, including the Human Rights Committee. Based on literature review and textual analysis, existing scholarly articles, primary sources such as international human rights standards, UN resolutions and guidelines issued by relevant UN agencies as well as national policies and laws are reviewed and analysed. Reports prepared by researchers appointed by the representatives of the ASEAN Intergovernmental Commission on Human Rights (AICHR, 2020a) will also be drawn upon. Finally, of the five countries identified for this paper (Indonesia, Malaysia, Singapore, Thailand, and Vietnam), preliminary online interviews were conducted in Malaysia, Thailand and Vietnam via email and telephone conversations.

The first section provides an introduction followed by an overview of the legislation prescribing the death penalty in ASEAN as well as an examination and analysis of the interpretations and practices of 'most serious crimes' by looking at the five selected AMS and identifying common grounds for its exercise in the region. Section 4 attempts to demonstrate that capital punishment as applied by AMS falls far short of international thresholds. Section 5 regards the array of crimes subject to the death penalty and the rationale behind such interpretations, the theories underpinning its use, and how 'Asian values' have helped define its implementation. It also examines concepts of 'crime' and the problems around interpreting the 'most serious crimes'. This paper concludes by outlining guidelines for a possible common regional interpretation of 'most serious crimes' and a regional norm.

2 Overview of the Legal Application of Capital Punishment in ASEAN

Southeast Asia remains a bastion of capital punishment, with eight out of ten Member States maintaining the death penalty. Two abolitionist States in ASEAN, namely Cambodia and the Philippines, have ratified the International Covenant on Civil and Political Rights (ICCPR) but only the Philippines is a party to the Optional Protocol aiming to abolish the death penalty. To reiterate what was described by Mark P. Capaldi in Chapter 1, most, if not all eight countries where the death penalty is still applied, have codified capital punishment in their respective penal or other types of criminal laws. In Brunei Darussalam, whilst the Criminal Procedure Code (Chapter 7) recognises the right to life, it further prescribes that such a right may be removed upon a guilty verdict in relation to certain offences. Moreover, in Brunei, the death penalty is also prescribed by Shariah Law (AICHR, 2020b). In Indonesia's criminal code, while Chapter II, Article 10 stipulates that capital punishment comprises part of the main framework of criminal sentencing, when imposed, it should also not deprive individuals of other additional rights (in captivity or otherwise) (AICHR, 2019a). In addition to the criminal code, capital punishment is also imposed in other laws. Law No 22 (1997) (later amended by Law No. 35 (2009)) on Drugs states that those who have processed, produced, procured, exported, given, or channelled drugs defined as 'Category 1' shall be subject to the death penalty (AICHR, 2019a). In Laos, Articles 82, 88, 89, 90, and 92 of the Penal Law prescribe that any person causing another person's death intentionally, negligently, or inadvertently shall be punished by house arrest, fine, deprivation of liberty, or the death penalty (AICHR, 2020c). In Malaysia, a mandatory death penalty was included in the Penal Code for various crimes from offences against the Yang di-Pertuan Agong's (King) person to terrorist acts resulting in death and murder. Other laws provide for discretionary death penalties such as the Strategic Trade Act 2010, the Water Services Act 2006, and the recent amendment to Section 39B of the Dangerous Drugs Act 1952. In addition, the Kidnapping Act 1961, the Firearms Act 1971, and the Armed Forces Act 1972 also enable its use (AICHR, 2019b).

In Myanmar, death as a punishment was prescribed by the Penal Code for offences such as high treason and acts causing death, murder, etc. The death penalty is also imposed by the Narcotic Drugs and Psychotropic Substances Law, and the Anti Trafficking in Persons Law (AICHR, 2020d). In Singapore, as in other territories, the constitution does not outlaw the use of the death penalty (AICHR, 2019c). Introduced in the late nineteenth century during the colonial era, in its quest for law and order, capital punishment has been an integral part of Singapore's criminal justice system. Thirty-two offences attract the death penalty, with some imposed as mandatory sanctions upon conviction (AICHR, 2019c). For example,

> [t]he Penal Code provides for the death sentence for at least ten different offences. The crimes of murder, attempted murder or endangering a person's life during an act of piracy and 'offences against the President's person' carry a mandatory death sentence. (Amnesty International 2004)

Other laws imposing the death sentence include the Hostage Taking Act, the Kidnapping Act, the Misuse of Drugs Act (which provides for mandatory death penalties), the Terrorism (Suppression of Bombings) Act, the Radiation Protection Act, the Internal Security Act, the Arms Offences Act, and the Singapore Armed Forces Act (AICHR, 2019c).

In Thailand, the death penalty is provided for by the Penal Code, the Military Code, the Prevention and Suppression of Prostitution Act BE 2539, the Firearms, Ammunition, Explosives, Fireworks, and the Equivalent of Firearms Act BE 2490, the Organic Act on Counter Corruption (No. 3) BE 2558, the Anti-Trafficking in

Persons Act (No. 2) BE 2558, the Act on Certain Offences Against Air Navigation BE 2558, and the Narcotics Control Act BE 2522 (AICHR, 2019d).

Like the majority of countries in ASEAN, the death penalty is explicitly stated in Vietnam's Penal Code and includes a number of crimes such as: infringement of national security; infringement upon human life, health, honour and dignity; infringement of economic management orders; drug-related offences; infringements upon public safety and public order; offences related to the abuse of power; undermining the peace; crimes against humanity; and war crimes (AICHR, 2020e). However, it is worth noting that the death penalty is not mandatory in Vietnam. In other countries, the death penalty can be both mandatory or discretionary depending on the crimes committed as provided by law.

The description above shows that in ASEAN, the death penalty is imposed for a large variety of crimes which can be grouped thus: (1) Offences against the person (murder, kidnapping, hostage-taking, trafficking); (2) Drug offences (trafficking, importation and exportation, and the manufacture of drugs); (3) Offences against State security (killing the head of state, terrorism, and offences directed against nuclear facilities, etc.); (4) Offences involving firearms or explosives; and (5) Other offences including economic crimes (corruption and bribery), and religious/moral interpretations.

With the exception of Thailand, the trend in most AMS has been to reduce the number of crimes attracting the death penalty. For example, the Thai Criminal Code of 1956 permitted imposition of the death penalty for a total of 31 different offences. In 2015, this number increased to 55. As of 2018, the number of offences warranting capital punishment has risen to 63 (AICHR, 2019d). Such figures can be contrasted against Vietnam where in 2015, the Penal Code imposed the death penalty upon only 18 crimes among a total of 314 (AICHR, 2020e). Similarly, another trend has been to reduce offences subject to mandatory death penalties. For instance, in 2012, the Government of Singapore adjusted its capital punishment regime by making the mandatory death penalty discretionary in specific situations. Thus, in drug trafficking and importation and exportation cases, where specific tightly defined conditions are met, the death penalty is no longer mandatory allowing courts to exercise their discretion. Nevertheless, out of 32 offences, 10 still remain mandatory in Singapore (AICHR, 2019c). In other countries such as Indonesia, the death penalty is not mandatory at all.

3 Interpretation of 'Most Serious Crimes' in Indonesia, Malaysia, Singapore, Thailand, and Vietnam

As already noted, all retentionist States in ASEAN apply capital punishment to a number of crimes especially drug-related offences, murder, those affecting State security, and crimes classified and provided for by international criminal and humanitarian laws such as genocide, crimes against humanity, etc. Seven out of eight countries apply the death penalty to terrorist acts, possession and use of weapons of mass destruction such as chemical weapons while six States (with the exception of Indonesia and Vietnam) prescribe it for acts of kidnaping and trafficking in persons. Four countries (Indonesia, Lao PDR, Thailand, and Vietnam) impose capital punishment for economic crimes including corruption and bribery, and the robbery of State assets. Following Rodrigo Duterte's ascendency to the presidency in 2016, the Philippines has pushed to reimpose the death penalty and withdraw from Optional Protocol II regarding abolition of the death penalty. A wide range of crimes was included in the proposed new draft Bill, particularly drug-related crimes. Furthermore, debates have been ongoing as to whether economic crimes such as plunder should also be listed.

This paper is particularly interested in how the 'most serious crimes' have been interpreted and applied in AMS especially Indonesia, Malaysia, Singapore, Thailand, and Vietnam.[1] These countries carry some common characteristics including: their classification as 'retentionist'; their tendency to sentence large numbers of drug-related offenders to death; their use of laws imposing capital punishment that cover the crimes studied in this paper; the high numbers of prisoners sentenced to death; their commitment to international human rights standards and the fact that ratification of international human rights treaties does not appear to have resulted in different behaviour as regards capital punishment.[2] In particular, the case of the Philippines will be mentioned when and where appropriate. Three categories of crimes shall be studied in order to identify some common concepts and paradigms behind 'the most serious crimes' as perceived by AMS.

3.1 Drug-Related Crimes

As already pointed out, all ASEAN retentionist States impose the death penalty for drug-related offences. These countries figure among a total of 35 States retaining the death penalty for drug-related crimes (Leechaianan & Longmire, 2013; OHCHR, 2018; Sander et al., 2020). Significantly, Indonesia, Malaysia, Thailand, Singapore, and Vietnam were classified by Harm Reduction International in its 2019 global report as States with a high application of the death penalty (Sander et al., 2020, p. 27). The same report indicates that 77% of 70 new death sentences handed down in Indonesia between October 2018 to October 2019 were directly related to drug offences. In total, 61% of the 271 people on death row in October 2019 were drug offenders (Sander

[1] According to the OHCHR Report issued in 2019, 3 countries in Southeast Asia (Cambodia, Philippines, and Timor-Leste) were classified 'abolitionist' for all crimes whilst Brunei Darussalam, Lao PDR, and Myanmar were deemed 'de facto abolitionist'. Five countries (Indonesia, Malaysia, Singapore, Thailand, and Vietnam) were held to be 'retentionist'.

[2] Indonesia, Thailand and Vietnam ratified ICCPR while Malaysia and Singapore are party to CRC and CERD which recognise right to life.

et al., 2020, p. 29). Similarly, according to official sources, as of 3 December 2019, 1,280 people were on death row in Malaysia. Research by Amnesty International reveals that over 70% were sentenced to death for drug offences, around half of whom were foreign nationals (Sander et al., 2020, p. 30). In Singapore, capital punishment is applied to a variety of offences, most commonly, drug trafficking. Between 2019 and 2020, about 50% of persons sentenced to death in Singapore were prosecuted for drug-related crimes (Harm Reduction International, 2021). In Thailand, official sources report that of the 312 people on death row as of 12 December 2019, 64% were convicted of drug offences. This reflects Thailand's broader approach to drug control: 79% (290,159 persons) of its total prison population are drug offenders (Sander et al., 2020, p. 31). In Vietnam, data and statistics on death row inmates are classified as state secrets forcing researchers to rely on media reports to estimate the true figures. According to these, Vietnamese courts handed down at least 75 death sentences in 2019, 74 for drug offences. Reflecting the reported surge of illicit drug markets in the region, a minimum of 30 defendants were convicted for transnational drug activities, including smuggling drugs to and from Lao PDR, Cambodia, and China (Sander et al., 2020, p. 32).

Interestingly, in Malaysia, after the 2018 general elections, the then Minister of Law in the Prime Minister's Department, the Hon Liew Vui Keong, publicly announced that the Cabinet intended to introduce a bill to Parliament in which 'All death penalty will be abolished' (Parliamentarians for Global Action, n.d.). This has since been watered down into a pledge to merely abolish its mandatory use. In email communications with Malaysia's former Representative to the AICHR, it was likewise revealed that a Special Committee had been appointed to prepare a reform proposal, the report of which was officially submitted to the government in February 2020. Said report proposed two categories of offences, namely: (11) offences with a mandatory punishment of death (if the acts result in death), and (23) offences with a discretionary punishment of death. Additionally, trafficking in dangerous drugs shall be punishable by death or life imprisonment and shall, if he or she is not sentenced to death, be punished by whipping of not less than 15 strokes. In other words, a compromise was made to change drug crimes from mandatory to discretionary death sentence offences whilst still considering such acts to be 'most serious crimes' (Personal communications, 2020).[3] It was confirmed that the proposal would be submitted to the Parliament in September 2022 for review.[4]

Around the world, debates have been raging over the application of the death penalty to drug-related crimes. While China was the first to impose capital punishment for drug offences after World War II, the list of countries adopting similar measures has increased over time.

> This sharp rise corresponded to both the entry into force of the 1988 United Nations Convention against Illicit Traffic in Narcotic Drugs and Psychotropic Substances, as well as a major

[3] Personal communications with a former Malaysian Representative to the AICHR, 22–28 May 2020.

[4] Personal communications with a former Malaysian Representative to the AICHR, 11 July 2022; UNOHCHR 2022.

> international political and law enforcement campaign against drug use and trafficking, often known as the 'war on drugs'. (Schabas, 2010)

In pursuit of a drug-free ASEAN, the ASEAN Declaration of Principles to Combat Abuse of Narcotic Drugs was adopted in Manila in 1976. Among other stipulations, it provided for several 'strategic' actions and mechanisms to achieve the goal, including strengthening justice systems and increased prosecutions of suspected drug-related crimes. Similarly, the Joint Declaration for a Drug-Free ASEAN was adopted in 2012 and also forms part of the ASEAN Vision 2025. Likewise, ASEAN 10 adopted various measures including, 'the review of jurisprudence related to illicit drug abuse and trafficking and [a] move for the passage of stricter laws on these crimes against society' (ASEAN, 2012). In all such actions and measures, ASEAN countries have allowed much discretion as to which means to employ. Countries like the Philippines under the Duterte regime, Indonesia and Thailand have waged a concerted 'war on drugs' for years. Heavy-handed law enforcement measures and the continued use of capital punishment suggests a little possibility for any progress in the near future.

As already mentioned, in all retentionist ASEAN countries, drug offenders comprise a major portion of those convicted, sentenced to death, and executed especially in Malaysia, Singapore, and Vietnam. Whilst the overall number of executions seems to be decreasing in some AMS such as Thailand, drug offences stubbornly remain on the list of crimes considered 'most serious' by all retentionist States. However, types of punishment and the application of laws may vary from one country to another.

> Drugs-related crimes for which the death penalty can be imposed include possession, production, trafficking or use of illicit narcotics. Generally, whether a person is sentenced to death or not depends on the type and quantity of drugs involved. In some countries possession of even a small amount of an illegal substance is punishable by death while in other countries drug possession per se is not a capital offence but may be construed as drug trafficking and hence subject to the death penalty. (International Commission Against the Death Penalty, 2013)

In Vietnam, the death sentence for drug crimes is not mandatory; punishments are made based on the 'seriousness of criminal behaviours' including the amount of drugs involved. Criminal law states that 'anyone found guilty of possessing more than 600 grams (21 ounces) of heroin, or more than 20 kilograms of opium, can face capital punishment' (Linh Pham, 2019). However, following an amendment of the criminal code, Vietnam abolished the death sentence for eight offences, including drug possession; nevertheless, other drug offences, such as manufacturing, transporting, and trafficking specific controlled substances, are still punishable by death (Girelli, 2019). Thailand is following a similar path to Vietnam. Its Narcotics Act (1979) allows for the discretionary imposition of the death penalty for 'Any person who produces, imports or exports the narcotics of category I … [if] committed for the purpose of disposal'. Section 66 stipulates that any person who 'disposes of or possesses for disposal' drugs classified as category I in excess of 20 grams is liable to receive the death penalty' (Narcotics Act).[5] The amended Narcotics Act of 2017 institutes five categories of drugs and only those included in category I[6] can receive the death sentence which is no longer mandatory. In Malaysia, under the Dangerous Drugs Act,

> anyone found with 200 grams (7.05 ounces) of cannabis, 1 kilogram (2.2 pounds) of opium, 40 grams (1.41 ounces) of cocaine, and 15 grams (0.53 ounces) of heroin or morphine face being charged with drug trafficking, which carries the death penalty. (Associated Press, 2019)

The above discussions demonstrate that governments in ASEAN continue to construct their own interpretations of 'most serious crimes' in contravention of current standards of international human rights law. Drug crimes form part of what retentionist countries perceive to be most serious crimes. With the exception of Indonesia, Malaysia, Singapore, Thailand, and Vietnam, all impose mandatory death sentences for drug-related offences. In all the countries studied, governments continue to hold a zero-tolerance mentality toward drug-related crimes. The most outspoken of all is Singapore. Its Ministry of Home Affairs Stated that,

> [T]he death penalty is applicable only for a very limited number of offences, involving the most serious forms of harm to victims and to society, such as intentional murder and trafficking of significant quantities of drugs. (Ministry of Home Affairs, 2021)

Said Ministry justified such imposition of the death penalty for its 'immense harm to drug abusers, families, and the community' (Ministry of Home Affairs, 2021).

3.2 Crimes Against the State and Military Codes

While most retentionist and several other States abolished the death penalty for ordinary crimes, they retained it for certain political offences, including offences against the State and public order, violations of military law in time of war, 'terrorist' acts, and acts of treason (International Commission Against the Death Penalty, 2013). Offences against the State fall into two categories. The first constitutes conduct inimical to the very existence of government including treason, sedition or advocacy to overthrow the government, and espionage. The second are offences affecting the orderly and just administration of public business, including perjury, bribery and corruption, and criminal libel and contempt by publication (Packer, 1962). Moreover, crimes against States, such as drug offences, have been expanded over time to include acts of terrorism, piracy, premeditated murder of a head of state or of a friendly State, betrayal of country, destruction of aircraft, possession and/or trading of illicit arms or ammunition, etc.

In all AMS where the death penalty remains, crimes against the State and military codes prescribe capital punishment. Thus, treason, sedition, sabotage, espionage,

[5] Narcotics Act, BE 2522 (1979), Ch 12, available at http://en.oncb.go.th/file/information_narcotics.html.

[6] That is, heroin, amphetamines, methamphetamines, MDMA (ecstasy), and LSD.

and terrorism are all punishable under national laws. In Indonesia, Criminal Code, Articles 104, 111, 123, 124, 140, 444, and 479 prescribe the death penalty for crimes against the State (AICHR, 2019a).[7] In Malaysia, mandatory death penalties are prescribed for discharging a firearm (the Firearms Act 1971, Sections 3 and 3A), offences against the Sultan (Penal Code, Section 121A), terrorist acts resulting in death (Section 130C), and other terror-related acts (Sections 130I, 130N, 130O, and 130QA) (AICHR, 2019b). In addition, offences providing for discretionary death penalties include the trafficking of arms (Section 7 of the Firearms Act 1971) and aiding or communicating with an enemy by a member of the armed forces (Sections 38 and 41 of the Armed Forces Act 1972). Other offences specified include those defined in the Arms Act 1960, the Water Services Industry Act 2006, the Strategic Trade Act 2010 (relating to illicit armed transactions) and waging war against the Sultan, to name but a few (AICHR, 2019b).

As mentioned previously, Singapore imposes capital punishment in cases of treason, national security, military crimes, war crimes, genocide, crimes against humanity, and offences against the State, etc. (AICHR, 2020a). In Thailand, 63 offences prescribe capital punishment including Articles 107, 108, 109 and 111 of the Penal Code which impose the death penalty or a life sentence for regicide and causing the death of the queen or the heir-apparent. Similarly, offences against national security, insurrection, terrorism and destroying or setting fire to public places will also result in the death penalty (AICHR, 2019d). In addition to State and national security-related offences specified by the Penal Code, the Military Code also contains a range of capital punishment offences ranging from prisoner of war, espionage, supporting the enemy, desertion of duties by military officials, to committing an act with intent to compromise military capacity or plotting to overthrow the government or to bring about change to the military's political or economic traditions (AICHR, 2019d). Such provisions are definitely in contravention of the Minimum Standards on the Use of the Death Penalty which clarifies that 'the death penalty should not be imposed as an act of political revenge in contravention of the minimum standards, eg, against coup plotters' (AICHR, 2019d). The death penalty is also imposed on some offences specified by the Act on Certain Offences Against Air Navigation BE 2558. It can therefore be seen that Thai laws prescribe capital punishment to a wide range of State and national security-related offences.

[7] Article 104: Attempts to foil the life, freedom, and capacity of the President or the Vice President to govern (*makar*); Articles 111(2) and 112: Any person colluding with a foreign government and to which such hostilities are produced into war or any person divulging information that he or she understands to be confidential towards a foreign power; Article 123: Any Indonesian who voluntarily enters into military service with a foreign power, knowing they may potentially be at war with that foreign power; Article 124(3): Any person who has betrayed the country to align with the enemy or 'destructs or damages a stronghold or post, which is reinforced or occupied, a means of communication, a storehouse, a military provision, or a military, naval or army chest or any part thereof, obstructs, prevents or frustrates a plan for inundation or another military plan devised or executed for defense or attack' or in the second degree 'causes or facilitates a revolt, mutiny, or desertion among the armed forces'; Article 140: Premeditated murder of a head of a friendly state; Article 444: Piracy resulting in the death of one of the persons on board; and Article 479(o)(2): Destruction of an aircraft resulting in death is also privy to capital punishment.

In the case of Vietnam, offences infringing national security are considered 'extreme serious crimes' deserving of the death penalty. In the Penal Code (which was amended in 2015 and entered into force in 2018), such crimes include high treason, activities against the government, espionage, rebellion, terrorist acts against the government, and the sabotage of government facilities. Interestingly, crimes against peace (wars of aggression), humanity, and war crimes which were incorporated into the Rome Statute also form part of a group of crimes undermining peace and security (AICHR, 2020e).

3.3 *Offences Affecting the Orderly and Just Administration of Public Business, and Economic Crimes*

Some 20 countries around the globe impose the death penalty for various economic crimes, including bribery and corruption of public officials, embezzlement of public funds, currency speculation, and the theft of large sums of money (Hood, n.d.). Of this number, four are members of ASEAN, namely, Indonesia, Lao PDR, Thailand, and Vietnam. In Indonesia, Article 2(2) of the Corruption Eradication Law permits imposition of the death penalty if the corruption is committed under certain circumstances (Budiman et al., 2020). As the COVID-19 pandemic continues to rage, pushes to impose the death penalty for corruption have intensified. Indeed, President Joko Widodo chose International Anti-Corruption Day 2019 to state that if the public supported the death penalty for perpetrators of corruption, the government would initiate revisions to include this provision in the draft Criminal Code (RKUHP) and the Corruption Eradication Law (Budiman et al., 2020, p. 31). This statement was later supported by ministers, including the Minister of Law and Human Rights and the Chairman of the Corruption Eradication Commission (KPK) who agreed that the 'KPK would demand the death penalty for corruption offenders in the COVID-19 pandemic handling budget' (Budiman et al., 2020, p. 31).

Likewise, the Criminal Code of Thailand prescribes the death penalty under 55 different articles for various offences including economic crimes. Other laws containing such provisions include the 1999 Anti-Corruption Law, the 2008 Anti-Trafficking in Persons Act, and the 2015 Act Regarding Offenses Relating to Air Travel. Corruption and bribery, as well as embezzlement in any form by officials of the three government branches (executive, legislative, and the judiciary), are punishable by death or imprisonment as prescribed by the Penal Code. In addition, the Organic Act on Counter Corruption (No. 3) BE 2558 also stipulates that a State official, an official of a foreign State or an official of an international organisation who illegally demands or accepts property or other benefits for oneself or for another person in order to or not to execute the power in his office will be punished by imprisonment, a fine, or death (AICHR, 2019d).

Nevertheless, Thailand has abolished the death penalty with regards to corruption committed by officials in its amended anti-corruption law (Muntarbhorn, 2021).

Finally, Vietnam applies capital punishment to acts of embezzlement or to those accepting bribes despite international standards which do not categorise such acts as 'most serious crimes'.

4 'Most Serious Crimes': The International Threshold

Previous sections have shown that all retentionist States in ASEAN continue to apply the death penalty to crimes not considered the 'most serious' according to international standards. This is exacerbated by the lack of a clear definition of the term which results in various challenges, the most critical of which are differing State party interpretations of the ICCPR. Article 6 stipulates:

1. Every human being has the inherent right to life. This right shall be protected by law. No one shall be arbitrarily deprived of his life.
2. In countries which have not abolished the death penalty, sentence of death may be imposed only for **the most serious crimes** in accordance with the law in force at the time of the commission of the crime and not contrary to the provisions of the present Covenant and to the Convention on the Prevention and Punishment of the Crime of Genocide. This penalty can only be carried out pursuant to a final judgment rendered by a competent court.

While Article 6(2) suggests the death penalty is not completely prohibited under international law, its imposition is only permissible if the nature of the offence satisfies the category of 'most serious crimes' and proper judicial procedures meet the standard requirements based especially on the due process of law, the right to a fair trial, and is conducted pursuant to a final judgment rendered by a competent court. However, since the phrase 'the most serious crimes' was not specifically defined at the time of drafting, much disagreement arose between States still retaining capital punishment, thus, it has been left to individual States to interpret the phrase according to their national laws and political complexities. The clear intention of Article 6(2) was articulated in Resolution 2857 of 1971 issued by the UN General Assembly which called for 'the progressive restriction of the number of offences for which capital punishment may be imposed, with a view to abolish this punishment in all countries' (UN General Assembly, 2007). The very notion of 'progressive restriction' makes it clear the degree of 'seriousness' that would justify the death penalty would need to be continuously evaluated and re-evaluated until the definition was so narrowed, de facto abolition would eventually be achieved (Hood, 2006). Consequently, relevant UN agencies, international NGOs, and international law experts have attempted to clarify and provide possible criteria for a certain level of common understanding and interpretation of 'the most serious crimes'.

The first attempt can be found in General Comment 5 (1982) of the UN Human Rights Committee which emphasised that the right to life was not to be interpreted narrowly. It noted:

> [W]hile it follows from Article 6(2) to (6) that State parties are not obliged to abolish the death penalty totally, they are obliged to limit its use and, in particular, to abolish it for other than the 'most serious crimes'.

Accordingly, States ought to consider reviewing their criminal laws in this light, and in any event, are obliged to restrict the application of the death penalty to the 'most serious crimes' (UN Human Rights Committee, 1994). Further, the Committee 'is of the opinion that the expression "most serious crimes" must be read restrictively to mean that the death penalty should be a quite exceptional measure' (UN Human Rights Committee, 1994). It also follows from the express terms of Article 6 that it can only be imposed in accordance with the law in force at the time of the commission of the crime and not contrary to the Covenant. Unfortunately, despite the above comments, a clear definition of the concept was not offered.

In 1984, the UN Economic and Social Council adopted the Safeguards Guaranteeing Protection of the Rights of Those Facing the Death Penalty (UN Economic & Social Council, 1984). This was further reiterated by the resolution adopted by the UN Commission on Human Rights in 2005 which states that its use should be limited to ensure also that the notion of 'most serious crimes' does not go beyond intentional crimes with lethal or extremely grave consequences and that the death penalty is not imposed for non-violent acts such as financial crimes, religious practice or expression of conscience and sexual relations between consenting adults nor as a mandatory sentence (UN Commission on Human Rights, 2005). These were later endorsed by the UN General Assembly and provided that:

> [I]n countries which have not abolished the death penalty, capital punishment may be imposed only for the most serious crimes, it being understood that their scope should not go beyond intentional crimes with lethal or other extremely grave consequences. (UN General Assembly, 2007)

This implies that 'most serious crimes' must be intentional crimes of violence with an immediate life-threatening effect. As such, capital punishment cannot be applied to non-violent financial crimes, non-violent religious practices or expressions of conscience, sexual relations between consenting adults, drug-related offences, illicit sex, vague categories of offences relating to internal and external security, or aggravated robbery where no death has ensued (Byrnes, 2007). Whilst States have some discretion in determining or interpreting the provisions of Article 6, nevertheless, they cannot simply designate a crime as most serious. Interpretation has to be made in light of international practice which demands a restrictive meaning of the term and which permits its use only as an exceptional measure. This concurs with the point made by the UN Special Rapporteur on extrajudicial, summary, or arbitrary executions that:

> It is clear that a subjective approach to this important issue is not viable, in the sense that a vast array of offences might understandably be classified by any given individual or Government as being among the 'most serious'. But such an approach would render the relevant international law standard meaningless. As a result, a systematic and normatively persuasive response is essential. (Alston, 2007)

Moreover, the UN Human Rights Committee also raised concerns over mandatory death sentences which it considered a violation of the right to life under Article 6(1) of the ICCPR. In addition, the Committee stated that conduct whose very criminalisation violates the Covenant, such as establishing opposition groups or offending a head of State, should never be subject to the death penalty (General comment No. 36, para. 36). The Human Rights Committee has established a significant jurisprudence interpreting the "most serious crimes" by consistently excluding offences that do not lead to loss of life from the imposition of the death penalty. According to the Committee, the use capital punishment for crimes such as: apostasy, abetting suicide, aggravated robbery with the use of firearm, robbery with violence, homosexual acts, illicit sex, espionage, evasion of military responsibility, economic crimes, offences against property, embezzlement by state officials, theft by force, misappropriation of state or public property, misuse of public funds, and crimes against the economy, in particular political crimes in general is inconsistent with Article 6 (2) of the ICCPR. The Human Rights Committee interprets the most serious crimes to mean "only intentional killings or attempted killings, and perhaps the intentional infliction of grievous bodily harm" (Miao, 2015). In 2013, the UN Secretary-General affirmed in his report to the Human Rights Council (HRC) that the death penalty should only be used for the 'most serious crimes' of murder and or intentional killing (Human Rights Council 2013). The HRC in fact made it clear since 2007 that drug-related offences, terrorism, and offences against the state are amongst those crimes that does not amount to 'most serious crimes' (Human Rights Council, 2007).

As demonstrated earlier, the meaning of the 'most serious crimes' has been clarified to refer to offences with intent to kill resulting in loss of life (International Commission Against the Death Penalty, 2013). In other words, not all homicide, for example, crimes of passion or crimes resulting in unintentional death (e.g. a robbery gone awry) should be included in its scope. Thus, the three categories of crimes discussed in the previous section, including drug-related offences (which boasts the highest number of prisoners on death row in all the countries under study), fail to meet the threshold of most serious crimes. This was reiterated by the UN High Commissioner for Human Rights in his open letter to the Philippines Congress dated 6 December 2016 which categorically stated that drug-related offences do not meet the threshold of 'most serious crimes'. He also emphasised that the International Narcotics Control Board which monitors State compliance with drug control treaties, 'considers that the use of the death penalty for drug crimes is incompatible under international law' (Sabillo, 2016). Accordingly, while drug-related crimes, especially drug trafficking, is clearly a 'serious crime', it cannot be characterised as 'most serious'. Indeed, Article 36(1) of the 1961 Single Convention on Narcotic Drugs only prescribes 'imprisonment or other penalties of deprivation of liberty'.[8] In

[8] '(a) Subject to its constitutional limitations, each Party shall adopt such measures as will ensure that cultivation, production, manufacture, extraction, preparation, possession, offering, offering for sale, distribution, purchase, sale, delivery on any terms whatsoever, brokerage, dispatch, dispatch in transit, transport, importation and exportation of drugs contrary to the provisions of this Convention, and any other action which in the opinion of such Party may be contrary to the provisions of this Convention, shall be punishable offences when committed intentionally, and that serious offences

the same way, the 1988 United Nations Convention against Illicit Traffic in Narcotic Drugs and Psychotropic Substances leads to an overwhelming inference that imposition of the death penalty is an inappropriate punishment in this regard (Rothwell, 2015).

In addition, by international standards, while some offences may involve loss of life and could therefore be construed as intentional murder, many are so broadly defined, they fail to meet the threshold for 'most serious crimes'. Others, such as activities against the government, could even be described as political offences. In written interviews with several respondents in Vietnam about crimes for which the death penalty is applicable, 4 out of 11[9] included offences against State and national security as one of the three 'most serious crimes' meriting capital punishment. It is worth noting the difficulty in finding death row statistics for State/national security-related crimes. Predictably, therefore, many governments continue to use the death penalty as a tool to suppress political dissent.

Although Malaysia and Singapore are not party to ICCPR these two countries are abided by other UN-based normative frameworks and declarations. They both are members of the General Assembly, the ECOSOC, the Human Rights Council, party to the CRC and CRPD as well as the UDHR which is considered as customary law. The inherent right to life is taken as a '*jus cogens*' implies restrictions on the scope of offences for which capital punishment may be imposed.

The challenges with defining such crimes lie in the State's critical role in creating legal categories. People are not inherently criminal and only become so when thus defined by political authorities through the criminal justice system. This practice is mirrored at the international level when the meaning of 'most serious crimes' is left to States to interpret in accordance with national laws and policies. Accordingly, attempts by international human rights bodies to clarify the concept have met with some resistance, particularly in ASEAN.

5 Unpacking the Concepts and Problems Around Various Interpretations of 'Most Serious Crimes'

As already demonstrated, drug-related offences, State security and military-related offences, as well as those affecting public order, public administration, and financial crimes fail to meet the threshold of 'most serious crimes' as explained by the international community and international law. Even though the UN Human Rights Committee, the UNODC, the UN General Assembly, and international law experts have tried to clarify the concept and offer interpretations of the term, none have attempted to specifically define 'most serious crimes' except clarifications as to its

shall be liable to adequate punishment particularly by imprisonment or other penalties of deprivation of liberty.'

[9] Respondents included 2 academics, 3 NGO staff, 1 staff member of an international organisation, 4 working in the judiciary system, and 1 representative of the Ministry of Justice.

scope which 'should not go beyond intentional crimes with lethal or other extremely grave consequences'.

Examination of all reports submitted as part of the thematic study of the AICHR reveals that not all AMS use the term, 'most serious crimes' in their national laws. In Vietnam, the phrase, 'especially or particularly serious crimes' refers to 'crimes that infringe national security, human life, drug-related crimes, corruption-related crimes and some other extremely serious crimes defined by [the Criminal] Code' (for example, crimes causing particularly serious harm to society with the maximum penalty being over fifteen years' imprisonment, life imprisonment, or the death penalty) (AICHR, 2020e). The death penalty was conceived as an exceptional sentence as claimed by Foreign Ministry spokeswoman, Le Thi Thu Hang, in accordance with the ICCPR (Anh Phan, 2019). Likewise, when criticised by Amnesty International, the Government of Singapore issued a statement asserting that it 'imposes capital punishment only for the most serious crimes' (Hor, 2004, p. 106). However, Hor (2004, p. 106) noted the same statement used the phrase, 'very serious crimes'. The Ministry of Home Affairs (2021) elaborated that the death penalty is applicable for a very limited number of offences involving the most serious forms of harm to victims and to society. It further explained that in deciding to impose it, the government takes into account

> [amongst other factors] three key considerations. First, the seriousness of the offence, in terms of the harm that the offence will cause to the victim and to society. Second, how frequent or widespread the offence is. Third, the need for a very high degree of deterrence. These considerations are considered in totality. (Ministry of Home Affairs, 2021)

So, most serious crimes or 'very serious crimes' were qualified by Singaporean authorities as emphasising the level of harm to individuals and society as well as the effect of deterrence. The other three countries (Indonesia, Malaysia, and Thailand) do not appear to qualify the 'most serious crimes' in their laws. In fact, in all countries, various offences tend to be ill defined and fluid subject to the vagary of the authorities.

Some common rationales behind the application of capital punishment in AMS can be found, at least among the five countries under study. These include:

(a) Reference to State Sovereignty. In response to Amnesty International, a spokeswoman at Vietnam's Ministry of Foreign Affairs, said, 'the application of the death penalty is a sovereign nation's prerogative and Vietnam only applies it for very grave crimes' (Linh Pham, 2019). She added further that 'execution of [the] death sentence is Vietnam's inalienable sovereign right [as is its right] to choose its legal and criminal judicial systems' [She also noted that the death sentence] 'is available in many countries all over the world' (Linh Pham, 2019). For its part, Indonesia also invoked the need to respect its legal system and to accept its much tougher drug laws.

> [Due to] the inter-linkage nature of human rights, the issue of [the] death penalty cannot be seen solely through one single lens. Moreover, there is no authoritative intergovernmental consensus on categories of offences that are considered serious crimes punishable by [the] death sentence. (Permanent Mission of the Republic of Indonesia to the UN, 2015)

Similarly, Singapore's Ministry of Home Affairs (2021) reiterates that

> every country has the sovereign right to decide for itself whether to impose capital punishment as part of its criminal justice system, depending on its own circumstances and in accordance with its international obligations. This sovereign right to impose the death penalty was reaffirmed most recently at the 75th United Nations General Assembly in 2020.

Moreover, in a proposed amendment to the 2020 UN resolution concerning a moratorium on the use of the death penalty, the Singapore delegation asserted the 'sovereign right of all countries to develop their own legal systems, including determining appropriate legal penalties' (Strangio, 2020).

It is because of the lack of a universally agreed definition of 'most serious crimes' at the international level that international agencies and other States are bound to respect national procedures. In ASEAN countries, where the principle of national sovereignty is frequently used as a tool to assure regional order, it is also seized upon to protect national interests thereby ensuring societal stability free from external interference in internal affairs. Indeed, this concept has been strictly adhered to by all AMS and is enshrined in the ASEAN Charter.

If it is true that all AMS are sovereign States, it is also true that Indonesia, the Philippines, Thailand, and Vietnam committed to accept and abide by the ICCPR. Although States may have some discretion in determining how to implement a treaty obligation in its particular national context, ultimately, it is for an international instance (a relevant international body) to make an objective and independent assessment in light of the text and context of the relevant treaty provision as to whether the obligation has been fulfilled. In other words, an individual State Party cannot generally be the sole judge of the meaning of a treaty obligation or whether it has been fulfilled in a particular case (Byrnes, 2007). At this juncture it seems appropriate to once again cite the words of UN Special Rapporteur, Professor Philip Alston (2007) when he said:

> It is clear that a subjective approach to this important issue is not viable, in the sense that a vast array of offences might understandably be classified by any given individual or Government as being among the 'most serious'. But such an approach would render the relevant international law standard meaningless.

In the end, a State cannot simply designate a crime as the 'most serious' and make its own assessment or classification; the crime in question needs to be looked at in the context of other crimes and its seriousness assessed not only in the social context but also in light of international practice.

(b) Predominance of retributive justice concept. As will be further discussed in Chapter 8, usual justifications for the death penalty focus on retribution and are based on the idea that those who commit wrongdoing, especially acts deemed serious, deserve to be punished, even to the point of being executed. All retentionist States in ASEAN apply the death penalty to murder and other acts resulting in loss of life. This practice of 'an eye for an eye, a tooth for a tooth' or *lex talionis* has always received popular support in the countries under study. The basic concept behind retribution by capital punishment is to ensure the offender is incapacitated by preventing him or her from committing further crimes. However, sometimes the line between punishment and revenge is blurred as the penalties imposed are not always proportionate to the crime committed. All retentionist States apply 'strict retribution' whereby the punishment is roughly equivalent to the kind of harm committed. In addition, ASEAN leaders, lawmakers, and the public, largely support retaining capital punishment for serious crimes as a deterrent. Thus, abolishing the death penalty would encourage unscrupulous robbers and killers to continue their lives of crime. In this case, punishment is conflated with prevention.

(c) Harm to society. Here, the concept of prevention is expanded to preclude harm to society by imposing the death penalty on offences not resulting in loss of life, such as drug-related crimes. Most, if not all retentionist States, argue that capital punishment must be imposed to counteract the nature and extent of the danger posed to society as a result of certain crimes. In Vietnam, for example, many crimes attracting the death penalty seek to violate national security and social order as prescribed in its constitution. Such acts are seen as a major threat to society as a whole, harming human health, causing offspring degeneration, degrading human dignity, disrupting family happiness, and gravely affecting social order, safety, and national security (Government of Vietnam, 2000). In the case of Indonesia,

> only those crimes committed with a certain gravity and severity and [having a] serious impact [on] society, will result in [a] death sentence. If we have to reintroduce [the] death penalty, it is simply because we are dictated by the aggravated situation affecting our society as a result of those crimes. (Permanent Mission of the Republic of Indonesia to the UN, 2015)

In the Philippines, one justification to re-impose the death penalty currently being debated in Congress as advanced by President Duterte in his 4th State of the Nation Address was the 'long way to go in ... fight[ing] against this social menace' (Acosta et al., 2019). This has led others to claim it as a compelling reason for re-imposing the death penalty to fight the country's widespread drug problem despite it being more of a social issue than a criminal one (Acosta et al., 2019). As mentioned above, the Singapore government imposes the death penalty based on the harm caused to both victim and society as a whole. Thailand has a similar perception. Its Corrections Department emphasised the government's policy to focus on the protection of society rather than the 'rights and freedom of wrongdoers'. A similar sentiment was echoed by Thailand's Prime Minister, Prayut Chan-ocha, when he said that Thailand required the death penalty to preserve peace and order in the country (Thai Examiner, 2018).

Addressing societal harm in the AMS as a whole by applying capital punishment is based on the presumption that any breach of law represents a threat to the order and functioning of society. As Luyen (2019) puts it:

> The death sentence can be considered as one [measure] to maintain social stability, protect the common interests of the community [and] the State, and protect people [by] punish[ing] those [committing] particularly serious offences [and] bringing justice to society.

The social harm paradigm is based on the utilitarianism theory of justice which stresses the benefits of punishment to the community and society as a whole. Accordingly, capital punishment is morally permissible if it serves the greater good of society. Greater good underscores the deterrent effect of crimes which discourages offenders from re-committing crimes whilst deterring other members of society from committing similar offences, thereby resulting in safer communities (Haist, 2009). However, the utilitarianism of the death penalty has a serious inherent shortcoming especially when it comes to its unique deterrent effect.

(d) Concerns over power. All retentionist countries in ASEAN are currently ruled by non-democratic and/or populist governments relying on the exercise of strong if not absolute power. Laws in these States include capital punishment for State/security-related offences such as acts against the King, Sultan, President, the government, spying, rebellion, infringing upon territorial security, conducting banditry activities, and defecting to the enemy, etc. It is believed the death penalty serves as an 'effective' mechanism to suppress dissenting voices including those of political dissidents and the opposition. This is clearly demonstrated in Vietnam where the penal law includes many provisions designed to maintain societal order and deter opposition to the socialist regime (Tran & Vu, 2019). In all countries, the death sentence is seen as a vital aid to protecting national security. Accordingly, national/State security is often conflated with the security of the country itself.

Greenberg and West (2008) argue that countries allowing little political space are more likely to apply capital punishment tending to use force or (even killing) to maintain order and control, or power. For example, statistics depict a trend that non-democratic governments are more likely than democratic governments to use capital punishment. Because leaders in ASEAN perceive crimes as social harm and a defiance of their authority, security of status, and power, a stringent response is therefore often demanded.

In other words, AMS attitudes to capital punishment could be said to reflect 'Asian values' as advanced by its leaders and the majority of the public. As such, social harmony, order, obedience to power/leaders, respect for State sovereignty, and community values over individual rights form the basis of 'good government' (rather than 'good governance') thereby ensuring stability, security, and economic development. Accordingly, societies must be protected from 'societal problems' such as drug use and soaring crime rates, to name but a few.

The UN Special Rapporteur on extrajudicial killings described in his 2007 report that

> capital crimes in domestic law include abetting suicide, adultery, apostasy, corruption, economic crimes, the expression of conscience, financial crimes, embezzlement by officials, evasion of military service, homosexual acts, illicit sex, sexual relations between consenting adults and religious practice; clearly allowing States to set their own standards makes a mockery of the notion of a 'most serious crimes' threshold, and quickly becomes a slippery slope towards major human rights violations. (Alston, 2007)

Permitting individual governments to set national standards on capital punishment allows administrations to rely on such 'values' to make sense of the serious dilemmas we are all confronted with. How can this situation be overcome?

6 Conclusion

It is undeniable that the prevention of homicide and other serious offences against the person, as well as the elimination of drug trafficking and other serious offences are legitimate and important social goals. Therefore, it is permissible for States to pursue these goals by means of criminal laws and sanctions. The key question is whether the death penalty is a proportionate and justifiable measure in the fight against serious crime especially when legislatures stray beyond the intentionality permitted by 'most serious crimes'. It is also recognisable that a crime is a socially harmful act or omission that breaches the values protected by a State. As events prohibited by law, such acts can thus be sanctioned by punishment on conviction. Moreover, it is within the discretion of a State to construe which acts require criminalisation and to incorporate such prohibitions into its respective criminal laws (Marchuk, 2013).

Nevertheless, the concept of crime may change over time and space. Crimes can be defined and analysed from different bases and paradigms; the most relevant to this study are social and legal definitions as well as behavioural and definitional paradigms. The legal definition of crime focuses on behaviour in violation of criminal law which therefore becomes liable for sanctioning by criminal justice agencies under the political authority of the State. From a theoretical perspective, it attributes to a behavioural paradigm which attempts to explain the causes of the behaviour in order to predict and control it. Since the late nineteenth century, positivist schools of criminology have been guided by the behavioural theory.

The definitional paradigm focuses on the processes which ensure certain actions and persons are selected and defined as criminal by political authorities. Developed and popularised in the early 1960s, it is known as the 'labelling theory' of deviance (Kramer, 1985). Here, the emphasis is put on the designation of specific behaviour as rule-breaking conduct which leads us to look at the responses of legal authorities. As such, attention shifted from criminal behaviour to the criminalisation process and the operation of the criminal justice system, where the social reality of crime is actually created. The definitional approach looks at how criminal laws are made, how legal theories are created, and how these categories are applied by legal control agents and how persons who are ascribed the legal status of convicted criminal are handled by the correctional system (Kramer, 1985). Finally, the general scope of criminology includes the processes of making laws, of breaking laws, and of reacting toward the breaking of laws. This is achieved by State authorities based on the assumption that crime is a socio-legal construction and they have the power to criminalise behaviour thus defined; hence, crimes are legal categories created by the State. Criminality is a legal status ascribed by legal actors in a legal process governed by specific procedural (legal) rules, again, created by the State (Kramer, 1985).

No one is suggesting that murderers or drug traffickers are not criminals. But, no behaviour or person is inherently criminal. They become criminal only when defined as such by political authorities. The point here is that the definition of 'most serious' crimes in ASEAN reflects the interests of those controlling political authority. It is crucial to evaluate the manner in which political authorities protect individual human rights from criminal harms but also to protect the rights of those accused or convicted from legalised oppression by criminal justice agents as well as the exercise of State power (Kramer, 1985, pp. 475–476). In the end, the State is not neutral but in many cases makes value judgments. As a result, criminal laws and the criminal justice system are not always objective and value-free, and may become allied to the State and serve its interests (Kramer, 1985, p. 475).

Justice Mahomed of the Constitutional Court of South Africa once said:

> [T]he death penalty sanctions the deliberate annihilation of life. It is the ultimate and the most incomparably extreme form of punishment [...] It is the last, the most devastating and the most irreversible recourse of the criminal law, involving as it necessarily does, the planned and calculated termination of life itself; the destruction of the greatest and most precious gift which is bestowed on all humankind. (Byrnes, 2007)

The fundamental principle around taking a life through the law's instrumentality is that

> it ought not to be done save in the rarest of rare cases when the alternative option is unquestionably foreclosed. [The] rarest of rare cases [is] when the collective conscience of the community is so shocked that it will expect the holders of the judicial power centre to inflict the death penalty. (Byrnes, 2007)

Therefore, the judiciary and legislative bodies should not only take into account the political preferences of political decision-makers. Those who support the death penalty do so because they believe punishment is necessary to maintain law and order in society. Yet it does nothing to maintain law and order in society. This is, in fact, tied to the ideology of using State violence and punishment as a means to exert social control through fear which is currently the norm in ASEAN countries. There is a real need for a more humanistic and human rights-based approach to capital punishment. As such, some guidelines/recommendations are proposed for consideration comprising a step-by-step approach towards establishing a common interpretation of the 'most serious crimes' in ASEAN, pertaining to the eventual abolition of the death penalty.

1. Reduce the number of crimes liable to capital punishment instead of pushing for its abolition. This is the trend in ASEAN;
2. Because mitigating factors in ASEAN are still absent in all retentionist countries, mandatory capital punishment should be completely removed;
3. Take all measures necessary to ensure it is limited to the most serious of crimes, such as acts carried out with the intention of killing;
4. Provide platforms for informed debates on issues relating to the death penalty and what constitutes the 'most serious crimes' in ASEAN and AMS to construct a 'common' basis for the region;
5. Undertake research to establish whether the different offences eligible for capital punishment actually contribute towards the management or reduction of that criminal act; and
6. As mentioned previously, no person is inherently criminal. Encourage a shift from labelling and categorizing crimes and corresponding punishments to analysing the reasons why people commit crimes.

This paper concludes by quoting Bardinter stating "the exclusion of the death penalty by the international courts for the most heinous crimes imaginable suggests that there is now no crime serious enough to warrant the death penalty" (Bardinter, 2004 cited in International Bar Association, 2008, p. 10). The most serious aspect of human beings and law is life not death.

References

Acosta, R., dela Cruz J. M., Nicolas, B., & San Juan, J. R. (2019, September 19). Death penalty: Deterrent or dilemma in PHL's war vs crime? *Business Mirror*. https://businessmirror.com.ph/2019/09/19/death-penalty-deterrent-or-dilemma-in-phls-war-vs-crime/. Accessed 11 October 2021.

AICHR. (2019a). *Thematic study on the right to life: Protection of the rights of personas convicted of the death penalty, Indonesia country report* (Unpublished report).

AICHR. (2019b). *Thematic study on the right to life: Protection of the rights of personas convicted of the death penalty, Malaysia country report* (Unpublished report).

AICHR. (2019c). *Thematic study on the right to life: Protection of the rights of personas convicted of the death penalty, Singapore country report* (Unpublished report).

AICHR. (2019d). *Thematic study on the right to life: Protection of the rights of personas convicted of the death penalty, Thailand country report* (Unpublished report).

AICHR. (2020a, April). *Thematic study on right to life: Protection of the rights of persons convicted of the death penalty, regional synthesis* (Unpublished report).

AICHR. (2020b). *Thematic study on the right to life: Protection of the rights of personas convicted of the death penalty, Brunei country report* (Unpublished report).

AICHR. (2020c). *Thematic study on the right to life: Protection of the rights of personas convicted of the death penalty, Lao PDR country report* (Unpublished report).

AICHR. (2020d). *Thematic study on the right to life: Protection of the rights of personas convicted of the death penalty, Myanmar country report* (Unpublished report).

AICHR. (2020e). *Thematic study on the right to life: Protection of the rights of personas convicted of the death penalty, Vietnam country report* (Unpublished report).

AICHR. (2021, April). *Right to life: Protection of the rights of persons convicted of the death penalty, thematic study commissioned by the AICHR* (Unpublished report).

Alston, P. (2007, January 29). *Report of the Special Rapporteur on extrajudicial, summary or arbitrary executions* (A/HRC/4/20). UN General Assembly. https://undocs.org/A/HRC/4/20. Accessed 18 December 2021.

Amnesty International. (2004, January). *Singapore—The death penalty: A hidden toll of executions*. https://www.amnesty.org/en/wp-content/uploads/2021/09/asa360012004en.pdf. Accessed 11 October 2021.

ASEAN. (2012). *Joint Declaration for a Drug-Free ASEAN*. https://asean.org/?static_post=joint-declaration-for-a-drug-free-asean. Accessed 11 October 2021.

Associated Press. (2019, June 28). *Malaysia plans to decriminalize drug use to battle addiction*. Associated Press. https://apnews.com/920550e2cc854b9a8123abcc0e4bf21d. Accessed 11 October 2021.

Budiman, A. A., Kamilah, A. G., Maya, G. A. K. S., Iftitahsari & Rahmawati, M. (2020, October). *Taking lives during pandemic: 2020 Indonesian death penalty report*. Institute for Criminal Justice Reform. https://icjr.or.id/wp-content/uploads/2020/12/Death-Penalty-Report-ICJR-2020.pdf. Accessed 22 February 2022.

Byrnes, A. (2007). *Drug offences, the death penalty, and Indonesia's human rights obligations in the case of the Bali 9: Opinion submitted to the Constitutional Court of the Republic of Indonesia*.

Series 44, Faculty of Law Research, University of New South Wales. http://www.austlii.edu.au/au/journals/UNSWLRS/2007/44.html. Accessed 18 December 2021.

Girelli, G. (2019, February). *The death penalty for drug offences: Global overview 2018.* Harm Reduction International. https://www.hri.global/files/2019/02/22/HRI_DeathPenaltyReport_2019.pdf. Accessed 11 October 2021.

Government of Vietnam, The Law on Preventing and Combating Narcotic Drugs, 2000. http://www.unodc.org/enl/showDocument.do?documentUid=2304&cuntry=VIE. Accessed 18 December 2021.

Greenberg, D. F., & West, V. (2008). Siting the death penalty internationally. *Law & Social Inquiry, 33*(2), 295–343.

Haist, M. (2009). Deterrence in a sea of just deserts: Are utilitarian goals achievable in a world of limiting retributivism? *Journal of Criminal Law & Criminology, 99*(3), 789–821.

Hood, R. (2006). *The enigma of the 'most serious' offences* (Working Paper No. 9). Center for Human Rights and Global Justice. https://chrgj.org/wp-content/uploads/2018/01/WPS_NYU_CHRGJ_Hood.pdf. Accessed 11 October 2021.

Hood, R. (n.d.). *Capital punishment in the early 21st century.* Encyclopedia Britannica. https://www.britannica.com/topic/capital-punishment/Capital-punishment-in-the-early-21st-century. Accessed 11 October 2021.

Hor, M. (2004). The death penalty in Singapore and international law. *Singapore Year Book of International Law, 8,* 105–117. http://www.commonlii.org/sg/journals/SGYrBkIntLaw/2004/6.pdf. Accessed 11 October 2021.

Human Rights Committee. (1994, July 24). *General Comment 6, Article 6 (Sixteenth session, 1982), compilation of General Comments and General Recommendations adopted by human rights treaty bodies* (HRI/GEN/1/Rev.1). https://undocs.org/en/HRI/GEN/1/Rev.1. Accessed 11 October 2021.

International Bar Association. (2008, May). *The death penalty under international law: A background paper to the IBAHRI resolution on the abolition of the death penalty.* https://www.ibanet.org/medias/Deathpenalty-Paper.pdf?context=bWFzdGVyfEhSSS1yZXBvcnRzfDE1NjM3NnxhcHBsaWNhdGlvbi9wZGZ8aDYzL2hmMy84ODAwNjgzNDkxMzU4L0RlYXRocGVuYWx0eV9QYXBlci5wZGZ8NGEzOWJiMTI1Yzk5YWI0YjJiZmM5ZGU1MzY4OWMwNzNiNjNmMTFlOTIyOGE2OGNkZmQ5NmU2MWFmZGYxNWQzMw&attachment=true. Accessed 10 July 2022.

International Commission Against the Death Penalty. (2013, January). *The death penalty and the "most serious crimes": A country by country overview of the death penalty in law and practice in retentionist states.* https://icomdp.org/wp-content/uploads/2020/10/Most-serious-crimes_final_6Feb2013.pdf. Accessed 11 October 2021.

International Covenant on Civil and Political Rights, December 16, 1966. https://www.ohchr.org/en/professionalinterest/pages/ccpr.aspx. Accessed 11 October 2021.

Kramer, R. C. (1985). Defining the concept of crime: A humanistic perspective. *Journal of Sociology & Social Welfare, 12*(3), 469–487. https://scholarworks.wmich.edu/jssw/vol12/iss3/4/. Accessed 18 December 2021.

Larasati, A., & Girelli, G. (2021). *The death penalty for drug offences: Global overview 2020.* Harm Reduction International. https://www.hri.global/files/2021/04/07/HRI_Death_Penalty_Report_2020_FINAL.pdf. Accessed 18 December 2021.

Leechaianan, Y., & Longmire, D. (2013). The use of the death penalty for drug trafficking in the United States, Singapore, Malaysia, Indonesia and Thailand: A comparative legal analysis. *Laws, 2*(2), 115–149. https://doi.org/10.3390/laws2020115

Luyen, T. V. (2019). Capital punishment in Vietnam, a study from the perspective of traditional and modern values. *Journal of Middle East and North Africa Sciences, 5*(6), 30–33. https://www.academia.edu/39265516/Capital_Punishment_in_Vietnam_a_Study_from_the_Perspective_of_Traditional_and_Modern_Values. Accessed 18 December 2021.

Marchuk, I. (2013). *The fundamental concept of crime in international criminal law.* Springer.

Miao, M. (2015). *A review of the progressive development of international human rights framework on capital punishment.* GlobaLex. https://www.nyulawglobal.org/globalex/Human_Rights_Capital_Punishment.html. Accessed 10 July 2022.

Ministry of Home Affairs. (2021, November 5). *The death penalty in Singapore.* https://www.mha.gov.sg/home-team-real-deal/detail/detail/the-death-penalty-in-singapore. Accessed 22 February 2022.

Morris, J., & Nguyen, S. (2018, December 21). *93% of Thai people want to see the death penalty put to use to curb shocking murders and drug gangs.* Thai Examiner. https://www.thaiexaminer.com/thai-news-foreigners/2018/12/21/death-penalty-thailand-thai-public-execution-foreigners-bang-kwang-death-row-murderer-drugs-monk/. Accessed 22 February 2022.

Muntarbhorn, V. (2021, April 22). Slowly moving away from the death penalty. *Bangkok Post.* https://www.bangkokpost.com/opinion/opinion/2103711/slowly-moving-away-from-the-death-penalty. Accessed 22 February 2022.

OHCHR. (2016, October 20). *Statement by the Special Rapporteur at the "Launch of the Parliamentary Fact Sheet on the Death Penalty and Terrorism-related Offences."* https://www.ohchr.org/en/NewsEvents/Pages/DisplayNews.aspx?NewsID=20800&LangID=E. Accessed 18 December 2021.

OHCHR. (2018, November). *Drug-related offences, criminal justice responses, and the use of the death penalty.* OHCHR Regional Office in South-East Asia. https://bangkok.ohchr.org/wp-content/uploads/2020/01/Drug-Related-Offences-2018.pdf. Accessed 18 December 2021.

Packer, H. L. (1962). Offences against the state. *Annals of the American Academy of Political and Social Science, 339*, 77–89.

Parliamentarians for Global Action. (n.d.). *Malaysia and the death penalty.* https://www.pgaction.org/programmes-and-campaigns/adp/mys.html. Accessed 11 October 2021.

Permanent Mission of the Republic of Indonesia to the UN. (2015, March 6). *Statement by the delegation of the Republic of Indonesia at the high level panel discussion on the question of the death penalty "regional efforts aiming at the abolition of the death penalty and challenges faced in that regard" at the 28th Session of the Human Rights Council.* https://mission-indonesia.org/2015/03/06/Statement-by-the-delegation-of-the-republic-of-indonesia-high-level-panel-discussion-on-the-question-of-the-death-penalty-regional-efforts-aiming-at-the-abolition-of-the-death-penalty-and/. Accessed 11 October 2021.

Pham, L. (2019, April 12). Vietnam affirms imposing of death penalty on absolutely severe crimes only. *Hanoi Times.* http://hanoitimes.vn/vietnam-affirms-imposing-of-death-penalty-on-absolutely-severe-crimes-only-607.html. Accessed 11 October 2021.

Phan, A. (2019, April 11). Vietnam only applies death penalty for "especially serious" crimes. *VN Express.* https://e.vnexpress.net/news/news/vietnam-only-applies-death-penalty-for-especially-serious-crimes-3908301.html. Accessed 11 October 2021.

Rothwell, D. (2015, April 27). *Law experts say Indonesian death penalty is illegal.* ANU. https://www.anu.edu.au/news/all-news/law-experts-say-indonesian-death-penalty-is-illegal. Accessed 11 October 2021.

Sabillo, K.A. (2016, December 8). UN: PH will violate int'l pact if it restores death penalty. *The Inquirer.* https://globalnation.inquirer.net/150445/un-ph-will-violate-intl-pact-restores-death-penalty#ixzz6OfJmuLzt. Accessed 11 October 2021.

Sander, G., Girelli, G., & Cots Fernández, A. (2020). *The death penalty for drug offences: Global overview 2019.* Harm Reduction International. https://www.hri.global/files/2020/02/28/HRI_DeathPenaltyReport2019.pdf, Accessed 18 December 2021.

Schabas, W. (2010, October). *The death penalty and drug offences.* Paper prepared by the Irish Centre for Human Rights and The International Centre on Human Rights and Drug Policy. https://www.hr-dp.org/files/wp-content/uploads/2010/10/Prof-Schabas-Death-Penalty-for-Drug-Offences-Oct-2010-EN.pdf. Accessed 18 December 2021.

Strangio, S. (2020, November 25). Explaining Southeast Asia's addiction to the death penalty. *The Diplomat.* https://thediplomat.com/2020/11/explaining-southeast-asias-addiction-to-the-death-penalty/. Accessed 22 February 2022.

Tran, K., & Vu, C. G. (2019). The changing nature of death penalty in Vietnam: A historical and legal inquiry. *Societies, 9*(3), 56. https://doi.org/10.3390/soc9030056

UN Commission on Human Rights (2005, April 20). *Human Rights Resolution 2005/59: The question of the death penalty* (E/CN.4/RES/2005/59). https://www.refworld.org/docid/45377c730.html. Accessed 18 December 2021.

UN Economic and Social Council. (1984, May 25). *Safeguards guaranteeing protection of the rights of those facing the death penalty, 21st plenary meeting* (E/RES/1984/50). https://undocs.org/en/E/RES/1984/50. Accessed 18 December 2021.

UN General Assembly. (1971, December 20). *Resolution 2857 (XXVI): Capital punishment.* https://www.unodc.org/documents/commissions/CCPCJ/Crime_Resolutions/1970-1979/1971/General_Assembly_Resolution-2857-XXVI.pdf. Accessed 18 December 2021.

UN General Assembly. (2007, December 18). *Promotion and protection of human rights: Human rights questions, including alternative approaches for improving the effective enjoyment of human rights and fundamental freedoms, 5 December 2007* (A/62/439/Add.2). https://undocs.org/en/A/62/439/Add.2. Accessed 18 December 2021.

United Nations Human Rights Council. (2007, 29 January). *Civil and political rights, including the questions of disappearances and summary executions* (A/HRC/4/20, para. 51). United Nations Documents.

United Nations Human Rights Council. (2013, 1 July). *Question of the death penalty: Report of the Secretary-General* (HRC/24/18, para. 24). United Nations Document.

Sriprapha Petcharamesree was a lecturer and senior advisor at the Institute of Human Rights and Peace Studies, Mahidol University in Thailand. She received her Ph.D. (Doctorat) in international politics from the University of Paris-X Nanterre, France. Sriprapha was awarded, in 2017, an Honorary Doctor by the University of Oslo, Norway for her contribution to human rights. From 2009–2012, she has served as the Representative of Thailand to the ASEAN Intergovernmental Commission on Human Rights (AICHR).

Her recent works focus, among others, on issues of citizenship, migration, refugees and asylum seekers as well as statelessness, human rights in international relations, and human rights education. She was entrusted by the AICHR (ASEAN Intergovernmental Commission on Human Rights) to synthesise the country reports on right to life focusing death penalty in ASEAN. She continues her research on the issues and advocates for the abolition of death penalty in the region.

Unpacking Dignity for Death Row Inmates in Southeast Asia

Patricia Rinwigati Waagstein

Abstract The concept of dignity is complex. For centuries, it has been widely shaped and debated by theologians, philosophers, jurists, and others as to its meaning, usefulness, and/or values. Nevertheless, a clear and solid understanding has yet to be reached. This chapter attempts to give meaning to the concept of dignity as regards death row inmates in Southeast Asia, particularly how their dignity has been perceived, treated, and respected. As such, the discussion highlights four different aspects of dignity. First, as a point of departure, it considers the meaning of dignity in ASEAN countries by examining their constitutions. Second, it contends that fully guaranteeing rights to the due process of law is necessary as a means to respect the dignity of the criminal justice system. Third, the validity of 'humane' executions is challenged and the hidden victims of capital punishment are revealed. In short, this chapter argues that despite its complexity, dignity should be defined as an intrinsic human value that can serve as a tool as well as a destination of human rights. Thus, protecting the human rights of death row inmates entails respecting the full integrity of their human dignity and that of their families.

1 Introduction

> I was kicked and hit during the investigation; they would not stop until I signed on the dotted line. The pain never went away. (AZ).[1]

Many such stories reveal the physical and psychological violence inflicted on suspects and prisoners: from sexual abuse to solitary confinement in darkened rooms to being housed next to the gallows within earshot of actual executions. Worse, it is not unusual for an inmate to be only informed of his or her imminent execution until

[1] Interview with an inmate facing the death penalty. For purposes of confidentiality, names have been withheld.

P. R. Waagstein (✉)
Faculty of Law, Universitas Indonesia, Depok City, Indonesia
e-mail: patricia.rinwigati@ui.ac.id

S. Petcharamesree et al. (eds.), *Unpacking the Death Penalty in ASEAN*,
https://doi.org/10.1007/978-981-19-8840-0_4

the last minute often causing intense suffering to family members unable to bid their last farewells. On top of enduring social stigma, relatives of death row inmates may also sink rapidly into poverty. Moreover, their children are often bullied in school, obliging them to abandon their studies, and as a result, they may fall prey to trauma and depression.

Aside from facing one's own imminent death, brutal conditions may subject death row inmates to a form of mental torture leading to an alternative kind of death preceding the date of his/her actual execution. This raises the question of how the dignity of such prisoners has been perceived, treated, and respected throughout.

For centuries, the idea of dignity has been widely shaped and debated by theologians, philosophers, jurists, and others as to its meaning, usefulness, and/or values (Habermas, 2010; Kasiri & Karimi, 2017; Valentini, 2017). International law, particularly with respect to human rights, generally views dignity as a fundamental aspect of one's humanity. Nevertheless, a clear and solid understanding has yet to be agreed upon. Hence, the need arises to at least clarify its meaning in the context of capital punishment.

Rather than discussing these debates in depth or passing judgement on the validity of each when all deserve supplementary study, this chapter shall attempt to unravel what it means to respect a person's dignity in light of a pronouncement of capital punishment, particularly in the context of Southeast Asia. Accordingly, this article draws on such data as regulations, articles, and other publicly available information. It is also supported by interviews with one death row inmate in Indonesia, his family members, lawyers involved in other death row cases, and guards at a correctional facility in Indonesia.

In short, this chapter seeks to examine the meaning of dignity and how it is reflected in the protection of their rights, methods of execution, and the integrity and welfare of their families. Finally, it will establish that the full appreciation and protection of human dignity requires abolition of the death penalty.

2 What Is Human Dignity?

2.1 Unpacking Dignity

The word, dignity, derives from the Latin, *dignitas,* which loosely means the inherent or unearned worth of human beings (Debes, 2018). Because the idea has been around for a long time and has been defined by and applied to various disciplines (Sulmasy, 2013), finding a common understanding can be challenging.

In the context of natural law, dignity is rooted in religious values which declare it a gift bestowed by God (Dramani, 2012; Sulmasy, 2013). As a religious and moral concept, philosophical and legal perspectives have also been applied to dignity laying the foundation for other norms such as the prohibition of contraception, abortion, and torture.

From a philosophical perspective, the meaning of dignity has evolved over time. Originally it can be traced back to Immanuel Kant who referred to human dignity as having an unconditional and intrinsic value and autonomy. Humanity should therefore be viewed not merely as a means but also an end (Dan-Cohen, 2014). This implies that humanity can only be achieved by respecting human dignity itself. Consequently, it entails not only the right to be treated with dignity but also an obligation to respect others.

Pertaining to human rights, dignity has been viewed as integral to one's full enjoyment of rights and fundamental freedoms. Article 1 of the Universal Declaration of Human Rights (UDHR) states that '*All human beings are born free and equal in dignity and rights.*' Likewise, the Preamble of the UDHR speaks to the interconnection of human dignity and human rights by reaffirming '*faith in fundamental human rights in the dignity and worth of a human person*'. Preambles in two other covenants and human rights treaties also recognise that: '*these [*human*] rights derive from the inherent dignity of the human person*' (United Nations International Covenant on Civil and Political Rights [ICCPR], 1966; United Nations International Covenant on Economic, Social, and Cultural Rights [ICESCR], 1966). Similarly, the ASEAN Human Rights Declaration (AHRD) acknowledges that all people are born free and equal in dignity and rights.

Dignity has also been associated with certain human rights and/or freedoms as articulated in various human rights instruments. The ICCPR, for example, mentions dignity particularly in reference to the treatment of detained individuals. Likewise, dignity is found in the context of detention, both in its nature and duration, education (ICESCR, 1966), right to privacy (African Charter on Human and Peoples' Rights, 1981), discrimination against women (United Nations Convention on the Elimination of All Forms of Discrimination against Women [CEDAW], 1979), all forms of exploitation and degrading treatment (CEDAW, 1979), particularly slavery, forced labour, the slave trade, torture, and cruel, inhuman or degrading punishment and treatment (United Nations Convention Against Torture and Other Cruel, Inhuman or Degrading Treatment or Punishment [CAT], 1984) including the death penalty (United Nations Economic Council, 1984).

This discussion speaks to several points. First, the concept of dignity is complex and multi-faceted. As mentioned earlier, numerous attempts have been made to define it in a variety of disciplines and legal instruments. However, its complexity means little agreement has been reached although all have something to offer as part of the emerging picture.

Second, dignity is defined as a crucial element of human beings; it signifies an inherent worth that belongs equally to all and is constituted by certain intrinsically valuable aspects. As a necessary and not contingent feature, it is therefore permanent and unchanging, not transitory or changeable. As such, certain limits can be set as to the justifiable treatment of humans. Therefore, dignity is of particular significance to morality, ethics, law, and politics as an extension of the Enlightenment-era concepts of the inherent and inalienable rights of man.

Third, in the context of human rights, dignity provides a moral basis for duty bearers to fully respect, promote, and protect such rights and freedoms in any context and at all costs. Highlighting its value, dignity was clearly spelled out in several instruments referring to certain rights which are regularly abused and violated such freedom from torture. In this case, dignity is considered to be a minimum prerequisite and a general defence of one's integrity. It is perceived as an ultimate goal of human beings, particularly in the context of rights violations and degrading treatment. Here, dignity as a moral value is transformed into a distinct legal principle, both as a minimal prohibition and a normative common denominator.

The fourth refers to its limitations. Is human dignity applicable equally and universally? The answer is no. Although man's nature (or his basic inherent features) is universal, the substance and character of human dignity are, more often than not, subject to political interpretation and compromised by cultural, social, and systemic factors. As such conditions evolve, so too do interpretations of dignity. For example, in the context of Europe, the term 'human dignity' only became a legal concept after World War II (Habermas, 2010). Habermas points out the historical development and conceptual connection between human rights and dignity in Germany, Italy, and Japan where the term, 'human rights' preceded human dignity as part of a consequence of a post-war moral evolution. Howard and Donnelly (1986) further examine six types of regimes using the five socio-political variables influencing the social definition of human dignity. They conclude that human dignity is a fundamental concept granted at birth regardless of social and political conditions. Nevertheless, its implementation is influenced by the values and commitments of specific regimes and communities as concomitant of one's particularly ascribed status.

2.2 The Concept of Human Dignity in Southeast Asian Countries

Southeast Asian countries consist of a diverse group of states and nations, mainly connected by colonial experiences. Different levels of economic development, political regimes, as well as socio-cultural traits further reinforce divergence within the region consisting of ten ASEAN Member States (AMS) and Timor-Leste. All these factors have a strong bearing on political, legal, and social worldviews, transactions, and systems existing within the region.

All Southeast Asian countries, except Singapore, clearly use the term human dignity, albeit interpreted differently, in their respective constitutions. In the constitutions of Thailand and Brunei Darussalam, dignity is connected to institutional status, which also requires an obligation to honour the dignity of the monarchy. In addition, dignity has been mentioned in the context of several State apparatuses such as the State Attorney (Constitution of the Kingdom of Thailand, 2017), judges (Constitution of the Republic of Indonesia, 1945), and the House of Representatives (Constitution of the Kingdom of Thailand, 2017). Here, dignity is an attribution reserved for high-ranking ceremonial and political officials. The nature may be permanent in the case of royal families, but temporary for other civilian government statuses.

The second meaning of dignity pertains to individual and collective integrity, viewed as an intrinsic quality of all human beings (Henry, 2011). Article 38 of the Constitution of Cambodia recognises the life, honour, and dignity of its citizens. Similarly, legal protection of dignity is stated in the constitutions of Thailand and Vietnam. Referring to collective integrity, Article 23 of Lao PDR's constitution prohibits any cultural and mass media activities which are detrimental to the national interests of the fine tradition of culture and dignity of its people.

Third, dignity is viewed as liberty or freedom. Cambodia's 1993 Constitution (amended in 2008) mentions dignity in the context of the protection of individuals against arbitrary legal enforcement. In this context, dignity is connected to freedom from any coercion and/or violations during judicial processes. Likewise, Thailand's Constitution provides for the protection of human dignity, rights, liberties, and the equality of its people. Moreover, any person can invoke human dignity or exercise his/her rights and liberties as long as it is not in violation of the rights and liberties of others or contrary to the constitution or good morals (Constitution of the Kingdom of Thailand, 2017). This includes the liberty to express opinions in writing, printing, publication, or expression by any other means. In Indonesia, dignity is protected in the context of rights to security and social protection, as well as rights to be free from physical abuse, fear, and torture (Constitution of the Republic of Indonesia 1945). This implies that dignity is also used to protect liberty particularly in judicial processes and instances of inhumane treatment such as torture, slavery, arbitrary coercion, and detention.

Hence, two conclusions can be reached. The first highlights two dimensions of dignity. While the universal dimension of dignity generally refers to the intrinsic worth of all human beings, its regional relative dimension provides an understanding of the external aspects of behaviour particularly on how to acquire dignity by certain behaviour in a diverse social environment. This article is not trying to provide a comprehensive definition of human dignity, it rather aims to give a comparative analysis of the legal development of dignity at the regional level which has very much been influenced by cultural, political as well as legal circumstances. In the end, it will confirm whether the regional interpretation of dignity may be in the line with the international instrument. Therefore, regionally, dignity is viewed through multiple lenses and interpretations. It is not a fixed category, but rather encompasses a series of meanings that may overlap and/or complement each other with human life as the centre point. Thus, respecting human dignity means to respect an essential part of life. Second, dignity in the context of liberty not only refers to a person or a group's 'freedom from' but also the 'capacity to choose' in the case of, for example, freedom of expression and other rights. In other words, dignity constitutes the ability to achieve autonomy (Dan-Cohen, 2014). As such, it is both an entitlement and an obligation to respect others.

In short, the Southeast Asian interpretation of human dignity is not unique, echoing as it does international sentiments. This implies that, throughout the region, dignity is perceived as an inalienable element of human beings, requiring minimum protections from the duty bearer.

2.3 *Dignity and Death Row*

It has been established in many parts of the world that the death penalty is a violation of the right to life. However, exceptions still exist albeit with strict limitations. Schabas argues that such exceptions are less and less clear due to progressive interpretations of the right to life now driving the abolition movement (Schabas, 1998). Unfortunately, due to the wide, loose, and in some cases broadening interpretation of 'most serious crimes', the death penalty still applies in certain cases as a common practice or exception in AMS.

The right to life refers to the entitlement of individuals to be free from acts and omissions that are intended or may be expected to cause their unnatural or premature death, as well as to enjoy their lives with dignity (United Nations Human Rights Committee, 2019). This is applicable to all human beings, including people suspected or convicted of even the most serious crimes. This article offers three ways to interpret dignity in the context of the death penalty.

2.3.1 Fully Protect Human Dignity by Requiring Abolition of the Death Penalty

There has been a global movement towards the abolition and progressive restriction of the death penalty. This is based on a growing recognition that, while each nation has the sovereign right to administer punishments of its own choosing, retention of the death penalty inevitably violates universally accepted human rights and human dignity (Hood & Hoyle, 2009, 2015). In other words, dignity can only be fully upheld if the death penalty is abolished.

Currently, whilst Cambodia and the Philippines have abolished capital punishment, the remaining eight AMS still retain such provisions despite an emphasis on the right to life in their respective constitutions. However, the wheels of progress have begun to spin within the region despite limitations and challenges. Lao PDR and Thailand are presently applying a moratorium on capital punishment. Other countries such as Malaysia, Myanmar, Indonesia, and Vietnam have also taken steps toward moratoriums and abolition; however, their positions on the latter remain unclear. Malaysia, for example, began to apply a moratorium while reviewing its laws to abolish the death penalty in 2018. Nevertheless, it appears the government has since shifted its stance of complete abolition to a more limited one of abolishing mandatory death penalties (Anti-Death Penalty Asia Network et al., 2021). Likewise, Myanmar has not carried out a judicial execution since 1988, although it still retains the death penalty and its courts have continued to sentence people to death prior to the coup. However, the situation was complicated when the military junta took power in February 2021 and passed the 2021 Martial Law. Currently, a significant increase in the number of death penalty sentences has raised fears of a return to active execution (Human Rights Watch, 2021; Reuters, 2021). At the same time, widespread reports of the escalating violence offered junta forces an excuse to repress the nationwide anti-coup movement (Henschke et al., 2021; Lone & Bhandari, 2021). In contrast to Myanmar, Vietnam and Indonesia are in the process of reforming their laws to limit application of the death penalty. Vietnam is in the process of comprehensively amending and supplementing its 1999 Penal Code to further reduce the death penalty by improving the effectiveness of prevention in dealing with offenders, and respecting and protecting the fundamental rights of its citizens. In Indonesia, progress has been made. The new Criminal Code which just recently was passed, could result in the capital punishment being side-lined as an alternative type of sentence for judges to rule upon, perhaps as a last resort (Indonesian Criminal Code, 2023). It would give judges the ability to confer an alternative verdict to the death penalty due to certain redeemable circumstances such as good behaviour, or other motions. However, since the new Criminal Code will only come into force in January 2026, it is not clear how the death penalty as an alternative punishment would be implemented.

2.3.2 Enable Human Dignity and the Death Penalty to Coexist with Extensive Regulation

Although international law still allows exceptions, retentionist countries are expected to reduce the number of criminals they execute and the crimes for which it may be imposed. (United Nations Economic and Social Council, 2015). These exceptions pertain to only the most serious crimes and exclude juvenile offenders whilst offering fair trial guarantees. Moreover, the judicial process imposing the death penalty needs to uphold fairness, equality, proper proportion, and parsimony which can be subsumed within a broader concept of respect for human dignity. The underlying principle is that dignity should be perceived as a minimum standard for penology. Consequently, evolving standards of decency must embrace and express respect for the dignity of a person and the punishment of criminals must conform to that rule.

2.3.3 Human Dignity also Means Living as a Respected Human Being in Relation to Oneself and Others

Dignity also entails being able to maintain one's identity, adapt to one's new situation, and feel connected to significant others whilst incarcerated. When one family member is treated badly by outsiders, his/her relatives may also feel under attack (Sharp, 2005). Because the nature of penology is personal, in the case of the death penalty, one could argue a significant burden is also imposed on family members. This leads to the infliction of double punishments which undermines the integrity of the individual as well as the collective dignity of his/her family.

3 Fully Guaranteeing Rights to the Due Process of Law in Light of Capital Punishment

The most important aspect related to the imposition of the death penalty is the due process of law. As such, capital punishment should only be considered and applied through a strict and transparent judicial procedure. Further, international human rights standards must be applied, such as prohibiting the death penalty pertaining to certain vulnerable groups such as minors, pregnant women, new mothers, and persons with disabilities. A fair procedure with a competent judicial institution is also expected, including full access to the right of appeal and commutation of sentence at all stages (United Nations Economic and Social Council, 2015).

Throughout Southeast Asia, the due process of law, including judicial processes are prescribed by law. Employing rights-based language, their criminal codes expressly provide for, at least in theory, the fair and equal enforcement of legal and judicial protections (AICHR, 2017). However, some gaps exist resulting in the risk that individuals or groups may be deprived of their constitutionally guaranteed rights as addressed below.

3.1 Protection Against Coercion

In pursuit of speedy results or in cases of faulty law enforcement, coercive measures are still being practised in the context of confessions and arbitrary arrest and detention, violating the basic rights of the accused including the right to remain silent. However, some Southeast Asian countries such as Brunei and Cambodia expressly prohibit the use of coerced confession as a form of evidence. These two countries clearly require that any confessions made must be voluntary. Moreover, evidence obtained under physical and mental duress is also prohibited. Similarly, in the Philippines, no one is compelled to bear witness against oneself. A person being investigated for an offence has the right to be informed of his/her right to remain silent. If he/she wishes to waive his/her right to remain silent or to counsel, his/her waiver must be made in writing and in the presence of counsel (Cohen et al., 2016). If the person has waived his/her right to counsel, the confession or admission should be signed in the presence of either his/her parents, elder brothers and sisters, spouse, mayor, judge, district school supervisor, or priest or minister of the gospel as chosen by him/her. In the case of Malaysia, there is no specific law governing torture nor the proper treatment of detainees; however, statements made by suspects are inadmissible by themselves. In this way, confessions, whether obtained by force or otherwise, are insufficient without a proper investigation. However, this does not rule out the use of force; for example, to extract information during an investigation (Bureau of Democracy, Human Rights and Labor, 2021; Human Rights Watch, 2014; SUHAKAM, 2021). Likewise, in Indonesia, confessions are no longer accepted as a sole form of evidence. Instead, Article 184 of the Criminal Procedure Law considers a defendant's testimony as merely one form of evidence. This means that defendants can freely provide information as long as such information has been given without undue pressure. This approach has brought about a major change in adjudication procedures, particularly the interrogation system. As confessions are no longer required, the practice of pressuring defendants to make involuntary confessions becomes unnecessary. Nevertheless, this does not mean coercion is no longer employed. Many reports reveal cases of non-compliance and the use of force to seek compelling information/evidence. Kicking, hitting, and threatening behaviour whilst armed are all common methods to expedite an investigation or obtain witness and offender confessions (KontraS, 2021).

In short, while safeguards from any forms of coercion are in place, challenges remain in the full implementation of these recent provisions. Moreover, the lack of resources and facilities for law enforcement officers may lead to the institutionalisation of coercion in judicial processes.

3.2 Protection Against Arbitrary Arrest and Detention

As pointed out by various sources, all countries in Southeast Asia guarantee the prohibition of arbitrary arrest and detention. Further, respect for dignity is regarded as a minimum standard in cases of deprivation of liberty.

Two challenges can be attributed to the context of Southeast Asia. First, some problematic provisions do allow arbitrary arrest and detention. These exceptions apply under certain situations depending on the punishment for the offence and the circumstances of the case. Singapore, Malaysia, and Brunei Darussalam, for example, permit detention without grounds for charge or trial when national security and public order are at stake (Cohen et al., 2016). Similarly, the Human Security Act in the Philippines, anti-terrorism legislation in Indonesia, and the Internal Security Act in Thailand have been criticised for violating due process of law and the right to equal protection under the law (Cohen & Lee, 2011; Cohen et al., 2016). Doubts arise as to whether existing mechanisms are sufficient to evaluate the current law and/or to provide remedies against non-compliance.

The second issue highlights loopholes in implementation, specifically related to wrongful arrests and detention as pointed out by various sources. In Indonesia, the 2020 Kontras Report disclosed that wrongful arrest and detentions involving coercion still persist (KontraS, 2021). Finally, in the Philippines, extra-judicial executions, revenge killings, enforced disappearances, torture, illegal arrest, and illegal search and seizures are still being regularly reported (Zawawi, 2019).

3.3 *Securing Impartiality of the Judiciary*

Judicial neutrality and impartiality are necessary for the sound delivery of justice and the protection of dignity. It has to be noted that judicial independence and impartiality are constitutionally mandated in all Southeast Asian countries. However, corruption, a lack of resources, and cracks within the judicial system impede realisation of these principles (Cohen et al., 2016).

Judicial corruption is one of the biggest threats against effective protection of rights since people depend on independent and impartial courts when claiming remedies for breaches of individual rights. As the ultimate upholder of individual rights, the judiciary is supposed to fight corruption, not be a part of it. A corrupted judicial system may further lead to violation of various human rights and impair the protection of dignity.

Combating corruption has proven to be an arduous battle across the region. While severe punishments have been established, corruption still remains systemically embedded in State apparatuses. For instance, despite capital punishment for some acts of corruption affecting finance or the economy in Indonesia, the practice still persists. It has also been noted that social status has a direct effect on one's access to justice. Impunity is generally enjoyed by the politically powerful and economically advantaged. On the other hand, as profiled by numerous organisations, many death row inmates live in poverty and are unable to hire lawyers or influence judicial decisions. The situation has been complicated by massive corruption which undermines the core of the administration of justice, generating a substantial obstacle to the right to an impartial trial, and severely undermining the population's trust in the judiciary. In the end, corruption is seen as an obstruction to dignified justice.

3.4 *Legal Aid for Death Row Inmates*

The right of a defendant to access legal aid exists in constitutional law, municipal/domestic law, or in governmental or judicial policies and practices throughout the region. However, differences arise in terms of the nature of the legal aid (mandatory or optional), the particular stage in criminal proceedings it is granted, and in who gives and receives the legal aid. Indonesia and Brunei Darussalam require mandatory legal aid for all offenders (whether citizens or non-citizens) charged with committing the most severe of crimes (AICHR, 2019). Singapore only grants free legal aid to its citizens particularly those hailing from low-income groups, those charged with capital punishment, and, to a certain degree, migrant workers. Lao PDR, Myanmar, the Philippines, Indonesia, and Thailand have specified eligibility criteria, such as financial situation and membership of vulnerable groups.

However, no definitive information has been collected as to whether death row inmates throughout Southeast Asia are able to enjoy free legal aid. Various national reports have highlighted the uncertainty of legal aid coverage, whether because aid is limited to trials and/or pre-trial (investigations) and/or only post-conviction procedures. In some AMS, since requirements are limited to only ensure the provision of legal aid at trials, accused persons may not have been legally represented during the investigation and interrogation stages, leading to possible due process violations (AICHR, 2019). This situation leads to uncertainty in respect of appeals for clemency. Malaysia, for example, allows legal aid for the application for pardon or clemency process. By contrast, Indonesia's free legal aid ends after the court decision is finalised (*in kracht van gewijsde*); hence, death row inmates must fund their own appeals for clemency, placing them at a significant disadvantage.

In addition to regulatory challenges, violations are still regularly reported such as a lack of access to legal counsel for persons facing the death penalty in Indonesia (Napitupulu, 2015), Vietnam (Vietnam Committee on Human Rights, 2016), and Myanmar (United Nations Human Rights Council, 2021b). Moreover, the quality of legal aid provided in the region is still very much in question (AICHR, 2019). For instance, in Indonesia, the legal counsel of Rusula Hia and Yusman Telaumbanua not only failed to offer an effective defence, he also recommended the death penalty to his clients.

In conclusion, proper due process of law and judicial procedures should allow suspects and the accused to claim their dignity. However, this requires a will to invest in the establishment of a fair, transparent and accountable system, training and adequate resources, and State commitment.

4 Is a 'Humane' Execution Even Possible?

Execution of a verdict is often considered to be the end of the criminal justice system meaning that once an inmate completes his/her punishment, justice is deemed to have been served. However, with respect to capital punishment, the severity of execution methods raises questions regarding the preservation of one's dignity. The use of stoning, injection of untested lethal drugs, gas chambers, immolation, immurement, and public executions are all considered violations of the prohibition against torture, inhuman, and degrading treatment (United Nations Human Rights Committee, 2019).

Nevertheless, execution is allowed albeit with strict limitations, particularly the requirement to minimise possible pain and suffering at all levels. The default method applied is commonly decided by the State. Thailand, Vietnam, and Lao PDR use lethal injections; Indonesia deploys firing squads; while Singapore and Malaysia employ hanging as an execution method. In Brunei Darussalam, methods of execution can either include hanging or beheading. Furthermore, for certain offences under Syariah Law, stoning becomes another option. However, public executions are no longer permitted.

The rationales behind the selection of methods of execution are both alarming and baffling. While condoning stoning, Brunei adheres to the principle of an immediate, painless, and respectable death (Syariah Courts Criminal Procedure Code Order 2018 of Brunei Darussalam). The application of stoning was criticised strongly in 2014 when a new law on capital punishment for gay sex was introduced. It was argued that stoning was considered a barbaric method and the law allowed for arbitrary punishment against lesbians, bisexuals, gays and transgender people in the country. The government rebutted the argument by declaring stoning to align with their values and that convictions would be rare as it required two men of 'high moral standing and piety' to witness the offence (Boffee, 2019).

By contrast, Singapore relies on death by hanging which it considers a more 'humane' mode of killing. However, the city-state has been heavily criticised for the manner it conducts executions rather than the method itself. Likewise, Japan argues that hanging is less cruel compared to other methods of execution such as beheading, shooting, electrocution, and lethal gas (Ong, 2020).

Over time, Vietnam has adopted several methods of execution from decapitation to lethal injection. During decolonisation, it utilised the guillotine, a method famously popularised by the French (Tran & Vu, 2019). However, following its independence in 1945, the Democratic Republic of Vietnam favoured use of the firing squad until the 2010 Law on Execution of Criminal Judgments when the State mandated execution by lethal injection. Although viewed as a more humane method by some (Vietnam Committee on Human Rights, 2016), it is not without its faults. For example, the unavailability of lethal substances poses a major problem forcing Vietnam to manufacture its own chemicals (Associated Press, 2013). At the same time, no clear evidence exists on the speed and efficiency of lethal injections.

Similarly, over time, Lao PDR and Thailand also switched their mode of execution from firing squad to lethal injection and for similar reasons.

In Indonesia, however, the method of execution remains the firing squad and this has never been questioned, the assumption being that it produces the most efficient results with the smallest margins of error.

Expanding this discourse on methods of execution brings to light several points of discussion.

4.1 All Methods Are Problematic

Primarily, the problem stems from treating people as objects in an experiment wherein effectiveness is measured by an expeditious death. Instant death means less pain; hence, it is considered more humane. However, can the notion of 'less pain' even be measured? Such concerns led Supreme Court Chief of Justice of India, K. G Balakrishnan to question the effectiveness of all execution methods: "*... how do you know that hanging causes pain? And how do you know that injecting the condemned prisoner with a lethal drug would not cause pain?*" (*Express*, 2009) These are difficult questions that may never be answered as it is rare for anyone to survive such an ordeal. Nevertheless, several cases in different jurisdictions have revealed the extreme suffering of inmates due to the failure of lethal injections or bullets to immediately kill. One priest who witnessed an execution in Indonesia stated that it took 7–8 min for an inmate to die after being shot (Kristanti, 2016). In another case, the head of a firing squad had to shoot an inmate twice as he failed to die for 15 min. These cases reflect that whatever the circumstances, an execution cannot help but inflict physical and mental suffering on an inmate. The humiliation and discomfort or even agony of the process itself can only be exacerbated by the physical pain suffered between one's execution and actual death. Hence, in no way can execution be said to serve humanity.

4.2 The Execution Protocol

Due to the extreme severity of the punishment, strict precautions are required by law. Inmates must be treated with clear respect, avoiding unnecessary measures and pain prior to his/her execution including the length of the notice period, the disclosure of information, and his/her treatment during the wait period on death row to name but a few.

As to the period of notice, no standards specifically prescribe a fair and humane wait time which is reflected across Southeast Asia. The time gap between the execution order and the execution itself ranges from a few hours (Thailand) to 72 h (Indonesia), in which everyone relevant to the inmates' interests is informed of his/her imminent demise (AICHR, 2017). This is problematic in two ways. First, in terms of practicality, such time may be insufficient for concerned family members to travel and pay their final respects. Indeed, even State authorities need 'enough time' to prepare. Second, violations often occur when remedies are lacking. In the case of Indonesia, while 72 h notification is required by law, in reality, the time frame can be much shorter (Erdianto, 2016). Failure to provide appropriate notification is considered inhumane and degrading as it undermines procedural safeguards surrounding the right to life (United Nations Commission on Human Rights, 2006).

Finally, full access to information is required as to the specifics of one's execution. While online platforms for accessing judicial documents are made publicly available in Indonesia, Brunei Darussalam, and Vietnam (Cohen & Lee, 2011), it is more difficult to get advance notice of the time, place, and personnel involved in executions. For example, details were kept confidential until the very last moment in Indonesia's most recent execution (KontraS, 2021). Similarly in Thailand, minimal advance notice was given to the family of the condemned in a 2018 execution (United Nations Human Rights Council, 2021a). Even bigger challenges are posed in Vietnam where the disclosure and release of any information regarding death penalties is prohibited. In fact, revealing information either intentionally or unintentionally is considered a crime and subject to penalties of up to 15 years imprisonment (Tran & Vu, 2019). This is also the case in Singapore where no public announcement is usually made prior to an execution. No clear explanations have been offered for these policies. Nevertheless, this lack of information regarding executions was highlighted in Singapore's 2011 Universal Periodic Review. As a result, it agreed to follow up on Finland's suggestion to make publicly available statistics and other factual information on its use of the death penalty (United Nations Human Rights Council, 2011). To date, however, Singapore has released no such pertinent information (United Nations Human Rights Council, 2021a).

5 Hidden Victims: The Family of Death Row Inmates

The intent of criminal punishment is usually to rehabilitate or inflict retribution on convicted individuals. However, the reality is often more complicated and wide-reaching. Oftentimes, the offender's family is dragged into a whirlwind of challenges. Many undergo severe trauma and suffer economically as a result of excruciatingly long legal processes and the ensuing protracted social stigma which they may carry for the rest of their lives. This is an aspect of capital punishment that existing laws have not fully appreciated nor addressed.

As revealed in interviews, the suffering of family members is all-encompassing, protracted, and can manifest in a myriad of ways. The first refers to the humiliation and stigma of simply being related to a death row inmate. In some cases, having been publicly shunned, families may consider themselves 'vicarious offenders' (Sharp, 2005). Even the act of walking into a courtroom for a trial can attract accusatory stares causing feelings of guilt, shame, and responsibility for the offender's actions, resulting in a desire to avoid all social situations (Sharp, 2005). Such fears can haunt family members long after the verdict has been reached or the execution carried out. In some cases, one may argue the hypersensitivity of relatives may be to blame and indeed, such feelings are entirely subjective. However, it is undeniable that the series of events from arrest to execution of a loved one can generate deep sorrow and pain. Thus, at the point of execution, family members too become victims of State policy.

The second issue faced by family members refers to economic impediments caused by the case. For example, when a family's main breadwinner is arrested and sentenced to death, other family members may struggle to survive. Economic difficulties faced during the trial often continue until the execution with families often unable to cover legal expenses and the expense of regularly visiting incarcerated loved ones. In some instances, costs may soar even higher due to corruption as a result of having to pay bribes, for instance, to ensure an inmate's protection or simply to facilitate visitation rights or deliver home-cooked food. The situation is further complicated when the death row inmate is a non-national. Visiting loved ones in a foreign prison or even constantly making expensive long-distance phone calls may become hugely burdensome. Hence, family members may be forced to prioritise survival. In such cases, death row inmates may be left alone without family support.

Third, the trauma suffered by children especially, untreated, can leave life-long wounds. Unlike any other criminal punishment, the execution of a parent severs the parent–child relationship irrevocably. The child faces first the threat, then the reality of a broken family amplified to the extreme when the parent is lost to a violent State-mandated death. As a result, the child experiences major physiological, emotional, and other trauma. While the loss of a parent is always traumatic and irreversible, when it is officially sanctioned, to a child, it becomes particularly confusing and frightening (United Nations Human Rights Council, 2013). Nonetheless, this issue is often neglected. Judicial or non-judicial systems may provide support to crime victims, but the children of death row inmates are always ignored. As indicated in interviews with the family of a condemned person in addition to a few lawyers defending death penalty cases, no acknowledgement or support for families is ever provided. This discrepancy has been highlighted several times by the Human Rights Council (Kearney, 2012). It has also been taken into consideration by the Committee Against Torture and the Committee on the Rights of the Child when addressing State reports on national implementation.

Fourth, many family members reported limited (or no) access to visits and/or limited information about the executions of loved ones (Bernie, 2019). Although all countries in Southeast Asia have provisions allowing visits to all inmates including those on death row, restrictions are applied such as limits on the number of visitors, times of visitations, and other requirements. The situation was further complicated by the COVID-19 pandemic which forced States to close their borders and introduce ever more restrictions. In Indonesia, for example, prisons halted all physical visitations during the pandemic, instead facilitating online Zoom calls. While understandable, problems often arose due to bad connections, inadequate digital devices, and limited internet quotas. As a result, only a small number of inmates and their families were able to use the new platform leaving many more in ignorance as to the condition of their loved ones during a frightening pandemic. Such a nightmare scenario only served to aggravate anxieties leading some to suffer mental and physical breakdowns.

The situation becomes even more complex prior to the execution. Each country in Southeast Asia requires death row inmates be given 2–4 days' notice of their impending executions. As mentioned earlier, this is to ensure sufficient time for preparation including the notification of family members. Despite this, examples abound of families being unable to bid farewell to loved ones due to late notifications.

Above are a few examples of the experiences faced by family members of death row inmates. Many more stories remain untold. While these accounts may vary in detail, two unifying ideas emerge: First, family members are victims which unfortunately have been suffering from institutional silencing. They have a right to speak and to be heard as well as to receive information and assistance so they can reclaim their power and have a voice in the aftermath of the trauma. Nevertheless, their rights have been violated; their dignity has been denied. They are victimised without being recognised as a victim. When a law is silent on this matter, respecting dignity should be viewed as a parameter on how to treat and regard others. Second, the situation of the death row inmate's family is inextricably linked with that of the death row inmate. The death row inmate's situation can thus not be seen in isolation - respect for human dignity should also be afforded to his or her family. In this case, a right to dignity leads to an obligation for the State as well as society to protect and respect it.

6 Conclusion

Although dignity is a universal concept, it is ill-defined due to its complexity and multi-faceted nature. The term has therefore continued to be used in a variety of ways depending on the context.

In the context of human rights, dignity encompasses a series of meanings referring to the dignity of life, equality, liberty, and attribution which may overlap and/or complement each other with human life as the centre point. It is both an entitlement as well as an obligation to respect others. Thus, respecting human dignity means respecting human life itself.

Therefore, in the context of the protection of the right to life, dignity is defined as an intrinsic human value implicating both oneself and others. In this way, dignity is reflected in three dimensions. First, full protection of human dignity necessitates the abolition of the death penalty. The death penalty is cruel, barbaric, and irreversible regardless of any execution method used and justifications because, at its core, the right to life is thoroughly denied. Second, towards abolition, human dignity is reflected in the extensive regulations controlling every step of the process. In this case, respecting dignity can serve as a core unifying principle of the right to life. The death penalty may be constitutional in a State but it does not mean a State has the right to take dignity away. Hence, it is argued that the concept of dignity extends beyond the law. Respecting dignity should be used as a tool to interpret due process and/or as a goal to fill the gap due to the absence of legal protection. In other words, dignity serves as a minimum set of standards for respecting the right to life. Finally, dignity demands respect for oneself and others reflecting the nature of humans as both individuals and an organ of society. This is reflected in the stories of family members of death row inmates above in which they suffer from traumatic and humiliating experiences because their loved one facing the death penalty. They are also deserved to be recognised in order to be able to voice their distress and claim their rights to speak, to be heard, and to receive information as well as assistance. Extinguishing life is not only the act of killing itself but the ultimate humiliation.

In short, dignity is an intrinsic value for a human being. Its existence does not depend on his/her action or that of others. Committing an extraordinary crime including committing murder does not justify indignity. Therefore, such ultimate dignity brings an obligation to respect it in any situation including the case of the death penalty.

References

African Charter on Human and Peoples' Rights, June 27, 1981. https://www.achpr.org/public/Document/file/English/banjul_charter.pdf. Accessed 1 January 2022.

Anti-Death Penalty Asia Network [ADPAN], et al. (2021, August 27). *Malaysia universal periodic review mid term.* https://www.ohchr.org/Documents/HRBodies/UPR/NGOsMidTermReports/ADPAN_Malaysia.pdf. Accessed 5 January 2022.

ASEAN Intergovernmental Commission on Human Rights [AICHR]. (2017). *Protection of rights of the death row inmates* (Draft).
ASEAN Intergovernmental Commission on Human Rights [AICHR]. (2019, July). *Thematic study on legal aid*. ASEAN Secretariat. https://aichr.org/wp-content/uploads/2019/09/AICHR-Thematic-Study-on-Legal-Aid-for-web.pdf. Accessed 5 January 2022.
Associated Press. (2013, May 16). Vietnam to produce lethal injection. *Bangkok Post*. https://www.bangkokpost.com/world/350340/vietnam-law-change-permits-domestically-produced-chemicals-in-lethal-injections. Accessed 5 January 2022.
Bernie, M. (2019, October 10). KontraS: Terpidana mati dipersulit bertemu keluarga & pengacara. *Tirto*. https://tirto.id/kontras-terpidana-mati-dipersulit-bertemu-keluarga-pengacara-ejxE. Accessed 1 January 2022.
Boffee, D. (2019, April 22). Brunei defends death by stoning for gay sex in letter to EU. *The Guardian*. https://www.theguardian.com/world/2019/apr/22/brunei-defends-stoning-death-gay-sex-letter-eu. Accessed 1 January 2022.
Bureau of Democracy, Human Rights and Labor (2021, March 30). *2020 country reports on human rights practices: Malaysia*. U.S. Department of State. https://www.state.gov/reports/2020-country-reports-on-human-rights-practices/malaysia/. Accessed 1 January 2022.
Cohen, D., & Lee, K. T. Y. (2011). *The rule of law for human rights in the ASEAN region: A base-line study*. Human Rights Resource Center.
Cohen, D., Tan, K., Nababan, A., & Kong, F. S. D. R. (2016, June). *Update on the rule of law for human rights in ASEAN: The path to integration*. Human Rights Resource Centre.
Constitution of Republic of Indonesia, 1945.
Constitution of the Kingdom of Thailand, B.E. 2560 (2017).
Dan-Cohen, M. (2014). Dignity, crime, and punishment: A Kantian perspective. In M. D. Dubber (Ed.), *Foundational text in modern criminal law* (pp. 101–118). Oxford University Press.
Debes, R. (2018, February 5). *A history of human dignity*. The Forum for Philosophy. https://blogs.lse.ac.uk/theforum/a-history-of-human-dignity/. Accessed 5 January 2022.
Dramani, A. (2012, April–June). Relativity of human dignity and the role of cultural diversity in international cooperation on human rights. *Global Journal of Management and Research*, 1–15.
Erdianto, K. (2016, July 31). *Kuasa hukum terpidana mati ungkap kejanggalan dan dugaan pelanggaran jelang eksekusi*. Kompas.com. https://nasional.kompas.com/read/2016/07/31/16325861/kuasa.hukum.terpidana.mati.ungkap.kejanggalan.dan.dugaan.pelanggaran.jelang.eksekusi?page=all. Accessed 5 January 2022.
Express. (2009). Indian court still favours hanging. *Express*. https://www.express.co.uk/news/world/112256/Indian-court-still-favours-hanging. Accessed 5 January 2022.
Habermas, J. (2010). The concept of human dignity and the realistic utopian of human rights. *Metaphilosophy, 41*(4), 464–480.
Henry, L. M. (2011). The jurisprudence of dignity. *University of Pennsylvania Law Review, 160*(1), 169–233. https://scholarship.law.upenn.edu/penn_law_review/vol160/iss1/3. Accessed 5 January 2022.
Henschke, R., Brown, K., & Aung, K. K. (2021, December 20). *Tortured to death: Myanmar mass killings revealed*. BBC News. https://www.bbc.com/news/world-asia-59699556. Accessed 5 January 2022.
Hood, R., & Hoyle, C. (2009). *The death penalty*. Oxford University Press.
Hood, R., & Hoyle, C. (2015). *The death penalty: A worldwide perspective*. Oxford University Press.
Howard, R. E., & Donnelly, J. (1986). Human dignity, human rights, and political regimes. *The American Political Science Review, 80*(3), 801–817. https://doi.org/10.2307/1960539
Human Rights Watch. (2014, April). *"No answers, no apology": Police abuses and accountability in Malaysia*. https://www.hrw.org/report/2014/04/01/no-answers-no-apology/police-abuses-and-accountability-malaysia. Accessed 5 January 2022.

Human Rights Watch. (2021, July 21). *Myanmar: Junta tribunals impose 65 death sentences*. Human Rights Watch. https://www.hrw.org/news/2021/07/21/myanmar-junta-tribunals-impose-65-death-sentences. Accessed 5 January 2022.

Indonesian Criminal Code. (2023). Law No. 1/2023.

Kasiri, M., & Karimi, A. (2017). Comparative study of observation of human dignity in death penalty in Iranian law and international documents. *International Journal of Law, 3*(4), 125–128.

Kearney, H. F. (2012, February). *Children of parent sentenced to death*. Quaker United Nations Office. https://www.quno.org/sites/default/files/resources/ENGLISH_Children%20of%20parents%20sentenced%20to%20death.pdf. Accessed 5 January 2022.

KontraS. (2021, June 25). *Laporan Situasi Praktik Penyiksaan dan Perlakuan atau Penghukuman lain yang Kejam, Tidak manusiawi, atau Merendahkan Martabat Manusia di Indonesia Periode Juni 2020–Mei 2021* [Report on the situation of torture and inhuman, cruel and degrading treatment and punishment in Indonesia June 2020–May 2021]. https://kontras.org/wp-content/uploads/2021/08/Final-Laporan-Penyiksaan-2021__Indonesia-Inggris.pdf. Accessed 5 January 2022.

Kristanti, E. Y. (2016, July 30). *Pengakuan saksi mata detik-detik eksekusi mati jumat dinihari*. Liputan 6. https://www.liputan6.com/global/read/2564818/pengakuan-saksi-mata-detik-detik-eksekusi-mati-jumat-dinihari. Accessed 5 January 2022.

Lone, W., & Bhandari, A. (2021, March 26). *More than 300 people killed Since Myanmar's coup*. Reuters. https://www.reuters.com/world/asia-pacific/more-than-300-people-killed-since-myanmars-coup-2021-03-26/. Accessed 5 January 2022.

Napitupulu, E. A. T. (2015). *Overview on death penalty in Indonesia*. Institute for Criminal Justice Reform. http://icjr.or.id/wp-content/uploads/2015/06/Overview-on-Death-Penalty-in-Indonesia.pdf. Accessed 5 January 2022.

Napitupulu, E. A. T. (2018, October). *Laporan kebijakan Hukuman Mati di Indonesia*. Institute for Criminal Justice Reform.

Ong, J. (2020, January 16). Rights group alleges barbaric, unlawful execution methods in Singapore. *Malaymail*. https://www.malaymail.com/news/malaysia/2020/01/16/rights-group-alleges-barbaric-unlawful-execution-methods-in-singapore/1828459. Accessed 5 January 2022.

Reuters (2021, April 10). *19 People sentence to death by Myanmar military*. CNN. https://edition.cnn.com/2021/04/09/asia/myanmar-coup-death-sentences-intl-hnk/index.html. Accessed 1 January 2022.

Schabas, W. A. (1998). International law and abolition of death penalty. *Washington and Lee Law Review, 55*(3), 797–844. https://scholarlycommons.law.wlu.edu/wlulr/vol55/iss3/10. Accessed 5 January 2022.

Sharp, S. F. (2005). *Hidden victims: The effects of the death penalty on families of the accused*. Rutgers University Press.

SUHAKAM. (2021, June 1). *Press Statement No. 20-2021—SUHAKAM is mortified to once again on the news of more deaths in custody*. https://suhakam.org.my/2021/06/press-statement-no-20-2021_suhakam-is-mortified-to-once-again-on-the-news-of-more-deaths-in-custody/. Accessed 5 January 2022.

Sulmasy, D. P. (2013). The varieties of human dignity: A logical and conceptual analysis. *Medicine, Health Care and Philosophy, 16*, 937–944. https://doi.org/10.1007/s11019-012-9400-1

Syariah Courts Criminal Procedure Code Order 2018 of Brunei Darussalam (2018).

Tran, K., & Vu, C. G. (2019). The changing nature of death penalty in Vietnam: A historical and legal inquiry. *Societies, 9*(3), 56. https://doi.org/10.3390/soc9030056

United Nations Commission on Human Rights. (2006, March 24). *Report of the Special Rapporteur on extrajudicial, summary or arbitrary executions: Transparency and the imposition of the death penalty*, E/CN.4/2006/53/Add.3. https://www.refworld.org/docid/45377b310.html. Accessed 5 January 2022.

United Nations Convention Against Torture and Other Cruel, Inhuman or Degrading Treatment or Punishment, December 10, 1984. https://www.ohchr.org/en/professionalinterest/pages/cat.aspx

United Nations Convention on the Elimination of All Forms of Discrimination against Women, December 18, 1979. https://www.ohchr.org/en/professionalinterest/pages/cedaw.aspx

United Nations Economic and Social Council resolution 1984/50, Safeguards guaranteeing protection of the rights of those facing the death penalty, E/RES/1984/50, May, 22 1984. https://www.unodc.org/pdf/criminal_justice/Safeguards_Guaranteeing_Protection_of_the_Rights_of_those_Facing_the_Death_Penalty.pdf. Accessed 5 January 2022.

United Nations Economic and Social Council. (2015). *Capital punishment and implementation of the safeguards guaranteeing protection of the rights of those facing the death penalty: Report of the Secretary-General*, E/2015/49. https://www.ohchr.org/Documents/Issues/DeathPenalty/E-2015-49.pdf. Accessed 5 January 2022.

United Nations Human Rights Committee. (2019, September 3). *General comment no. 36, Article 6 (Right to Life)*, CCPR/C/GC/36. https://undocs.org/CCPR/C/GC/36

United Nations Human Rights Council. (2011, July 21). *Report of the working group on the universal periodic review: Singapore*, A/HRC/18/11. https://www2.ohchr.org/english/bodies/hrcouncil/docs/18session/A-HRC-18-11_en.pdf. Accessed 5 January 2022.

United Nations Human Rights Council. (2013, December 18). *Summary of the panel discussion on the human rights of children of parents sentenced to the death penalty or executed: Report of the United Nations High Commissioner for Human Rights.* https://www.ohchr.org/Documents/Issues/Children/Summaryparentssentencedtodeath_Dec2013.pdf. Accessed 5 January 2022.

United Nations Human Rights Council. (2021a, September 15). *Question of the death penalty: Report of the Secretary-General (Advance unedited version)*, A/HRC/48/29. https://www.ohchr.org/Documents/Issues/DeathPenalty/A_HRC_48_29_AUV_2021.docx. Accessed 5 January 2022.

United Nations Human Rights Council. (2021b, September 16). *Written updates of the Office of the United Nations High Commissioner for Human Rights on the situation of human rights in Myanmar*, A/HRC/48/67. https://reliefweb.int/sites/reliefweb.int/files/resources/A_HRC_48_67.pdf. Accessed 5 January 2022.

United Nations International Covenant on Civil and Political Rights, December 16, 1966. https://www.ohchr.org/en/professionalinterest/pages/ccpr.aspx

United Nations International Covenant on Economic, Social, and Cultural Rights, December 16, 1966. https://www.ohchr.org/en/professionalinterest/pages/cescr.aspx

Valentini, L. (2017). Dignity and human rights: A reconceptualisation. *Oxford Journal of Legal Studies, 37*(4), 862–885. https://doi.org/10.1093/ojls/gqx011

Vietnam Committee on Human Rights. (2016, June 21–23). *The death penalty in Vietnam: Report compiled for the 6th World Congress against the death penalty, Oslo.* https://www.fidh.org/IMG/pdf/2016_-_report_on_death_penalty_in_vietnam.pdf. Accessed 1 January 2022.

Zawawi, S. (2019). *The Philippines' Anti-torture law: Ten years on, what now?* Association for the Prevention of Torture. https://www.apt.ch/en/blog/philippines-anti-torture-law-ten-years-what-now. Accessed 5 January 2022.

Patricia Rinwigati Waagstein S.H., MIL, PhD, is a senior lecture at the faculty of law, University of Indonesia. She has also been a practicing attorney and consultant who has worked in Timor Leste, USA, Sweden, and ASEAN countries for over fifteen years. She has extensive experience and expertise in human rights, business and human rights issues, criminal justice, and international law. She holds a bachelor degree in law from University of Indonesia (1996), a Master's Degree in Public International Law from Lund University, Sweden (1999) and a Doctoral Degree in law from Uppsala University, Sweden (2009).

In addition to being a lecturer, she is currently the director of Djokosoetono Research Center managing 22 research units at the Faculty of Law, University of Indonesia including Human Rights Center. Areas of research interest: human rights, humanitarian law, criminal law, and international law.

Authoritarian Regimes and the Media: How They Shape Perception and Support for Capital Punishment in ASEAN

Ma. Ngina Teresa V. Chan-Gonzaga

Abstract This chapter examines the ways by which authoritarianism and the media affect public perception and support for capital punishment in the ASEAN region by outlining and discussing its tenacious, oft perplexing, support there. Despite the worldwide trend towards the abolition of the death penalty, ASEAN Member-States still seemingly support retentionist principles and policies. This paper, however, illustrates that public support and political stances in its favour are, in reality, neither unconditional nor unnuanced. Drawing from past studies and considering current realities on the ground, this chapter investigates the complex interplay among the issues of capital punishment, authoritarianism, and the media. As observed in recent years, authoritarianism, in one form or another, has crept into the ASEAN region, stifling dissent and threatening the media—which may either be State-controlled or, at the very least, State-suppressed. Following an analysis of such interplay, this chapter then explores various alternatives for framing the capital punishment discourse with the ultimate goal of working against its retention and re-imposition in the long run.

1 Introduction

While it appears that there is indeed a global trend progressively inclined towards the abolition of capital punishment as reflected in the December 2018 UN General Assembly (UNGA) where about 63% of Member-States (121 of 193) voted in favour of a moratorium with presumably a view to complete abolition, it cannot be denied that the picture in Southeast Asia does not quite reflect this development (UNGA, 2018a, 2018b). Only two ASEAN Member-States (AMS) supported UNGA Resolution 73/175 on the moratorium on the use of the death penalty (Cambodia and Malaysia), while two were clearly against it (Brunei Darussalam and Singapore) (UNGA, 2018a, 2018b). The remaining six abstained (UNGA, 2018a, 2018b).

Malaysia's 2018 stance may have been the consequence of a pronouncement by the (then) newly elected government to completely abolish the death penalty; but, as

Ma. N. T. V. Chan-Gonzaga (✉)
School of Law, Ateneo de Manila University, Makati City, Philippines

S. Petcharamesree et al. (eds.), *Unpacking the Death Penalty in ASEAN*,
https://doi.org/10.1007/978-981-19-8840-0_5

observed in succeeding months, the government backtracked on this intention, citing public opinion and a lack of public support as its excuses (Girelli, 2019).

On the other hand, the Philippines, ostensibly an abolitionist State, having erased capital punishment from its statute books in 2007, did not vote in favour of the 2018 resolution, instead simply abstaining (UNGA, 2018a). Whilst it had voted in favour of a similar resolution in 2014 (UNGA, 2014, 2015, p. 722) during the administration of former President Benigno Aquino III, since 2016, it has abstained due to former President Rodrigo Duterte's very vocal intention to restore the death penalty (Al Jazeera, 2016; UNGA, 2017, p. 779, 2019, p. 911).

Eight of ten AMS still legally allow capital punishment (FIDH, 2016, p. 5). While it can be argued that at least half have been *de facto* abolitionist for the last few years, one cannot discount how easily such a situation could change as occurred in Thailand when, after nearly a decade of restraint, the government carried out an execution in June 2018 (*Bangkok Post*, 2018). Moreover, so long as capital punishment is legal in a State, the concomitant issues (e.g., affecting prisoners on death row) persist.

So despite the global trend, why do most AMS maintain retentionist principles and policies? Traditional theories on criminal justice, particularly the retributive and utilitarian kinds, are still central to most policies; as well as a stubborn insistence, despite inconclusive findings on the subject, that it deters serious crime.

Moreover, it does seem that, in one fashion or another, there is apparently popular and public support for capital punishment in the region. However, whether the support and opinions are based on educated positions is a different matter altogether.

This chapter primarily aims to discuss the tenacious, and oft perplexing, support for the death penalty in AMS. The impact of current conditions, experiences, and circumstances of authoritarianism and the media in several AMS are likewise examined.

Section 2 analyses the complexities and nuances related to the ostensible "popular" support for capital punishment in the ASEAN region and seeks to determine if there is, in reality, support for it, or if the support is only superficial or apparent. Section 3 then discusses the attitudes of regimes towards capital punishment in Southeast Asia. With authoritarianism becoming more pronounced in AMS in recent years, it also points out the more opaque and obscure reasons behind capital punishment in these increasingly autocratic countries and their consequences. Thereafter, Sect. 4 explains the interplay among the death penalty, authoritarianism, and the media. Next, an overview of the state of the media in the region is presented followed by an examination of how the media and its underlying aspects affect public perceptions especially with regard to capital punishment. Section 5 proffers concluding points and observations that entertain new possibilities—which are equally effective, if not more persuasive—in the fight against the retention and re-imposition of the death penalty in the long run. A synthesis of the points discussed herein concludes the chapter.

2 Popular Support in the Region: Apparent or Real?

When the Vietnamese government abolished the death penalty for five of originally 22 capital crimes in 2018, news reports and online polls showcased apparently negative public reactions and claims that support for the death penalty was still the majority stance. In an online poll taken by *VnExpress* carrying the question: "*Should Vietnam abolish the death penalty?*", about 52% (an estimated 231 of 444 votes) of respondents said no (*VnExpress*, 2017). An article in the Vietnamese-language edition of *VnExpress* also allegedly garnered over 80 comments expressing vehement disagreement with the amendment (Luong, 2017).

In Malaysia, after the May 2018 elections saw a new government installed, an announcement was made regarding the intention of the cabinet to push for the abolition of the death penalty.[1] Datuk Liew Vui Keong, the *de facto* law minister in the Prime Minister's Department, said in October 2018 that: "[The] [d]eath penalty will be abolished. Full stop" (Lai, 2018). Online polls conducted soon after by Berita Harian Online, Harian Metro, and the New Straits Times Online, claiming 22,000 Facebook and Twitter users as its base, yielded a result of 82% votes opposed to the intended abolition (Kamarudin, 2018). While these social media polls are suspect, being statistically unreliable with less than rigorous methodology, not to mention being influenced by the framing of the issues which were more nuanced than presented, it is undeniable that such perceived public opinion has been cited as a basis for tempering moves towards abolition. Asked in April 2019 why they were not completely abolishing capital punishment as promised, Datuk Liew said that they were simply listening to the voice of the people (Bedi, 2019).

So ostensible "deference" to the will of the people has been cited as a reason why Malaysia, as well as Indonesia, retains the populist policy that both administrations continue to pursue.

In 2017, when asked about the possibility of a moratorium, President Joko Widodo of Indonesia cited a 2015 survey said to have found that 85% of Indonesians continue to support capital punishment for drug trafficking (*The Straits Times*, 2017). Saying he would consider it if it were the will of the people, Widodo insisted that it would be difficult to obtain the support of Parliament without clear public backing (*The Straits Times*, 2017). In reaction to these comments, Ricky Gunawan from pro-abolition group Community Legal Aid Foundation told the press that the President's comments were a good sign but that "the downside is he leaves it to the people to decide, and a good leader should [t]ake a stance instead of leaving [it] to the people to decide" (*The Straits Times*, 2017). Consequently, he urged French President Francois Hollande then scheduled to visit Indonesia in March 2017, to advocate for abolition in talks with Widodo (*The Straits Times*, 2017). Aside from the presence of a French national on death row, France had itself abolished the death penalty even when the public clearly

[1] A more recent development, as far as Malaysia is concerned, is the government's pledge in June 2022 that it intends to submit legislation to Parliament in order to confer judges the discretion to impose other penalties in lieu of the death penalty for eleven (11) crimes (Death Penalty Information Center, 2022; UNOHCHR, 2022).

supported it (*The Straits Times*, 2017). While not conclusive, these comments seem to concede certain public support for the death penalty. As an aside, Hollande and Widodo did not discuss the issue at all during that State visit (Halim, 2017).

In Singapore, where the government has been staunchly pro-retentionist and seemingly inflexible in this position even on the international stage, the Ministry of Home Affairs conducted a survey in late 2018 to study, *inter alia*, Singapore residents' support for the government's anti-drug policies (Singapore Ministry of Home Affairs, 2019). With 2,000 residents interviewed, the Ministry reported very strong public support for the current policies, with close to 98% agreeing that Singapore should continue to maintain a tough legal regime for drugs and approximately 70% agreeing that the death penalty was an appropriate punishment for drug trafficking on a large scale (Singapore Ministry of Home Affairs, 2019).

In Thailand, days after the execution of murder convict Theerasak Longji in 2018 (the first execution since 2009), public opinion polls showed an approval rating of more than 90% for the death penalty for "cruel murderers" (FIDH, 2018). Further, anti-death penalty advocates who spoke out against the execution and called for statutory abolition were reportedly targeted on social media (FIDH, 2018). As in other neighbouring countries, the Thai government also uses public support as justification for its retention of capital punishment (FIDH, 2018).

In the Philippines, a perfunctory appraisal of various online polls and social media comments on news items on the issue of capital punishment prompts the perception that the majority of Filipinos do seek re-imposition of the death penalty. Similarly, politicians and congressional representatives who have also expressed support for re-imposition bills, past and present, consistently cite public opinion and support. For example, when House Bill No. 4727, seeking to re-impose capital punishment, was overwhelmingly passed in the (lower) House of Representatives in 2017 (Cepeda, 2017),a number of congressmen and women again pointed to public opinion for their vote (Republic of the Philippines Congressional Record, 2017). And indeed, surveys conducted that year appeared to back up the justification. A Pulse Asia Research survey in early 2017 showed a majority of Filipinos in favour of re-imposition, although it dropped to 67% from 81% the year before (Rappler, 2017). In the survey, 97% of respondents said that rape should be punished capitally, 88% said the same for murder, and 71% thought drug dealing also warranted the death penalty (Rappler, 2017). Moreover, in the first quarter of 2017, in a survey conducted soon after the vote on House Bill No. 4727, the Social Weather Station (SWS) found that 61% of Filipinos approved of a measure seeking to re-impose the death penalty for certain drug offences (Social Weather Stations, 2017).

Be that as it may, legitimate questions have been raised over the very basis of this so-called popular support and the possibility that it is, in fact, overstated. While such support may be sweepingly cited in the media and by government officials, there have been calls to analyse the basis for such claims. Concerns have been raised regarding the methodologies employed, the framing of survey questions, and the sample sizes utilised, among others, usually in surveys and studies conducted by either government offices or private polling companies.

In 2012, Oxford Professor, Roger Hood (2013), undertook a study for the UK-based Death Penalty Project and the Malaysian Bar on capital punishment in Malaysia (p. viii). At the outset, the majority of respondents (>1,500) appeared to support the death penalty in theory: 91% for murder and between 74% and 80% for drug trafficking offences (Hood, 2013, pp. ix, 5, & 24–25). However, when details were shared and respondents were asked to confront and evaluate specific case scenarios regarding capital offences, opinions markedly changed and support for execution in specific cases drastically dropped (pp. viii-xii). Only three of six murder scenarios (two of which had aggravating circumstances) generated more than 50% support for the death penalty (the highest being 65%) (p. xiv). All drug-related scenarios generated less than 30% support for death penalty decisions (pp. ix & x). There was also no consensus on mandatory sentences, although 56% favoured it for murder (pp. xiii & xiv).

Even in Singapore, where the death penalty is seemingly firmly entrenched, the perception of popular support has been called into question. In 2016, a survey conducted by the government's Reaching Everyone for Active Citizenry @ Home (REACH) department reportedly showed that 80% of 1,160 respondents supported retaining capital punishment and 82% agreed with the statement that capital punishment is an important deterrent of serious crimes (Singapore REACH, 2016, pp. 1 & 2). However, another study in the same year undertaken by a team led by Professor Chan Wing Cheong of the National University of Singapore indicated that opinions were not as clear-cut (Chan et al., 2018, pp. xv–xix). In a survey designed and patterned after the Roger Hood study in Malaysia, Chan found that while the majority of Singaporeans still supported the death penalty as a general proposition, it was not a strongly or unconditionally held position (Chan et al., 2018, pp. iii & xix). It appears that public opinion is influenced by factors such as mitigating circumstances, actual deterrent effects, and the strength of the belief that implementation was error-free and did not affect innocent lives (Chan et al., 2018, pp. xvii–xviii & 42). It appears that when confronted with the details and factual circumstances surrounding particular cases, a lower percentage of those asked supported the death penalty:

> When asked to choose between measures which respondents thought would be most effective in reducing violent crimes leading to death and illegal drug trafficking, about three-quarters ranked 'greater number of executions' last. Furthermore, if there was evidence that innocent persons had been executed, support for capital punishments dropped dramatically by more than 60%. It would therefore be misleading to say, without qualifications, that there is public support for the death penalty in Singapore. (Chan et al., 2018, pp. v, xix, & 4, underscoring added)

Ms. Braema Mathi of MARUAH has opined that Singaporeans have been "conditioned" to accept that the only way to effectively deal with the drug situation is to execute the drug traffickers (Tang, 2018). Advocates for abolition have maintained that public support might also be attributed to a lack of knowledge or understanding beyond the superficial oft-parroted claims (Tang, 2018). In the 2016 NUS survey, nearly two-thirds (2/3) of the 1,500 individuals asked admitted knowing very little or next to nothing about the application of capital punishment in Singapore (Tang, 2018).

Meanwhile, in the Philippines, the Commission on Human Rights, the country's independent national human rights institution, commissioned the SWS in 2018 to undertake a national survey on public perceptions regarding the death penalty (Gomez-Dumpit, 2019). Described as the country's "first survey … to explore thought processes and disentangle layers of perceptions about the death penalty[,]" (Gomez-Dumpit, 2019) and with a base of 2,000 respondents, the survey revealed that there was moderate agreement at 59% on the part of respondents (42% strongly and 17% somewhat) to reinstate the death penalty "for [people] who were proven by the courts to have really committed heinous crimes" (Social Weather Stations, 2018). But for six out of seven serious drug crimes—President Duterte's preferred target of capital punishment—only 33% or less demanded the death penalty when given other sentencing options. Rape under the influence of drugs was the only exception where 47% thought the death penalty should apply (Social Weather Stations, 2018). Even the latter finding though falls short of a majority. Dr. Mahar Mangahas, SWS President, opined that the most significant revelation or the strongest finding of the 2018 survey was that alternatives to capital punishment are preferred by many Filipinos and, when offered options or a range of penalties, a majority would not choose the death penalty for any drug crime (Gavilan, 2018). Another interesting observation that came to light is the shallow extent of awareness of most individuals on issues involving capital punishment. For instance, when asked whether they knew that the Supreme Court of the Philippines had overturned about 72% of capital punishment cases for violation of due process in the last decade before the repeal of the death penalty, around two-thirds (2/3) of those asked expressed ignorance of that fact (Social Weather Stations, 2018).

In any case, "public support" or "popular opinion" may, in some cases, be more apparent than real. General or simplistic questions about favouring retention or re-imposition impair the health of the debate as there are obviously complex aspects of the discourse (e.g., support for mandatory death sentencing or judicial discretion) and a lack of awareness of the key factors (e.g., rate of wrongful convictions in a jurisdiction) on the part of those who "support" or who are asked for their "opinion."

In a recent analysis of public opinion surveys which took particular account of those conducted in five key Asian countries—including Malaysia, Thailand, Singapore, and the Philippines—Harm Reduction International claims that public support (a) "is much more complex and nuanced than often depicted;" (b) appears to be based on trusting that the death penalty deters crime, and in the belief that the criminal justice system works; and (c) appears to be "abstract" where even those who claim to support the death penalty theoretically were more tempered in response when confronted with actual cases (Girelli, 2019).

3 Capital Punishment and the Attitude of Regimes in the Region

Amnesty International (AI) has pointed out that strong public support for capital punishment, where it is claimed to exist, is often associated with and linked to "a lack of reliable information," and important factors on how the death penalty is applied are often not fully comprehended and considered in formulating an opinion (e.g., the weakness of the criminal system, inherent bias against poor sectors, the risk of convicting innocent individuals) (Amnesty International). Such information—particularly in AMS which claim that security concerns prevent them from providing full access to data on death penalty implementation—is unlikely to be available to the general public. Therefore, a full debate on the matter is inhibited, constricted, and lacking transparency, and, as can be noted in the surveys conducted in the region, demonstrate the public's lack of awareness and seeming disinterest in proactively acquiring a deeper understanding of the issues—even as the public still expresses support for the measure. But AI has also posited that "the decision to execute someone cannot be decided by public opinion [and that] [g]overnments must lead the way" (Amnesty International).

In a series of global panel discussions on the abolition of the death penalty organised by the Office of the High Commissioner on Human Rights (OHCHR) in 2012, the crucial role of moral as well as political leadership was underscored by narratives that showcased how such leadership had been and could be used to shift and shape public opinion (UNOHCHR, 2012, pp. 15–16). Moreover, countries such as Canada, France, Germany, and the UK were cited as jurisdictions where abolition occurred even when public opinion seemingly favoured the death penalty (UNOHCHR, 2012, p. 16). Making the observation that "public opinion is based on emotion rather than rationale, but criminal justice should serve public safety and rehabilitation of the offender, not feelings of vengeance[,]" Mr. Cousin Zilala observed that in the case of South Africa, it was the Constitutional Court which struck down capital punishment, declaring it incompatible with the country's human rights culture and stating that it was crystallising "what is right, not what is popular" (UNOHCHR, 2012, p. 16).

Whether the governments of AMS can or will "lead the way" is another question.

In recent times, it is unfortunately undeniable that most governments in ASEAN have settled (if one were to subscribe to the authoritarian-democratic dichotomy) on the authoritarian side of the spectrum leading Dan Slater of the University of Michigan to write, "Southeast Asia is and always has been well on its way to being a democratic abyss" (Barber, 2018, p. 54). From the decidedly closed authoritarian kind exemplified by Brunei Darussalam, to the hegemonic authoritarian regimes of Cambodia and Vietnam, to once liberal democracies like Indonesia and the Philippines which elected autocratic-leaning populist leaders, Southeast Asia is not shaping up to be a democratic collection of States (Morgenbesser, 2019). Indeed, authoritarianism in Southeast Asia has instead become more sophisticated, opines Dr. Leo Morgenbesser, with competitive elections and opposition parties as well as troll armies to spread propaganda (Morgenbesser, 2019).

Even Indonesia, the Philippines, and Thailand, liberal democracies in the not-so-distant past, have taken decidedly authoritarian turns. And for at least Indonesia and the Philippines, authoritarian inclinations have been coupled with and brought about by populism. Populism, operationally defined as "the charismatic mobilisation of a mass movement in pursuit of political power" (Kenny, 2018, p. 9), is evident in how autocratic populist leaders have positioned themselves as distinct from traditional politicians who may have caused collective dissatisfaction, disenfranchisement, and frustration on the part of the general populace who viewed these political elitists as failing on important matters such as social services as well as law and order. The Philippines' Duterte and Indonesia's Widodo did not operate as entrenched members of problematic political parties and this perhaps was part of their refreshing appeal to tired electorates. They strategically positioned themselves as alternative outsiders and problem-solvers where weak democratic mechanisms were perceived to have failed, never mind if these solutions also included violent and despotic methods which emasculated democratic institutions, weakened the rule of law, and undercut constitutional checks and balances (Kurlantzick, 2018).

The common thread found in populist authoritarian regimes is the bannering of policies that are supposed to be tough on crime—and unfortunately, this rhetoric is often also the justification for capital punishment. Indeed, observations were made in 2014 that President Widodo's government executed several drug traffickers to bolster diminishing popularity and to project a firm anti-drug stance (Bayuni, 2015).

While it is perhaps true that the majority of ASEAN countries are presently refraining from executing death sentences or have some sort of unofficial moratorium in place for a sustained number of years, it is perhaps too optimistic to declare a trend in the region towards abolition mirroring the global trend. Death sentences are still judicially imposed. For instance, Myanmar may not have carried out an execution since 1988 but death sentences continue to be meted out by tribunals to this day (The ASEAN Post Team, 2018). Moreover, the present rise of populism and/or authoritarianism may also negatively affect whatever strides that may already have been gained (The ASEAN Post Team, 2018).

In abolitionist Philippines, the re-imposition of the death penalty ranked very high on the previous administration's legislative agenda (BBC News, 2016). In fact, the very first bill filed in the 17th Congress by members of the (lower) House of Representatives sought the return of capital punishment. Filed by pro-administration representatives, the bill's explanatory note states how the Philippine system of criminal justice "has had to make do with penal laws that are perceived to be less than dissuasive" and points out the "need to reinvigorate the war against criminality by reviving a proven deterrent coupled by its consistent, persistent, and determined implementation" (Republic of the Philippines House Bill No. 1, 2016, explanatory note). Pro-Duterte senators had also filed bills in the Senate to re-impose the death penalty for various crimes, primarily drug-related, with at least one senator being very vocal about his motivation—because the President wanted it (Rey, 2019).

While the former Philippine President had no qualms about declaring his personal preference for capital punishment, Indonesian President Widodo's pronouncements retain a seeming deference to public clamour. Widodo, described as someone "who nurtures his power and political legitimacy mostly from public opinion, perhaps more than any other president before him because he does not control any political party" (Bayuni, 2015), has referred to the death penalty as "important shock therapy" for those convicted of drug-related crimes (Kine, 2017). In 2017, he said that a moratorium could be put in place if he had the backing of the people: "If my people say OK, they say yes, I will start to prepare" (Kine, 2017). In December 2019, he again spoke on an issue relating to capital punishment, but this time on the possibility of applying it to corruption offences (*The Jakarta Post*, 2019). While conceding that such laws do not carry the death penalty for graft charges (except during national disasters), he again spoke of considering amendment or revision of the 2001 Corruption Law "if it is the people's will" (*The Jakarta Post*, 2019).

Authoritarian regimes in the region, for the most part, resort to simplistic and sweeping messaging on (1) the death penalty being an effective deterrent; (2) public support being in favour of the death penalty; and (3) capital punishment as a hallmark of public order and being "tough on crime."

The more evolved surveys of recent times, however, show that this much-touted public support is not unconditional nor unnuanced. When details are given, when sentencing options are provided, or when due process violations are discussed—opinions change. However, the problem, as alluded to earlier in this chapter, is that data and information on matters surrounding actual cases are hard to come by.

Statistics on the implementation of the death penalty are even considered State secrets in one-party Vietnam (Tran & Vu, 2019, p. 20). Similarly, Singapore's Official Secrets Act serves to gag the various protagonists and characters in capital cases (Han, 2019). In the case of Singapore, this difficulty in obtaining information, states Kirsten Han, has resulted in the issue being "distant and abstract," of being "out of sight and out of mind" for the average Singaporean (Han, 2019).

The lack of transparency and access to defendants, the difficulty in getting official data, and the absence of a freedom of information law are also factors contributing to the opaque and obscure picture of the true state of affairs (e.g., the number of convicts currently on death row, the number of trial court convictions in any given year) even in countries not expressly disallowing access to information (Han, 2019).

One disturbing consequence of such a dearth of information is that news media is forced to rely on the little official data supplied and the pronouncements of key official government informants, and, in most instances, recite the government messaging.

4 Capital Punishment and the Media

The interplay among the issue of capital punishment, authoritarianism, and the media is by no means a simple one. Law professor Susan Bandes has observed that "[l]aw and media exist in a complex feedback loop" (Bandes, 2004, p. 585) and precisely the way these two concepts react and interact in that loop is affected by even more variables such as the state of media independence in authoritarian regimes; the "newsworthiness," importance, and framing given by media to certain issues; the importance given to media by those holding executive power as well as those in positions to legislate changes, etc. As Bandes asserts: "Certainly the media [is] just one factor in the complex interplay of ideological, political[,] and social forces that give capital punishment such alarming resonance and staying power in this country. Nevertheless, they are a significant factor, and surely more than just a mirror or a messenger" (Bandes, 2004, pp. 596–597). She may have made the assertion with the United States of America (US) in mind, but it is posited that her statement also has global relevance.

4.1 The State of the Media in the Region

Authoritarianism has historically had a very hostile relationship with freedom of the press and, in a region currently filled with authoritarian markers, the outlook is dismal. In the 2020 World Press Freedom (WPF) Index of 180 countries published by Reporters Without Borders (RSF), no AMS ranked in the top 100 (RSF, 2020). Eight States languish in the bottom quarter with only Malaysia (101st) and Indonesia (119th) faring better (RSF, 2020).

In closed and hegemonic authoritarian regimes, it is not surprising that media and the press would be owned or under the strict control of ruling authorities. For instance, the State and the royal family either own or control all media in Brunei Darussalam. Self-censorship is *de rigueur* and RSF reports that, while authorities are free to intervene in journalistic activities, this is uncommon because "repressive legislation, rendered even harsher by the introduction of a very strict version of the Sharia, suffices to deter any comments that could be interpreted as blasphemy or criticism of the Sultanate" (BBC News, 2019a; RSF, 2021a). Notably, the English-language Laotian Times—styling itself as "[t]he leading English language news website in Laos" (The Laotian Times)—is the only news website not listed by the BBC as "state-run" or "state-owned" (BBC News, 2019b). In Laos, the government owns most mainstream media outlets and the ruling party reportedly exercises absolute control over the media (BBC News, 2018a; RSF, 2021b). This is true too of Vietnam where the media is, for the most part, held and controlled by the State and the Communist Party (BBC News, 2018b; RSF, 2021c). In Cambodia, RSF reports that citizens can only access mainstream news from major media groups with ties to Prime Minister Hun Sen, amidst reports of many radio stations being silenced (BBC News, 2019c; RSF, 2021d).

In the cases of Cambodia and Vietnam, bloggers as well as independent journalists do still strive to serve as critics and sources of independent information, the internet being less susceptible to governmental restraint (BBC News, 2018b, 2019c; RSF, 2021c, 2021d). However, these groups have seen members of their ranks prosecuted and imprisoned for alleged violations of laws (BBC News, 2018b, 2019c; RSF, 2021c, 2021d). In Vietnam, articles in the Criminal Code dealing with, amongst other issues, "anti-[S]tate propaganda" and "abus[e] [of] the rights to freedom and democracy to threaten the interests of the [S]tate" have been wielded against critics (RSF, 2021c).The military has also reportedly created a cyber-warfare department to defend the Communist Party and to counter online dissent, and a new law directs that all foreign online platforms must store Vietnamese-related user data in servers within Vietnam and surrender such data when required by the authorities (RSF, 2021c). Such censorship is by no means confined to Vietnam. Cambodia also has commonly used defamation and *lèse-majesté* laws to curb dissent (Kennedy & Southern, 2021; Tsang, 2021).

Moreover, other countries in the region have been backsliding on the matter of press freedom. Following a period of brief promise after the 2016 elections, media freedom has been declining in Myanmar (RSF, 2021f; BBC News, 2017). Another turn for the worse was recorded by RSF in Singapore which dropped seven places in the 2020 WPF Index compared to the year prior (BBC News, 2020a; RSF, 2019, 2020, 2021h). The Singaporean government has even been compared to China in terms of its desire to inhibit free press, as evidenced by the government's penchant for suing or pressuring journalists for defamation or sedition and the power of the Media Development Authority to exercise censorship (RSF, 2021h). Furthermore, the two most dominant media corporations—Singapore Press Holdings (SPH) and MediaCorp—both have ties to the State and control virtually all mainstream media (BBC News, 2020a). Two of the three major dailies are published by SPH and the third is published by MediaCorp which also operates the main television and broadcast radio stations (BBC News, 2020a). According to Reuters Institute, both have also begun to dominate online media platforms (BBC News, 2020a).

In the remaining AMS, media and the press may not be controlled by the government to the same extent as in the examples just discussed, but government encroachment into the fourth estate and repressive turns, both executive and legislative, have been observed across the board. In Indonesia, authoritarian measures have resulted in a diminution of free speech, even as players are not restricted to government-owned or controlled outfits (BBC News, 2020b; RSF, 2021e). Authorities have reportedly restricted media access and disabled internet connections in certain areas during tension-filled times and the military has also taken to intimidating journalists who cover military abuses (BBC News, 2020b; RSF, 2021e). RSF has cited increasing self-censorship of journalists due to threatened prosecution under anti-blasphemy legislation and the Electronic and Information Transactions Law (BBC News, 2020b; RSF, 2021e). Former Minister of Finance, Rizal Ramli, has written that part of President Widodo's apparent public appeal is due to a "subservient local media industry" and that media outfits are dominated by conglomerates who wish to preserve and expand business by ensuring that they stay on the right side of the president and his government (Ramli, 2019). In the Philippines, ABS-CBN, the largest privately-owned conglomerate—which displeased President Duterte and became the subject of his tirades after the 2016 elections for perceived slights during the campaign—went off the air in 2020 when its legislative franchise was not renewed by the Philippine Congress (Malindog-Uy, 2020; RSF, 2021g). Other worrying developments in the Philippines include journalists becoming the target of extra-judicial killings and independent media outlets seemingly becoming the target of prior restraint as well as questionable subsequent punishment (BBC News, 2019d; RSF, 2021g). Also in 2020, Maria Ressa, editor of web-based news outlet, Rappler, was convicted of cyber libel in a case which had arguably already prescribed (Panganiban, 2020; Ratcliffe, 2020).

In Thailand, like the Philippines, most print media is privately owned, and it appears that the State also controls the major national television and radio networks (BBC News, 2014; RSF, 2021i). Press freedom in Thailand ranked lower than the Philippines and even Myanmar in 2020, with RSF identifying a 2019 cyber-security law giving the executive branch even more powers potentially posing another threat to online opinions (BBC News, 2014; RSF, 2020, 2021i). Moreover, Thailand still retains *lèse-majesté* laws in its statute books (BBC News, 2014; RSF, 2021i).

While Malaysia significantly improved in the WPF Index by 22 places in 2020, RSF still expressed reservations regarding restrictive laws such as the 1948 Sedition Act, the 1972 Official Secrets Act, and the 1998 Communications and Multimedia Act, all of which pose significant threats to media practitioners (BBC News, 2020c; RSF, 2019, 2020, 2021i).

4.2 The Interplay of Media, Politics, and Public Opinion

To summarise the immediately preceding section, media is heavily State-controlled in several countries in the region. In others where the press is ostensibly free and independent, there are currently major challenges and difficulties brought about by, among other issues, increasingly authoritarian regimes which view freedom of expression and a free press as subservient to their version of public order and national security.

Because of this, when dealing with media coverage of capital punishment, the influence of government in terms of messaging cannot be underestimated. And when the government in question is authoritarian in nature with an overall policy of communicating messages that are tough on crime, coupled with an insistence that capital punishment is an effective deterrent, the input into public instruction and education (whether express or subtle) is decidedly pro-death penalty.

News articles that find their way into print or broadcast commonly deal with either one of two subjects: (1) any move on the part of the State to institute a policy (e.g., legislative proposals to review the death penalty or aspects of it such as mandatory sentences or covered crimes, executive steps to formalise a moratorium on executions), or (2) coverage of particular cases where the death penalty had been meted out (e.g., judicial sentencing especially in sensational cases including actual executions of individuals).

Outside the internet and blogosphere, coverage of these subjects in countries where the media is largely State-owned or controlled will likely not be critical of government action. In countries where the press is free and independent to any extent, there will be instances of op-ed pieces advocating both positions and more diverse features, but since the majority of available and preferred sources of the mainstream press are governmental, the treatment of the subject in news reporting will still not be predominantly or overtly anti-government or anti-capital punishment.

The answer to the query of whether media really affects the way the public views current events and issues seems rather obvious. While most of the scientific research regarding this particular subject has been done in a different jurisdiction (i.e., the US), the psychology of the findings is such that they are also of value when looking at our own context because media, especially broadcast and online media, has been a pervasive inescapable feature of Southeast Asia. Ray Surette makes the observation that: "[o]ver time people tend to perceive things the way the media portray them" (Surette, 1992 p. 76, cited in Lipschultz & Hilt, 1999, pp. 249–250). For good or bad, the media does not only report, it actually defines (Surette, 1992 p. 76, cited in Lipschultz & Hilt, 1999, pp. 249–250). Likewise, depictions in media "construct social reality" (Lipschultz & Hilt, 1999, p. 240) and, as Gaye Tuchman observed, "the act of making news is the act of constructing reality itself rather than a picture of reality" (Tuchman, 1978 p. 12, cited in Lipschultz & Hilt, 1999, p. 240).

In arguing for a more studied focus on media and its aspects (i.e., its limitations, potential, grammar, and logic), Bandes points out that such issues have implications for the construction and delivery of justice since most of what the public knows about the workings of the criminal justice system does not come from direct experience, but from media portrayal (Bandes, 2004, p. 585). Moreover, it is not only individual opinions and social relations that are thus affected, but also political movements and even government policy due to the feedback loop (Bandes, 2004, p. 591). So the way media covers an issue over time has far-reaching consequences which may not always be apparent; and when an issue like the death penalty is oversimplified and consistently framed in a particular manner, it does impel a certain bias or view. In a study by Elisabeth Noelle-Neumann in 1995, it was observed that "where media messages are consonant, it is possible that the content will have the effect of influencing people" (Noelle-Neumann, 1995, cited in Lipschultz & Hilt, 1999, p. 240).

In a study on executions in Nebraska, Jeremy Harris Lipschultz and Michael L. Hilt made the observation that, even as television aids in creating a social reality regarding the death penalty as well as the concomitant public attitude about it, the State has the power to "manipulate events" (Lipschultz & Hilt, 1999, p. 250). In that study, the observation referred to the inescapable drama of the execution coverage given the selection of sources as well as the routine of local television networks (Lipschultz & Hilt, 1999, p. 250). However, this statement—about the power of States to manipulate or influence events—actually rings true in our context, albeit not exactly in the same way.

Aside from the obvious cases of media outfits under the total control of (authoritarian) States, governments can impel certain journalistic predispositions in more complex and oblique ways. As mentioned earlier, in most countries in the region, data and statistics about death penalty cases can be hard to access. In Vietnam, statistics on capital cases are State secrets; similarly in Singapore, one has to contend with the Official Secrets Act (Han, 2019). So what may be considered as "verified fact" for news reporting depends on what authorities deem proper to share. This can result in a reiteration of the government message (or the necessary news soundbite) becoming the constant and recurring theme. Conditioning over time is not a far-fetched supposition. In the case of Singapore, for instance, considering the dearth of information available to advocates against capital punishment for drug offences, the government has further been accused of imposing its own narrative on the anti-drug campaign through openly distributed propaganda by the Central Narcotics Bureau without a strong counter (Han, 2019).

Even with more open access to sources in capital cases, government offices and officials will still be the primary sources for media coverage. When reporting is "occurrence-driven," it is for the most part linked to landmark events dictated by government authority (e.g., arrests, trials, and executions) so pertinent pieces of information will still be governmental (e.g., police blotters, mug shots, indictments, and judicial orders, etc.) (Bandes, 2004, p. 590). Inevitably, the content of news articles will be significantly influenced by officially available material (Bandes, 2004, p. 590). More often than not, the defendant's "side of the story" will not be exhaustively covered beyond the information found in official submissions and public documents, especially when the defendant is detained or has already been convicted (Bandes, 2004, p. 590). Accessing such individuals while imprisoned can also be hampered by so many restrictions and constraints, journalists may be reluctant to report the story unless special circumstances prevail (Bandes, 2004, p. 590). It is also not uncommon for journalists highlighting the plight of prisoners on death row to be accused of siding with the criminal element or of belittling the grief and anguish of victims (Bandes, 2004, p. 590). Moreover, Bandes points out that, without the trappings of an occurrence or crime, journalists may be reluctant to write independently on the issue of capital punishment as a social problem: "Such a role conflicts with their perception of themselves as impartial chroniclers. The upshot is a severe imbalance in the guise of neutrality. The reliance on occurrence becomes a reliance on the voice and priorities of government institutions," making journalists, as David Protess put it, 'unwitting governmental partners'" (Protess, 1997, cited in Bandes, 2004, pp. 590–591).

Another way death penalty coverage is exploited by authorities is to use it as supporting "evidence" of a regime's tough stance on crime—usually to deflect attention from current events that may be the subject of public criticism or denunciation, such as those involving governmental ineptitude and corruption.

In Indonesia, for instance, the media attention, which followed in the wake of the execution of convicted drug traffickers in early 2015, was called out as "reinforc[ing] a myth that it serves as a panacea for a social illness" (Wibowo, 2015). The media coverage during that period saw the government's argument about capital punishment being an effective deterrent being reiterated without scientific support but replete with quotes from not only academics but also celebrities and religious organisations in support of the death penalty (Wibowo, 2015).

Deasy Simandjuntak (2015) observed that capital punishment also serves a political function in Indonesia and that the intensity of the coverage "may have been used to politically consolidate and boost the government's waning popularity in light of problems in other pressing issues, such as corruption" (p. 1). The role of media was key in disseminating the message and the "making" of public opinion; Simandjuntak opines that amplified media reporting on the issue at that time may have been used to (1) distract the public and to avert attention from other critical issues of the day, i.e. deficiencies in other policy areas; and (2) portray the Indonesian government as taking a stand to protect its sovereignty from the pressures of foreign powers attempting to influence its processes (Simandjuntak, 2015, pp. 3 & 6–7).

5 Final Points and Observations

While authoritarianism to one extent or another is prevalent in the region, and while the current state of the media is far from ideal, it is important for those aspiring to become more liberal democracies with a vibrant free press not to lose hope in gaining (and regaining) ground.

While authoritarianism affects and utilises media coverage of important issues like the movement for abolishing capital punishment in ASEAN jurisdictions, media coverage, in turn, creates and influences public opinion on these issues. Thus, public support gives a semblance of legitimacy to authoritarian messaging on the need for the death penalty as a crucial deterrent to crime. As Bandes has pointed out, it is, in fact, a feedback loop (Bandes, 2004, p. 591), although one which hopefully can be disrupted on a number of fronts.

In conclusion, three points are proffered:

(1) A reframing of the key points in the death penalty discussion may have value and should be considered.
(2) The internet and social media can potentially be a strategic front for abolition advocates in the region who must grapple with authoritarian strangleholds on the more traditional media outlets.
(3) Public instruction and education on key aspects of the death penalty issue, whether through media partners or other channels like communities and schools, must continue. In connection with this, more nuanced surveys similar to the Roger Hood-led one in Malaysia which go beyond simplistic questions should be encouraged.

5.1 The Conflict-Displacing Innocence Frame as a Pragmatic Alternative

In a seminal study by Frank E. Dardis et al. (2008) on media framing of capital punishment, the authors wrote of the advent of a novel conflict-displacing "innocence frame" in the death penalty discourse in the US which highlighted the imperfections of the criminal justice system, and how it greatly impacted individual cognitive responses, ultimately resulting in a decline of public support for capital punishment (p. 134).

Historically, discussions on the death penalty in the US have predominantly involved constitutional or cost issues (Hayes, 2013) with the main frame of the debate being morality (or religion)-based (Baumgartner et al., 2008, p. 6). This changed in the mid-1990s when the media started paying attention to wrongful convictions and exonerations (partly brought about by advancements in DNA testing) (Baumgartner et al., 2008, p. 42; Dardis et al., 2008, pp. 125–126). As Dardis et al. asserted, this new media frame did not hew along traditional lines but instead came at the discourse from "a completely different point of evaluation[—]whether the system works as advertised" (p. 133).

This new approach led to a significant reduction of public support for the death penalty perhaps because Americans were conflicted or ambivalent in the first place—many believing it to be justifiable but also feeling anxious about innocent people being subjected to the ultimate penalty (Hayes, 2013). It is posited by a number of writers that, since media coverage focused on exonerations and wrongful executions, more individuals have (slowly and gradually) come to the realisation that the death penalty is potentially unfair (Hayes, 2013).

The study presented two results of interest: (1) that the discourse on the death penalty has been transformed by the "new and unprecedented media focus" on potential mistakes and gaps in the system (which are decidedly irreversible); and (2) that the new frame differs from its predecessors as "it serves to readjust the structure of the debate by introducing an entirely new set of considerations that are not necessarily contradictory to any existing arguments" (Dardis et al., 2008, p. 118).

Whereas previous frames such as the morality-based one potentially reinforced those who already had a position on the issue, reasoning along these lines did not do much to convince those already taking a stand on the other side of the issue to change their minds. These "conflict-reinforcing" frames, asserts Dardis et al. (2008, p. 118), did not reframe discourse but "simply encourage[d] polemic within a specific, existing frame of reference." Not so with conflict-displacing frames which focus on innocence and which not only highlight claims of innocence but also the imperfections of the criminal justice system—the latter being an issue which is all too familiar in ASEAN (Dardis et al., 2008, p. 125):

> The most remarkable thing about the innocence frame may be what it does not ask of those who are opposed to it. It does not ask them to re-evaluate their own core moral or religious background and values; rather, it simply asks people to focus on the question of whether a human-designed institution processing thousands of cases can be expected to do so perfectly, without a single error. Most people probably would say that this is very unlikely. (Dardis et al., 2008, pp. 133–134)

The value of abolition advocates and media partners cohesively strategizing and working on angles to amplify miscarriages of justice and the innocence frame may be worth exploring. Engaging in the debate on moral and religious grounds, or even reticently that there is no concrete proof of the death penalty being an effective deterrent, indeed have led to an impasse more often than not. This is not to say that the innocence angle is being ignored by advocates in the region, only that it does not appear to be the most prominent frame used. While perhaps the more principled attitude would still be to insist on the inherent right to life of every human being, it is submitted that a conscious and committed reframing might be the more pragmatic move.

5.2 The Internet and Social Media as the New Strategic Front

A survey of the media situation shows authoritarian attacks and strangleholds on the more traditional media outlets in several AMS. While it is by no means suggested that the fight to uphold press freedom in whatever platform should ever be relinquished, exigencies may require that new fronts and platforms be explored.

For example, the internet has become a convenient alternative for more traditional print and broadcast media. Newspapers seeing print circulation fall have also taken to online portals. Moreover, this shift or auxiliary platform has been utilised by broadcast companies as well. As a result, for millions in the region, smartphones have become the hub for all information (and entertainment).

At the end of June 2021, more than 70% of citizens in eight of the ten AMS were online, while 50% used the internet in the remaining two (Internet World Stats, 2021). Brunei boasted the highest penetration and Myanmar the lowest (Internet World Stats, 2021). In terms of pure numbers, Indonesia (at 76.8%) had the most users (212,354,070 of 276,361,783) (Internet World Stats, 2021).

Studying how social media tools and the internet can be optimised should remain a priority, especially as the rate of users in the region will continue to rapidly increase. This also includes being aware of how several States in the region block access and censor content for reasons usually bannered as "public order" or "national security." Moreover, authoritarian regimes themselves have weaponised the internet and social media to serve their own ends. "Troll armies," although unofficial, are reportedly used by Philippine President Duterte to counter criticism on Facebook and Twitter (Etter, 2017, cited in Kurlantzick, 2018). Vietnam, on the other hand, has created a cyber unit informally named "Force 47" which aims to counter online criticism and spread pro-government propaganda (Hiep, 2019, p. 5). Reportedly 10,000-strong, this cyber unit was created in 2016 as a tool to maintain a "healthy" online atmosphere and safeguard authorities against information deemed toxic and hostile to the "Vietnamese revolution" (Hiep, 2019, p. 5). Some assignments given to this unit include gathering information on social media, reporting accounts and sites disseminating negative statements or fake news, as well as actively engaging in debates exhibiting unfavourable opinions.

But even in Communist Vietnam, the internet has proved its worth in the fight against capital punishment when a farmer on death row for killing three men and injuring several others because of a land dispute had his sentence considered by the People's Supreme Court after it was confirmed in appellate court. This occurred after 3,500 individuals signed an online petition in less than a week asking the President for executive clemency. While the last report available did not say that this was granted, his lawyers did receive an order from the People's Supreme Court to provide more information in support of his request for a trial by cassation (Tran, 2019).

Still, while taking advantage of its virtues, it is prudent to be aware of the internet's shortcomings including the fact that informational legitimacy—something often taken for granted in more traditional forms of news reporting—is not readily apparent in many internet sources. It is still, for the most part, open unregulated media.

5.3 Public Education as an Enlightening Tool

Mr. Justice Thurgood Marshall, in his concurring opinion in the landmark US case of *Furman v. Georgia* (which dealt with the issue of whether the death penalty was prohibited by the Eighth Amendment as a cruel and unusual punishment), observed that: "the question with which we must deal is not whether a substantial proportion of American citizens would today, if polled, opine that capital punishment is barbarously cruel, but whether they would find it to be so *in the light of all information presently available*" (*Furman v. Georgia*, J. Marshall concurring opinion, p. 362, emphasis supplied). And he was confident in his assumption that, if armed with such information, the people would conclude that capital punishment was indeed immoral and thus unconstitutional (*Furman v. Georgia*, J. Marshall concurring opinion, p. 363).

While perhaps not rising to the level of Marshall's confident assumption, fairly recent surveys in a few AMS (e.g., Malaysia, Singapore, the Philippines) have revealed surprising revelations about the level of awareness that our own citizens have on the issue of capital punishment. The majority of the public, whose support is often flaunted as a key factor in retaining capital punishment, appear to know very little about the issues surrounding it. And while findings in the survey still show a great number expressing approval of the death penalty in abstract terms, such approval rates decline in the face of hypothetical (but reality-based) scenarios possible under the current state of legislation. The purported strength of such support is therefore suspect and opinions are seen to be altered when situations are expounded on and questions no longer oversimplified.

Continued public information dissemination on the state of death penalty legislation and application, the inclusion of this issue in appropriate fora and awareness campaigns, conducting like studies or surveys to the extent possible—all these can contribute to challenging the government's sound bytes on the state of public support in media—and with any luck, this will inform and shape elements that go into the law and media feedback loop.

6 Conclusion

Despite the worldwide trend towards the abolition of capital punishment, the ASEAN region has indubitably taken steps in the wrong direction. This chapter analysed its seemingly widespread support for the death penalty. However, as studies, articles, and reports have shown, the public's support for the death penalty is ultimately more apparent than real. That notwithstanding, with authoritarianism sweeping the ASEAN region in recent years, the death penalty is revealed to be bucking the global trend and is possibly gaining more widespread support in the ASEAN. This is primarily brought about by tendencies of authoritarian regimes to stifle dissent and impair the freedom of the press. At the same time, this chapter has shown that the media plays a crucial role in influencing public opinion and support for or against the death penalty. Ultimately, the ways authoritarian regimes and the media shape public perception and support for capital punishment in the ASEAN region cannot be taken for granted.

That said, there is a need to explore possibilities for framing the capital punishment discourse with the view of working against its retention and re-imposition in the long run. Hopefully, these insights and observations may prove helpful in continuing the efforts to assert the right to life.

References

Books and Articles

Al Jazeera. (2016, May 16). Philippines' Rodrigo Duterte recommends death penalty. *Al Jazeera*. https://www.aljazeera.com/news/2016/5/16/philippines-rodrigo-duterte-recommends-death-penalty. Accessed 5 December 2021.

Amnesty International. (n.d.). *The death penalty—Your questions answered*. https://www.amnesty.org/en/what-we-do/death-penalty/the-death-penalty-your-questions-answered/. Accessed 5 December 2021.

Bandes, S. A. (2004). Fear factor: The role of media in covering and shaping the death penalty. *Ohio State Journal of Criminal Law, 1*, 585–597. https://doi.org/10.2139/ssrn.413385

Bangkok Post. (2018, June 20). Death penalty 'here to stay'. *Bangkok Post*. https://www.bangkokpost.com/thailand/general/1488498/death-penalty-here-to-stay. Accessed 5 December 2021.

Barber, B. (2018). Authoritarianism gains in Southeast Asia. *American Foreign Service Association, The Foreign Service Journal, 95*(4), 51–54. https://www.afsa.org/sites/default/files/fsj-2018-05-may.pdf. Accessed 5 December 2021.

Baumgartner, F. R., De Boef, S. L., & Boydstun, A. E. (2008). *The decline of the death penalty and the discovery of innocence*. Cambridge University Press.

Bayuni, E. (2015, January 23). Commentary: Capital punishment and public opinion. *The Jakarta Post*. https://www.thejakartapost.com/news/2015/01/23/commentary-capital-punishment-and-public-opinion.html. Accessed 5 December 2021.

BBC News. (2014, June 2). Thailand profile—Media. *BBC News*. https://www.bbc.com/news/world-asia-15639421. Accessed 5 December 2021.

BBC News. (2016, May 16). Philippines: Duterte vows to bring back death penalty. *BBC News*. https://www.bbc.com/news/world-asia-36297583. Accessed 5 December 2021.

BBC News. (2017, May 2). Myanmar profile—Media. *BBC News*. https://www.bbc.com/news/world-asia-pacific-12991727. Accessed 5 December 2021.

BBC News. (2018a, July 24). Laos country profile. *BBC News*. https://www.bbc.com/news/world-asia-pacific-15351898. Accessed 5 December 2021.

BBC News. (2018b, November 20). Vietnam profile—Media. *BBC News*. https://www.bbc.com/news/world-asia-pacific-16567840. Accessed 5 December 2021.

BBC News. (2019a, August 27). Brunei profile—Media. *BBC News*. https://www.bbc.com/news/world-asia-pacific-12990064. Accessed 5 December 2021.

BBC News. (2019b, December 2). Laos profile—Media. *BBC News*. https://www.bbc.com/news/world-asia-pacific-15353971. Accessed 5 December 2021.

BBC News. (2019c, August 13). Cambodia profile—Media. *BBC News*. https://www.bbc.com/news/world-asia-pacific-13006543. Accessed 5 December 2021.

BBC News. (2019d, January 21). Philippines profile—Media. *BBC News*. https://www.bbc.com/news/world-asia-15527446. Accessed 5 December 2021.

BBC News. (2020a, February 17). Singapore profile—Media. *BBC News*. https://www.bbc.com/news/world-asia-15966553. Accessed 5 December 2021.

BBC News. (2020b, February 17). Indonesia profile—Media. *BBC News*. https://www.bbc.com/news/world-asia-pacific-15105923. Accessed 5 December 2021.

BBC News. (2020c, February 17). Malaysia profile—Media. *BBC News*. https://www.bbc.com/news/world-asia-pacific-15384221. Accessed 5 December 2021.

Bedi, R. S. (2019, April 5). Liew: Process of abolishing death penalty ongoing, more time needed after moratorium. *The Star*. https://www.thestar.com.my/news/nation/2019/04/05/liew-process-of-abolishing-death-penalty-ongoing/. Accessed 5 December 2021.

Cepeda, Mara. (2017, March 7). Death for drug convicts: House passes bill on final reading. *Rappler*. https://www.rappler.com/nation/163495-drug-convicts-philippines-death-penalty-bill-final-reading/. Accessed 5 December 2021.

Chan, W. C., Tan, E. S., Lee, J., & Mathi, B. (2018, February). *Public opinion on the death penalty in Singapore: Survey findings* (NUS Law Working Paper 2018/02). https://law.nus.edu.sg/wp-content/uploads/2020/04/002_2018_Chan-Wing-Cheong.pdf. Accessed 5 December 2021.

Dardis, F. E., Baumgartner, F. R., Boydstun, A. E., De Boef, S., & Shen, F. (2008). Media framing of capital punishment and its impact on individuals' cognitive responses. *Mass Communication & Society, 11*(2), 115–140. https://doi.org/10.1080/15205430701580524

Death Penalty Information Center. (2022, June 12). *Malaysian government pledges to end mandatory death penalty*. Death Penalty Information Center. https://deathpenaltyinfo.org/news-brief/malaysian-government-pledges-to-end-mandatory-death-penalty. Accessed 11 July 2022.

Etter, L. (2017, December 7). What happens when the government uses Facebook as a weapon? *Bloomberg*. https://www.bloomberg.com/news/features/2017-12-07/how-rodrigo-duterte-turned-facebook-into-a-weapon-with-a-little-help-from-facebook. Accessed 5 December 2021.

FIDH. (2018, October 10). Thailand: Still dragging feet on death penalty. *FIDH*. https://www.fidh.org/en/issues/death-penalty/thailand-suffered-a-massive-setback-on-the-road-to-the-abolition-of. Accessed 5 December 2021.

Gavilan, J. (2018, October 10). SWS: Less than 50% of Filipinos want death penalty for 7 drug-related crimes. *Rappler*. https://www.rappler.com/nation/213959-filipinos-death-penalty-drug-related-crimes-sws-survey-march-2018/. Accessed 5 December 2021.

Girelli, G. (2019, October 17). The death penalty for drugs: What public opinion surveys in Asia teach us. *Filter*. https://filtermag.org/death-penalty-drugs-public-opinion-asia/. Accessed 5 December 2021.

Gomez-Dumpit, K. S. (2019). *Statement before the House of Representatives Committee on Justice' 18th Congress 1st Regular Session, 24 September 2019*. https://chr.gov.ph/statement-of-commissioner-karen-s-gomez-dumpit/. Accessed 5 December 2021.

Halim, H. (2017, March 30). Jokowi and Hollande did not discuss death penalty: Foreign Minister. *The Jakarta Post*. https://www.thejakartapost.com/news/2017/03/30/jokowi-and-hollande-did-not-discuss-death-penalty-foreign-minister.html. Accessed 5 December 2021.

Han, K. (2019, December 20). Things we don't know about the death penalty in Singapore. *Popula*. https://popula.com/2019/12/20/thingsdon'tdont-know-about-the-death-penalty-in-singapore/. Accessed 5 December 2021.

Hayes, D. (2013, March 17). How the media is killing the death penalty. *The Washington Post*. https://www.washingtonpost.com/news/wonk/wp/2013/03/17/how-the-media-is-killing-the-death-penalty/. Accessed 5 December 2021.

Hiep, L. H. (2019). The political economy of social media in Vietnam. *ISEAS Perspective* 77, 1–7. https://www.iseas.edu.sg/images/pdf/ISEAS_Perspective_2019_77.pdf. Accessed 5 December 2021.

Hood, R. (2013). *The death penalty in Malaysia: Public opinion on the mandatory death penalty for drug trafficking, murder, and firearms offences*. The Death Penalty Project. https://www.deathpenaltyproject.org/wp-content/uploads/2018/02/Malaysia-report.pdf. Accessed 5 December 2021.

International Federation for Human Rights [FIDH]. (2016). *Going backwards: The death penalty in Southeast Asia*. https://www.fidh.org/IMG/pdf/asie682apdmweb.pdf. Accessed 5 December 2021.

Internet World Stats. (2021). *Internet usage in Asia 2021: Internet users, Facebook subscribers & population statistics for 35 countries and regions in Asia*. https://www.internetworldstats.com/stats3.htm. Accessed 5 December 2021.

Kamarudin, F. (2018, October 11). Online poll reveals majority of netizens opposed to death penalty abolition. *New Straits Times*. https://www.nst.com.my/news/nation/2018/10/420315/online-poll-reveals-majority-netizens-opposed-death-penalty-abolition. Accessed 5 December 2021.

Kennedy, L., & Southern, N. P. (2021, February 10). Cambodia's post-pandemic law and order. *Foreign Policy*. https://foreignpolicy.com/2021/02/10/cambodia-law-public-order-hun-sen-pandemic-control-dissent/. Accessed 5 December 2021.

Kenny, P. D. (2018). *Populism in Southeast Asia*. Cambridge Elements in Politics and Society in Southeast Asia. Cambridge University Press.

Kine, P. (2017, March 29). *Indonesian death penalty moratorium needs presidential push*. Human Rights Watch. https://www.hrw.org/news/2017/03/29/indonesian-death-penalty-moratorium-needs-presidential-push. Accessed 5 December 2021.

Kurlantzick, J. (2018, November 1). *Southeast Asia's populism is different but also dangerous*. Council for Foreign Relations. https://www.cfr.org/in-brief/southeast-asias-populism-different-also-dangerous. Accessed 5 December 2021.

Lai, A. (2018, October 11). Liew: Death penalty to be abolished. *The Star*. https://www.thestar.com.my/news/nation/2018/10/11/liew-death-penalty-to-be-abolished-moratorium-on-all-pending-capital-punishments-as-well-says-minist/. Accessed 5 December 2021.

Lipschultz, J. H., & Hilt, M. L. (1999). Mass media and the death penalty: Social construction of three Nebraska executions. *Journal of Broadcasting & Electronic Media, 43*(2), 236–253. https://doi.org/10.1080/08838159909364487

Luong, D. (2017, October 24). Death penalty still the public's answer to solving social downfall in Vietnam. *VnExpress*. https://e.vnexpress.net/news/news/death-penalty-still-the-public-s-answer-to-solving-social-downfall-in-vietnam-3660448.html. Accessed 5 December 2021.

Malindog-Uy, A. (2020, July 16). Why did Congress deny ABS-CBN a franchise? *The ASEAN Post*. https://theaseanpost.com/article/why-did-congress-deny-abs-cbn-franchise. Accessed 5 December 2021.

Morgenbesser, L. (2019, October 23). *The rise of sophisticated authoritarianism in Southeast Asia*. https://medium.com/the-machinery-of-government/the-rise-of-sophisticated-authoritarianism-in-southeast-asia-a42742c4bdeb. Accessed 5 December 2021.

Noelle-Neumann, E. (1995). Public opinion and rationality. In T. L. Glasser & C. T. Salmon (Eds.), *Public opinion and the communication of consent* (pp. 33–54). The Guilford Press.

Office of the United Nations High Commissioner for Human Rights [UNOHCHR]. (2022, June 20). *Malaysia: UN experts welcome announcement to abolish mandatory death penalty* [Press release]. https://www.ohchr.org/en/press-releases/2022/06/malaysia-un-experts-welcome-announcement-abolish-mandatory-death-penalty. Accessed 11 July 2022.

Panganiban, A. V. (2020, June 21). Cyberlibel and Maria Ressa. *Philippine Daily Inquirer*. https://opinion.inquirer.net/130986/cyberlibel-and-maria-ressa. Accessed 5 December 2021.

Protess, D. (1997). Last chance for the condemned: Do media matter in Gubernatorial Clemency decisions? *Chicago Policy Review, 2*, 93.

Ramli, R. (2019, January 9). Widodo Administration's authoritarian measures continue to weaken Indonesian democracy. *The Business Times*. https://www.businesstimes.com.sg/opinion/widodo-administrations-authoritarian-measures-continue-to-weaken-indonesian-democracy. Accessed 5 December 2021.

Rappler. (2017, May 5). Filipinos' support for death penalty wanes—Survey. *Rappler*. https://r3.rappler.com/nation/168939-filipinos-support-death-penalty-wanes-pulse-asia. Accessed 5 December 2021.

Ratcliffe, R. (2020, June 14). Trial of journalists to deliver 'existential moment' in Philippines. *The Guardian*. https://www.theguardian.com/world/2020/jun/14/trial-of-journalists-rappler-philippines. Accessed 5 December 2021.

Rey, A. (2019, July 2). Pacquiao, Bong Go file bills on death penalty for illegal drugs cases. *Rappler*. https://www.rappler.com/nation/234434-bong-go-files-death-penalty-bill-illegal-drugs-plunder/. Accessed 5 December 2021.

Reporters Without Borders (Reporters Sans Frontières) [RSF]. (2020). *2020 World Press Freedom Index*. https://rsf.org/en/ranking/2020. Accessed 5 December 2021.

Reporters Without Borders (Reporters Sans Frontières) [RSF]. (2019). *2019 World Press Freedom Index*. https://rsf.org/en/ranking/2019. Accessed 5 December 2021.

Reporters Without Borders. (2021a). *Brunei: Self-censorship on politics and religion*. https://rsf.org/en/brunei. Accessed 5 December 2021.

RSF. (2021b). *Laos: Muted online criticism*. https://rsf.org/en/laos. Accessed 5 December 2021.

RSF. (2021c). *Vietnam: State violence v. bloggers and journalists*. https://rsf.org/en/vietnam. Accessed 5 December 2021.

RSF. (2021d). *Cambodia: Ruling party eliminates critical media*. https://rsf.org/en/cambodia. Accessed 5 December 2021.

RSF. (2021e). *Indonesia: Press freedom still pending in Jokowi's second term*. https://rsf.org/en/indonesia. Accessed 5 December 2021.

RSF. (2021f). *Myanmar: Set back ten years*. https://rsf.org/en/myanmar. Accessed 5 December 2021.

RSF. (2021g). *Philippines: Holding the line against Duterte's attacks*. https://rsf.org/en/philippines. Accessed 5 December 2021.

RSF. (2021h). *Singapore: An alternative way to curtail press freedom*. https://rsf.org/en/singapore. Accessed 5 December 2021.

RSF. (2021i). *Thailand: Gen. Prayuth and monarchy in ever greater control*. https://rsf.org/en/thailand. Accessed 5 December 2021.

RSF. (2021j). *Malaysia: Back to harassment, intimidation and censorship*. https://rsf.org/en/malaysia. Accessed 5 December 2021.

Simandjuntak, D. (2015). Spectacle of the scaffold? The politics of death penalty in Indonesia. *ISEAS Perspective* 46, 1–8. https://www.iseas.edu.sg/images/pdf/ISEAS_Perspective_2015_46.pdf. Accessed 5 December 2021.

Singapore Ministry of Home Affairs. (2019, May 17). *Very strong support for Singapore's anti-drug policies* [Press Release]. https://www.mha.gov.sg/mediaroom/press-releases/very-strong-public-support-for-singapore's-anti-drug-policies/. Accessed 5 December 2021.

Singapore REACH. (2016, October 6). *Findings of poll on attitudes towards the death penalty*. https://www.reach.gov.sg/-/media/reach/reach-files/news-and-press-releases/2016/press-release/reach-poll-on-attitudes-towards-death-penalty.ashx. Accessed 5 December 2021.

Social Weather Stations. (2017, April 25). First quarter 2018 Social Weather Survey. *Social Weather Stations*. https://www.sws.org.ph/swsmain/artcldisppage/?artcsyscode=ART-20170425085448. Accessed 5 December 2021.

Social Weather Stations. (2018, October 10). *March 2018 national survey on public perceptions on the death penalty: 33% or less demand the death penalty for 6 of 7 crimes related to illegal drugs.*

https://www.sws.org.ph/swsmain/artcldisppage/?artcsyscode=ART-20181010122553. Accessed 5 December 2021.
Surette, R. (1992). *Media, crime & criminal justice: Images and realities*. Brooks/Cole Publishing Company.
Tang, L. (2018, November 30). The big read: Capital punishment—A little more conversation on a matter of life and death. *Today*. https://www.todayonline.com/big-read/big-read-capital-punishment-little-more-conversation-matter-life-and-death. Accessed 5 December 2021.
The ASEAN Post Team. (2018, October 11). Is ASEAN close to abolishing the death penalty? *The ASEAN Post*. https://theaseanpost.com/article/asean-close-abolishing-death-penalty. Accessed 5 December 2021.
The Jakarta Post. (2019, December 10). Death for graft convicts? Possible if public wants it: Jokowi. *The Jakarta Post*. https://www.thejakartapost.com/news/2019/12/09/death-for-graft-convicts-possible-if-public-wants-it-jokowi.html. Accessed 5 December 2021.
The Laotian Times. (n.d.). https://laotiantimes.com/. Accessed 5 December 2021.
The Straits Times. (2017, March 28). Indonesia's president Joko Widodo says open to death penalty review. *The Straits Times*. https://www.straitstimes.com/asia/se-asia/indonesias-president-joko-widodo-says-open-to-death-penalty-review. Accessed 5 December 2021.
Tran, K., & Vu, C. G. (2019). The changing nature of death penalty in Vietnam: A historical and legal inquiry. *Societies, 9*(3), 56. https://doi.org/10.3390/soc9030056
Tran, Q. (2019, February 20). Death-row inmate Dang Van Hien may get a second chance at life. *The Vietnamese*. https://www.thevietnamese.org/2019/02/death-row-inmate-dang-van-hien-may-get-a-second-chance-at-life/. Accessed 5 December 2021.
Tsang, D. W. (2021, January 6). Asia's lèse-majesté laws are a futile attempt to stifle dissent. *Fair Observer*. https://www.fairobserver.com/region/asia_pacific/dai-wei-tsang-lese-majeste-laws-asia-thailand-protests-censorship-news-14251/. Accessed 5 December 2021.
Tuchman, G. (1978). *Making news*. The Free Press.
VnExpress. (2017, October 25). Should Vietnam abolish the death penalty. *VnExpress*. https://e.vnexpress.net/news/perspectives/should-vietnam-abolish-the-death-penalty-3660987.html (poll found when clicking "Result"). Accessed 5 December 2021.
Wibowo, K. A. (2015, February 6). Indonesian media reinforce death penalty as answer to drug crisis. *The Conversation*. https://theconversation.com/indonesian-media-reinforce-death-penalty-as-answer-to-drug-crisis-36951. Accessed 5 December 2021.

Legal Sources and Materials

Furman v. Georgia, 408 U.S. 238 (Supreme Court of the United States) (1972) (J. Thurgood Marshall, concurring opinion).
Republic of the Philippines, House of Representatives, House Bill No. 1. (2016). House Bill No. 1: An Act Imposing the Death Penalty on Certain Heinous Crimes, Repealing for the Purpose Republic Act No. 9346, Entitled "An Act Prohibiting the Imposition of Death Penalty in the Philippines" and Amending Act No. 3815, as Amended, Otherwise Known as the "Revised Penal Code", and Other Special Penal Laws, House Bill No. 1, 17th Congress, 1st Reg. Session (2016). https://hrep-website.s3.ap-southeast-1.amazonaws.com/legisdocs/basic_17/HB00001.pdf. Accessed 5 December 2021.
Republic of the Philippines, House of Representatives, Congressional Record. (2017). Congressional Record: Vol. 4, No. 79, 17th Congress, 1st Regular Session (March 7, 2017). https://hrep-website.s3.ap-southeast-1.amazonaws.com/legisdocs/congrec/17th/1st/17C1RS-VOL4REC79-20170307.pdf Accessed 5 December 2021.
United Nations General Assembly [UNGA]. (2014). United Nations General Assembly Resolution, Moratorium on the Use of the Death Penalty. U.N. Doc. A/RES/69/186 (18 December 2014). https://undocs.org/A/RES/69/186. Accessed 5 December 2021.

UNGA. (2015). Resolutions and Decisions adopted by the General Assembly during its sixty-ninth session, Volume 1, Resolutions, 16 September – 29 December 2014, U.N. Doc. A/69/49 (Vol. I). https://undocs.org/A/69/49(Vol.I). Accessed 5 December 2021.

UNGA. (2017). Resolutions and Decisions adopted by the General Assembly during its seventy-first session, Volume 1, Resolutions, 13 September – 23 December 2016, U.N. Doc. A/71/49 (Vol. I). https://undocs.org/en/A/71/49(Vol.I). Accessed 5 December 2021.

UNGA. (2018a). Moratorium on the use of the death penalty. U.N. Doc. A/RES/73/175 (Dec. 17, 2018). https://undocs.org/A/RES/73/175. Accessed 5 December 2021.

UNGA. (2018b). Draft Resolution, Third Committee of the General Assembly, Promotion and protection of human rights: human rights questions, including alternative approaches for improving the effective enjoyment of human rights and fundamental freedoms, Report of the Third Committee, ¶ 162, Draft Resolution XIII (Moratorium on the use of death penalty), 73rd Session of the General Assembly, U.N. Doc. A/73/589/Add.2 (Dec. 4, 2018). https://undocs.org/A/73/589/Add.2. Accessed 5 December 2021.

UNGA. (2019). Resolutions and Decisions adopted by the General Assembly during its seventy-third session, Volume 1, Resolutions, 18 September – 22 December 2018, U.N. Doc. A/73/49 (Vol. I). https://undocs.org/en/A/73/49(Vol.I). Accessed 5 December 2021.

United Nations Office of the High Commissioner for Human Rights [UNOHCHR]. (2012). *Moving away from the death penalty: Lessons from national experiences.* United Nations. https://www.ohchr.org/Lists/MeetingsNY/Attachments/27/moving_away_from_death_penalty_web.pdf. Accessed 5 December 2021.

Ma. Ngina Teresa V. Chan-Gonzaga is currently Professor and Associate Dean for Academic Affairs of the Ateneo de Manila University School of Law. Her areas of interest include human rights, political law, civil law, and legal ethics. Prior to joining Ateneo Law full time, she served as Commissioner of the Philippine Presidential Commission on Good Government. Previous professional commitments include engagements with Romulo Mabanta Buenaventura Sayoc & De Los Angeles Law Office and the Ateneo Human Rights Center. She was also Program Officer of the Working Group for an ASEAN Human Rights Mechanism.

She obtained her Juris Doctor degree from the Ateneo Law in 2002 and obtained her Magister Juris from Oxford University in 2008. She has been teaching at Ateneo Law since admission to the Philippine Bar in 2003 and served as the Civil Law bar examiner for the Philippine National Bar Examinations in 2018.

Religions and the Death Penalty in Southeast Asia

Khemthong Tonsakulrungruang

Abstract Southeast Asia is a religiously diverse region, representing significant portions of the three major world religions: Buddhism, Islam, and Christianity. As such, religion plays an important role in public discussions on policy *vis-à-vis* law and justice. Concerning the death penalty, all religions recognise the sanctity of life and condemn murder. Yet, most Southeast Asian States have kept the death penalty on their penal codes. This chapter asks how religions reconcile their dogma with the seemingly contradictory nature of their State praxes by analysing the three case studies of Thailand, Malaysia, and the Philippines which together cover the three major religions. It explores the idea of life, violence, and secular law in each faith before examining debates concerning the death penalty within all three jurisdictions. Finally, it asks on what basis can a religion approve, condemn, or distance itself from such a controversial topic.

1 Introduction

Southeast Asia is a truly religiously diverse place (Human Rights Resource Center, 2015). Indeed, the region represents all the major religions. In mainland Southeast Asia, Myanmar, Thailand, Laos, and Cambodia, are considered the stronghold of Theravada Buddhism, while Vietnam is a Mahayana Buddhist country. On the peninsular and archipelago, Malaysia, Brunei, and Indonesia embrace Islam. The latter is actually the world's largest Muslim country. The Philippines, on the other hand, boasts the planet's third largest Roman Catholic community while Singapore showcases how all these religions coexist in peace. Religions not only have enormous influence over the hearts and minds of more than 600 million people, but also influence how governments formulate public policy.

Yet religious teaching is not law. The two are not one and the same. No Southeast Asian nation fully embraces religious teaching as law. Instead, their legal systems

K. Tonsakulrungruang (✉)
Faculty of Political Science, Chulalongkorn University, Bangkok, Thailand
e-mail: khemthong.t@chula.ac.th

S. Petcharamesree et al. (eds.), *Unpacking the Death Penalty in ASEAN*,
https://doi.org/10.1007/978-981-19-8840-0_6

have been influenced by western legal culture through colonisation and modernisation. Even the penal codes of most Muslim-majority nations in Southeast Asia have not embraced Islamic or Syriah law. Even the only exception, Brunei, put full implementation of its Syriah-inspired penal code on hold after much controversy. However, the absence of religion in a penal code does not render it irrelevant. Rather, religious influence operates at a deeper level, shaping the views of policymakers and the morality of voters alike.

All major religions including Buddhism, Islam, and Christianity, accept the sanctity of life. For various reasons, life, especially human life, is precious and inviolable. Therefore, religious dogma preaches against the taking of life. Accordingly, the act of killing a person is considered immoral. Nevertheless, religions differ in their treatment of the death penalty. While for some, homicide is absolutely forbidden, others may allow capital punishment under certain circumstances, for specific purposes, and in accordance with particular procedures. Most Southeast Asian nations maintain the death penalty although several tend towards leniency or apply a moratorium; nonetheless, officially the punishment continues to linger on the statue books. Indeed, religious leaders and communities are often strong advocates of the death penalty despite its seeming contradiction with religious dogma leading to heated debates.

This chapter asks how religions shape the death penalty debate in Southeast Asia, a region that is only partially secularised and where religion's presence in the public sphere is acceptable, or even encouraged. Unfortunately, due to the availability of materials and word count limits, this chapter cannot properly cover all ten jurisdictions comprising Southeast Asia. Instead, three countries have been selected as together they represent the three major religions: Thailand (Buddhism), Malaysia (Islam), and the Philippines (Catholicism). By choosing these countries, this study does not claim a true representation of how these faiths regard the death penalty as religions are far from monolithic. These are simply variants, of the sheer diversity, of how that religion may respond to such a difficult topic. This chapter by no means offers a comprehensive comparative review of religions and the death penalty in Southeast Asia since that is beyond the scope of a single chapter.

The death penalty differs from other homicides as it is State-sanctioned. Thus, it becomes necessary to explore beyond the fact of death. Rather, one must ask about a religion's teaching on the ideal role of the State, human life, and violence. Why is human life deemed so precious? Can violence ever be justified? How do these viewpoints affect one's thinking about the death penalty?

Ultimately, this chapter is concerned with two themes. First, as religion is a mix of canon and religious authority interpretation of said canon, how does religious text understand the death penalty and has this interpretation evolved? Second, which authority, State or religious leaders, dominates the debate and which should take precedence? The following sections trace how such opinions, either to propagate or negate the death penalty, were either adopted or rejected in three local contexts.

2 Thailand: Theravada Buddhism

Mainland Southeast Asia, covering Myanmar, Thailand, Laos, and Cambodia, is the stronghold of Theravada Buddhism. An orthodox school of Buddhism, Theravada prides itself on its strict preservation of ancient traditions. It has also remained politically active unlike the Mahayana school in East Asia comprising China, Taiwan, South Korea, and Japan, where Buddhism's political influence has greatly diminished (Keyes, 2016, p. 41).

Waves of Indian merchants probably introduced Buddhism to this region more than a thousand years ago (Assavavirulhakarn, 2010, pp. 56–68). Ancient kingdoms warmly embraced the new religion, incorporating its sophisticated system of beliefs into their animism. Over the centuries, Buddhism became part of the cultural landscape, inspiring arts, literature, and ceremonies. But most importantly, it was a force that shaped people's morality, and therefore on some level, State policies on law and justice.

Although the arrival of Europeans in the 19th century dismantled these ancient Buddhist kingdoms, the religion itself was never entirely uprooted. Instead, the new nation-states born after independence declared themselves ardent Buddhists (Swearer, 2010). Demographically, mainland Southeast Asia represents the world's largest Buddhist community, with more than 150 million followers. At more than 90%, an overwhelming majority of Thailand's population is also Buddhist (Office of International Religious Freedom, 2021b).

Politically, Buddhism remains a principal ideology in the region, often guiding public morality. As such, several constitutions of Southeast Asian nations reflect its prominent role in the political sphere. For example, Buddhism is a State religion of Cambodia[1] and is granted special status in the constitutions of Myanmar[2] and Thailand.[3] In Thailand, although the State guarantees religious freedom and equality, it pays particular heed to Buddhism over other religions making it the country's *de facto* national religion (Tonsakulrungruang, 2018). This is why remarks from Buddhist monks and intelligentsia often dominate public discussions on policy *vis-à-vis* law and justice, e.g., abolition of the death penalty, gambling, and alcohol consumption.

2.1 *Buddhism's View on Law and Authority*

Despite wielding enormous influence on public policy, Buddhism offers few laws for "mundane" (or ordinary/worldly) followers. Lord Buddha was not a political leader. He saw the world as separated between the mundane and the spiritual (Ishii, 1986, pp. 8–9). Although he led the latter world, he also paid respect to worldly

[1] Constitution of the Kingdom of Cambodia 1993 (rev. 2008), art 43.

[2] Constitution of the Republic of the Union of Myanmar 2008, art 361.

[3] Constitution of the Kingdom of Thailand 2017, art 67 para 2.

authority and took responsibility for the former. Notwithstanding, he never imposed a legal code upon his lay disciples but did promulgate *vinaya* or a monastic code of discipline for life in such communities (Kiefer-Pulz, 2014). Even so, he issued rules only when necessary, instead, placing great emphasis on self-control. Initially, when monks reached enlightenment, *vinaya* was unnecessary because self-control was deemed to liberate individuals from man-made rules. It was only after his followers grew in number and disputes arose between ordinary monks that he invented *vinaya* piece-meal, corresponding the rules to specific circumstances.

However, monks still had to accept the authority of political rulers as *vinaya* was limited to the confines of their monasteries. Therefore, monks still had to comply with the secular law of the land. If the two laws (*vinaya* and mundane) conflicted, Buddha deferred to the wishes of the ruler, allowing his monks to alter their *vinaya* accordingly (Chotisthayangura, 2010, p. 30).

Yet Buddhism once inspired a cult of Buddhist law known as *dhammasastra*, which spread across mainland Southeast Asia (Huxley, 2002, pp. 205–206). From the 14th to the 19th centuries, local rulers cleverly borrowed the aura of this religion and the model of *vinaya* to improve their own indigenous legal systems. The result were more sophisticated legal codes, believed to be derivatives of *dhamma* or the cosmic law of the universe. The era of *dhammasastra* ended with the period of colonisation when European legal codes replaced ancient ones. However, it is possible the Buddhist legal ethics of *dhammasastra* remain the basis for legal thinking in the region (Tonsakulrungruang, 2021, pp. 60–61).

2.2 Buddhism's Justification of Violence

Buddhism believes in reincarnation, meaning that sentients go through endless cycles of birth and rebirth (Harvey, 2000, pp. 12–14). One's behaviour, good and bad, conditions one's next life. Good deeds elevate one into a higher life form, and *vice versa*. Within this scheme, humans are the highest possible life form on earth (King, 2011, p. 107). Yet, if a man commits an evil act, he will be downgraded into a lower life form in the next. Accordingly, a person may have been a king, a pauper, a dog, an elephant, and a bird amongst countless other possibilities. Even the Lord Buddha had past lives as an elephant, a lizard, a bird, as well as a prince, sage, and king (Baker & Phongpaichit, 2019).

Belief in rebirth reminds Buddhists that life is precious. Human life is particularly precious as beings must accumulate high levels of merit to be born thus (King, 2011, p. 107). Moreover, humans have the potential to understand *dhamma*, practice meditation, and reach nirvana. Nevertheless, other lives are also precious because they too have the potential to be human. This belief leads to the first rule of Buddhism or *sila*—that one shall not take a life (Gethin, 1998, p. 110).

Hence, the first precept forbids killing without exception; Buddha himself did not differentiate between the lives of humans and animals. *All* life shall not be taken.

Vinaya goes further, prohibiting monks from even uprooting a plant. But how practical is this teaching? Can a government run a country without any type of violence?

Buddha envisaged an ideal system of governance, one that ruled with mercy. In such a place, the greatest king (known as *cakkavattin*) would not defeat his foes by force alone but by *dhamma*.[4] While he may command a vast army, he imagined this man would conquer the world by charisma alone derived from observing *dhamma*. Further, he would eradicate theft by giving everyone enough to live on. At the same time, Buddha warned that violence begets violence so using deadly force against criminals would escalate situations inevitably causing chaos (Somboon, 2008, p. 46).

Buddhism also preaches taking the middle way and avoiding extremity. While a precept (or *sila*) governs a person's behaviour, it does not constitute a law. Therefore, a person choosing not to follow a precept may still be considered a Buddhist but may not be on the path to enlightenment. Buddha understood the difference between monastic *vinaya*, which is strict, and the *sila* of the mundane. Accordingly, he refused to compel his monks to become vegetarian, explaining that if one lives by begging from the locals, one should not be too demanding.[5] This implies that Buddha tolerated killing as long as the monk recipient was not directly involved.[6] However, this juxtaposition leads to an ambiguous stance on violence and killing—while Buddhism rejects the act of killing, it is also aware that lay persons may be unable to avoid it.

In reality, administering a kingdom can hardly avoid violence. One exemplary and greatly admired king, Ashoka of Mauriya, committed many atrocities in war before he embraced Buddhism (Obeyesekere et al., 1972, p. 29; Tambiah, 1976, p. 60). As such, his kingdom was undeniably founded upon earlier acts of violence that eradicated his potential enemies, thus enabling him to rule peacefully. Likewise, the Singhalese kings of Lankan crushed their enemies with deadly force while claiming the meritoriousness and necessity of such acts to protect the faith (Jerryson, 2016, p. 151). In the same vein, the Buddhist kings of Ayutthaya and the kingdoms of Burma waged war to claim the title of Buddhist kings.[7] Moreover, such monarchs have sporadically carried out purification of the faith by executing those monks failing to recite the Buddha's teachings perceiving them to be false and therefore a taint on the religion (Tambiah, 1976, pp. 164–178). Under such precepts were executions of criminals and torture commonplace.

Dhammasastra, despite its claim to derive from *dhamma*, accepted not only the death penalty but also other forms of cruel punishment. For example, a proprietor could be caned, have his skull cut open, or suffer a kick by an elephant (Boonchalermvipas, 2016, pp. 99–100). Although doubtful that all such gruesome punishments were ever implemented, *dhammasastra* clearly embraced violence. It is interesting to note that these punishments mirror the description of hell in Theravada Buddhism.

How does Buddhism react to violence? The best solution might be to pragmatically distance oneself from such an act, deeming it belongs to another realm beyond one's

[4] Sutta Pitaka Vol 3: Sutta. Tī. Pā. Cakkavattisuttaṃ.

[5] Devathata's proposal in Vinaya Pitaka Vol 7: Vinaya. Culla (2).

[6] Vinaya Pitaka Vol 5: Vinaya. Mahā (2).

[7] See Ling (1979).

capacity to intervene. Another solution might be to justify the act for meritorious causes such as protecting the faith.

2.3 Thai Buddhism's Deferral on the Death Penalty

Debates on the death penalty within Thai Buddhism have been few and far between, possibly due to the Sangha's (Thailand's Buddhist order) particular organisation. Another reason could be the Sangha's acceptance of the necessity of the death penalty and violence to preserve the Thai nation.

The Thai Sangha has long been under the State's close control (Na-Rangsi, 2002, p. 59). Thai kings appoint trusted abbots to the Sangha Council, the governing body that oversees monastic affairs including Tipitaka (the Buddhist canon) interpretation and the expulsion of deviant monks. All monks must belong to the order or face criminal liability.[8] This total control discouraged any dissent to State policy. As such, it was advisable for monks to remain distant from political matters to avoid controversy and the wrath of the ruler. When King Rama VI decided to send troops to fight alongside the allies in World War I, one senior abbot, Phra Thepmoli, expressed his disagreement by delivering a sermon on the detrimental effect of war on human life. Although the message reflected canon, it was in conflict with His Majesty's policy who ordered Phra Thepmoli to be demoted and detained for a year (Visalo, 2009, pp. 42–43). Such are the reasons why the Sangha Council has repeatedly issued resolutions forbidding monks from commenting on political issues.

Thai Buddhism has a record of endorsing State-sanctioned violence. An infamous example occurred in 1976 when Buddhist monk, Kittivudho ignited a firestorm by saying that killing communists was not an act of evil—a comment regarded by many as a licence to kill (Keyes, 1978, pp. 153–155). As a result, right-wing militias galvanised and stormed Thammasat University where they killed a score of left-leaning students in an incident later known as the 6 October massacre. Nevertheless, Kittivudho was not disciplined for breaking the non-political engagement rule suggesting the Sangha finds some violence acceptable, for example, to protect Buddhism and the monarchy. Over the years, such nationalistic justifications have been echoed again and again by other monks.

One even tried to go further than the pragmatic silence of his peers. Buddhadasa was a well-known Buddhist scholar who taught a rational interpretation of the Tipitaka (Jackson, 2003) which appealed particularly to middle-class urban populations. In a sermon to newly appointed judges, Buddhadasa argued that judges could avoid committing a sin as a result of sentencing a convicted felon to death if he or she acted without malintent such as hatred or anger (Leelasophit, 2010, pp. 56–57). Thus, judges following his advice were simply delivering kammic consequences to a person who had already committed a heinous crime. Under this precept, a judge is a medium and the death penalty is karma. Consequently, Buddhadasa's sermon

[8] The 1962 Sangha Act [Thailand], sec. 43; The Penal Code, sec. 208.

helped justify the death penalty to judges and other parties personally involved in the justice system. However, the monk failed to mention problems of wrongful convictions or over-sentencing, both common criticisms of capital punishment. Unsurprisingly, Buddhadasa's explanation became the mainstream answer for judges seeking to justify the death penalty and as a result, they have recited his sermon ever since.

2.4 *Buddhist Kingship and the Death Penalty*

One mechanism mitigating the seriousness of the death penalty debate in Thailand is the royal pardon. According to Buddhist kingship, monarchs are supposed to demonstrate the virtues of mercy and justice whilst seeking a balance between displaying forgiveness and showing respect for law and order. It is therefore His Majesty's prerogative to pardon the condemned at his full discretion. Any death row inmate may petition for clemency.[9] In such cases, the Correctional Department first screens their application before passing it, along with its recommendation, to the king. If successful, a prisoner's death sentence will usually be commuted to life imprisonment.

Despite not implementing any death sentences since 2009, Thailand finally executed Theerasak Longji (convicted of aggravated murder) in 2018 when King Rama X rejected his petition, breaking its *de facto* moratorium (Laothong, 2018).

3 Malaysia: Islam

Southeast Asia is located in a strategic location, serving as a route connecting the two civilisations of India and China (Aljunied, 2019, pp. 24–28). As a result, the archipelago was an important trading route that fell under the influence of the Indic civilisation for over a thousand years. Situated where the ancient kingdoms of Hindu-Buddhist traditions, such as the Sri Vijaya and Majapahit empires lay (p. 22), it later embraced the Islamic civilisation then dominated the archipelago. Muslim merchants began to arrive in the late first millennium but intense Islamisation only commenced around the 11th to 13th centuries (pp. 30–37). Islam first took root in the port towns before moving inland. The faith then swept across what is now southern Thailand, Malaysia, Singapore, Indonesia, and Brunei. Eventually, Islam was incorporated into the syncretism of Hindu-Buddhism and animism as practised by the locals.

The 18th century witnessed the arrival of the British who gradually co-opted local rulers on the Malay peninsula and Borneo to successfully build a settlement under its rule (Aljunied, 2019, pp. 111–116). In doing so, the British sought the cooperation of local rulers by leaving Islam untouched. Other parts of the archipelago fell to the Dutch Empire.

---

[9] Criminal Procedure Code [Thailand], sec. 262.

Malaysia was born in 1957 when the British agreed to the independence of Malaya, North Borneo, Sarawak, and Singapore (Chang et al., 2014, pp. 34–35). By then, half the nation was Muslim. The rest comprised of Chinese, Indians, and indigenous people mostly practicing Buddhism, Hinduism, and animism—in other words, a considerable diversity of race and religion existed in this newborn nation. During the drafting of its constitution, one crucial question arose regarding the status of Islam. What would recognition of Islam in the constitution mean?

While drafters were inclined to prepare a more inclusive charter, arguing that the clause was purely symbolic, many Muslim Malay politicians campaigned for the establishment of Islam. The local rajas opposed such a call, fearing they could lose traditional control over the faith (Chang et al., 2014, p. 116; Aljunied, 2019, p. 164). However, the Reid Commission which was tasked with preparing the federal constitution, stated clearly that such recognition was for ceremonial purposes only (Chang et al., 2014, pp. 116–117). Accordingly, Malaysia was declared a secular rather than a theocratic State. Hence, while Article 3 of the 1957 Constitution recognised Islam as the federal state religion, it also guaranteed the rights of other religions to practice in peace and harmony.[10] Further, sultans were declared the heads of Islam within each state.[11] Indonesia's constitution shows a similar restraint in establishing Islam as its State religion. Article 29 simply declares that Indonesia is based on a monotheistic belief without specifying a particular religion.[12] Such measured constitutional arrangements distinguish Islam in Southeast Asia from the Muslim-majority nations of other regions whose constitutions often recognise Islam as both the State religion and the supreme authority (Temperman, 2010, pp. 50–62). However, the implications of such a move can be seen in Brunei where the absolute monarchy's recognition of Islam as the State religion gradually led to the implementation of Syriah therein (Office of International Religious Freedom, 2021a, pp. 3–4).

By contrast, due to its political history, Malaysia's legal system is influenced mainly by British law. Islamic law constitutes only a small enclave, covering personal and religious matters as listed in the index to its Constitution.[13] Each state can operate its own Syriah law and courts although as regards criminal law, Syriah merely covers offences against Islam and punishment is limited to caning.

Currently, about 60% of Malaysians profess Islam (Human Rights Resource Center, 2015, p. 236). Another 19% identify as Buddhists. The rest are Hindus, Taoists, and others. However, despite an arrangement that tries to balance secularism and Islam, Malaysia has recently witnessed growing religious tension (Human Rights Resource Center, 2015, pp. 277–281; Liow, 2021). As a result, it now ranks very highly on the 2018 Pew Government Restriction Index, similar to Indonesia and Brunei (Pew Research Center, 2020).

---

[10] Federal Constitution of Malaysia 1957 (rev 2007), art 3.1.

[11] Federal Constitution of Malaysia 1957 (rev 2007), art 3.2.

[12] Federal Constitution of Malaysia 1957 (rev 2007), art. 29.

[13] Federal Constitution of Malaysia 1957 (rev 2007), List II, Schedule 9

3.1 *Islam's Concept of Authority and Law*

Contrary to Buddhism, which clearly demarcates the monastic and mundane worlds, Islam admits no such concept of separation as demonstrated by the life of the Prophet Muhammad who was both a political and religious leader. Thus, while relaying the words of Allah to the world, he also founded a Muslim empire (Lapidus, 1996, p. 8). Subsequent Islamic empires followed in his footsteps. As such, those caliphs claiming to be successors of the prophet and vice-regents of God, also simultaneously sought to be administrators and defenders of Islam.[14]

This distinct feature of Islam—the absence of separation between church and State—results in an amalgamation of law and morality making Islam a legalistic religion. Allah does not only reveal the path to salvation but also provides Muslims with a divine and complex law, known as Syriah, to deal with worldly matters from marriage to property, criminal justice to slavery.

What constitutes Syriah? Of its four sources, the most authoritative is the Qur'an (Tellenbach, 2014, pp. 248–249). As the central religious text of Islam, the Qur'an is believed to be a revelation from Allah as dictated to the Prophet Muhammad. However, it contains very little about law, even less about criminal law. The second source of Syriah is *sunnah*, a body of social and legal customs and practices based on the Prophet's actions and teaching. These comprise two sources of Syriah *stricto sensu*. The remaining two count as supplements: consensuses of the Islamic community covering legal questions known as *idjima*, and *qiyas* or analogical reasonings as applied to juridical principles from the first two sources. Together, they form a very complex set of laws that Muslim legal scholars have studied and debated for centuries.

3.2 *Syriah and the Death Penalty*

In Islam, human life is to be respected but this is not absolute. As the Qu'ran states, a man cannot be deprived of his life unless by due process (Schabas, 2000, p. 230)[15] Thus, the death penalty is allowed provided appropriate procedures are followed. Mostly, death is permissible to protect something more valuable (which outweighs an individual's life) such as Islam's five core values, namely: (1) religion, (2) life, (3) property, (4) honour and dignity, and (5) lineage (Aziz, 2015, p. 68). Because such values protect individual interests whilst benefiting society, infringements, for example, attacks on Islam or property rights, are subject to punishment.

Regarding criminal law, Syriah delineates three types of offence. Each requires its own standard of procedure, proof, and sentencing. As a consequence, the death penalty in each type of Syriah criminal law is governed by different sets of rules.

---

[14] See in general, Lapidus (1996).

[15] Qu'ran, verse 6:151.

Hadd or *hudud*, in its plural form, is a crime against Allah and the foundation of Islam (Tellenbach, 2014, pp. 251–252). This is the most serious crime and is outlined both in the Qur'an and *sunnah. Hadd* cannot be changed or abolished. The purpose of *hadd* punishment is first, deterrence, and second, retribution. Three other offences punishable by death are adultery, apostasy, and *hirabah* (Aziz, 2015, p. 77). The latter refers to highway robbery, sometimes translated as brigandry or piracy. Further, a robbery involving murder can subject an offender to crucifixion. A fourth offence eligible for the death penalty is *baghj* or an armed resistance to lawful authority (Sharif, 2006, pp. 292–294). *Baghj* is considered particularly serious because it can lead to other crimes and poses a threat to Islam. Nonetheless, some jurists do not include *baghj* in *hadd* (p. 295).

A person can only be convicted of a *hadd* crime under very stringent standards of proof, either by confession or eyewitness testimony, both of which are covered by specific procedures (Tellenbach, 2014, pp. 254–256). Crimes must be proven beyond doubt (p. 256). In some instances, women are exempted from the death penalty as they are considered too weak to threaten Islam (p. 253). Moreover, death is not the sole recourse because in many cases, God prefers repentance: hence, those who repent and show remorse shall be forgiven (Aziz, 2015, p. 79).[16]

Qisas is a crime against life and one's body which includes homicide (Tellenbach, 2014, pp. 258–259). Although these punishments are designed to exact vengeance (a life for a life), sentences must be proportionate (equal for equal). So while murder is punishable by death, unintentional manslaughter is not. However, the standard of proof is less stringent requiring conviction beyond any reasonable doubt and circumstantial evidence is permissible (p. 260). Again, death is not mandatory. In such cases, the victim's family has a choice since the injury was done to them whether to insist on punishment, opt for blood money (*diyah*), or offer forgiveness, which Allah encourages (Aziz, 2015, pp. 79–80; Tellenbach, 2014, pp. 260–261).

The remaining offences are *ta'zir* which is at the discretion of the State to promulgate. This is a man-made law and can be altered. However, it is debatable whether *ta'zir* can be punishable by death. Should the punishment for *ta'zir* be less than that of *hadd*? Can a man be executed for a crime not explicitly permitted by Allah? (Aziz, 2015, pp. 81–82; Tellenbach, 2014, p. 260).

Theoretically, although the death penalty is permissible in Islam, it has to be carried out only for certain causes and with extreme care. Procedural safeguards are supposed to be high. Death is but one of many choices such as compensation, repentance, or forgiveness.

Although no modern State adopts Syriah law in its entirety, many grant it jurisdiction over specific disputes, especially family and inheritance matters. Moreover, other countries may not claim to use Syriah directly but point to Islamic legal doctrine as a source, or even *the* source of their legislation (Temperman, 2010, pp. 50–62). The application of Islamic criminal law is even rarer due to the influence of western legal thought from the 19th century onward (Tellenbach, 2014, p. 249). Specifically,

[16] Surah 5 Al-Ma'idah, ayat 33–34

while French criminal law significantly influenced the penal codes of Muslim countries in the Middle East and North Africa, Anglo-Saxon legal theory had the same effect on former colonies in the Far East, including Malaysia.

A notable correlation between Muslim countries and the death penalty can be seen. Excluding China, those carrying out the highest numbers of executions are mostly the Muslim-majority States, namely, Iran, Saudi Arabia, Iraq, Pakistan, and Yemen (Amnesty International, 2021, pp. 55–56). Despite Islam's propensity for forgiveness and repentance, a majority of Muslims indicate considerable support for the death penalty (Asif, 2021). As a result, experts admit the topic of abolition is only discussed in narrow circles of scholars (Tellenbach, 2014, p. 267).

3.3 Malaysia's Secular Criminal Law

Malaysia's criminal law is mainly secular due to the influence of British common law (Shuaib, 2012). Upon independence, it was agreed that the federal government would confer power as regards certain listed matters to promulgate Islamic law by allowing individual states to establish Syriah courts to which the sultan would appoint judges. Non-Muslims, however, are only subject to federal law.

Syriah is applicable to most private and personal matters: marriage, divorce, custody, and inheritance. In addition, it regulates religious affairs including the "creation and punishment of offences by persons professing the religion of Islam against precepts of that religion" (Shuaib, 2012, pp. 94–96). Each state may enact its own version of Islamic law as applied by its Syriah courts as long as it does not run counter to federal law. Punishments are limited to fines and no more than six strokes of the cane.

The death penalty in Malaysia is part of a larger package to unlock the limits placed on Syriah law. Since the 1980s, following waves of Islamic revitalisation across the globe, Malaysia too witnessed demands for a greater application of Syriah law. All political parties seemed to ride this wave, calling for the Islamisation of Malaysia, the making of *negara Islam* or an Islamic State (Hung, 2016, p. 3; Liow, 2021, pp. 4–5). However, a difference in strategy can be noted between the government, led by the UMNO coalition front, and PAS, the main opposition party. The former preferred a gradual and more conventional approach excluding the death penalty and other draconian punishments, and the latter advocated more radical methods (Liow, 2021, p. 4). In 1993, the state legislature of Kelantan passed the Syriah Criminal Code (II) Bill 1993, known as the Hudud Bill, to implement Syriah criminal law including *hudud* and *qizas*. The *hudud* covers *hirabah* and adultery which are punishable by crucifixion and stoning respectively (Kamali, 1998, pp. 204–206). Upon enactment, the Kelantan legislature and the Chief Minister were fully aware the bill could not come into effect without amending the Federal Constitution (p. 205). In other words, the Hudud Bill exceeded the jurisdiction of Syriah as granted by the Federal Constitution. In 2002, the Terenganu State legislature followed Kelantan's lead by passing another *hudud* bill, which again could not be implemented due to constitutional challenges (Kamali, 2019, pp. 254–255). Therefore, these bills seemed to be more about making statements than enforcing laws. Both were controversial and were initiated by PAS rather than UMNO. However, these bills have not been repealed. Indeed, PAS has continued to push revised *hudud* bills in both states (Hung, 2016, pp. 6–7). In 2017, the government even allowed PAS's bill into the legislature, a calculated move of then PM Najib Razak to appeal to Muslim voters to repair the damage done to his popularity by a series of corruption scandals (Reuters staff, 2017). The bill sought to raise the limit of Syriah punishment albeit without introducing the death penalty. Although it gained considerable support (as well as criticism), the bill was eventually rejected (U.S. Department of State, 2017).

So far, the majority of the public, non-Muslim as well as Muslim leaders, have expressed their opposition to the *hudud* bill idea (Hung, 2016, p. 12; Kamali, 2019, p. 258). However, this opposition is getting smaller and weaker as religious leaders voice their support. Those opposing the motion have even been denounced as *kafir* or heretics (Hung, 2016, p. 9).

Syriah encompasses justice as well as mercy so the debate on the *hudud* bill could go either way. The difference between proponents and opponents of the bill seems to be a difference in how one reads and understands Syriah law. As a response to the Kelantan *hudud* bill in 1993, one prominent scholar, Kamali (2019, pp. 233–234), expressed his disagreement citing contextual concerns. His criticism centred around the Kelantan government's literal interpretation of Syriah which, he contends, misunderstands its purpose and fails to consider its true goal and subsequent developments. Malaysia is still a pluralistic society and he felt such an approach would generate fear and fail to achieve the real goal of Syriah whereas a more compassionate and humanitarian reading would cast Islam in a better light. According to Kamali, more liberal ways of interpreting Syriah could avoid the death penalty entirely.

An attempt to compromise human rights and *hudud* can be seen in the topic of apostasy. A broader interpretation argues that a correct reading of the Qu'ran limits the death penalty to cases where an apostate is contemptuous and hostile to Islam. Therefore, those silently renouncing the faith should be excluded (Adil, 2007). Still, it is doubtful whether this represents the majority view of Muslim Malaysians.

3.4 Court Cases against the Death Penalty

Perhaps the most unexpected involvement of Islamic law in the capital punishment debate concerns how it was used to oppose the death penalty. Malaysia retains a mandatory death penalty for certain crimes, including drug and firearms offences leaving the court no discretion in sentencing. In the *Che Omar bin Che Soh v. Public Prosecutor* case of 1988, three men were charged under either firearms or drug offences. They appealed to the Malaysian Supreme Court claiming that mandatory death sentences were un-Islamic and so unconstitutional, violating Article 3 of the Malaysian Constitution denoting Islam as the State religion. Also, as these crimes were neither *huddud* nor *qisas*, judges were allowed discretion in handling the sentences. However, the Supreme Court rejected the appeal. As such, this case had the effect of defining the scope of Article 3—that while Islam was the State religion of Malaysia, Malaysia was not an Islamic State (Moustafa, 2018, pp. 138–141). Accordingly, Islamic moral and legal principles could not be a source of its legislation. Further, because Malaysia's sovereignty stems from earthly rulers, its laws must also gain effect from secular legislative processes.

This stance was confirmed in 2020 when the Supreme Court again upheld a mandatory death sentence (Malay Mail, 2020). The power to amend such a law rests in parliament where the people's representatives may discuss the topic more thoroughly, not, it held, within a court of law.

In 2009, the Malaysian government announced upon submitting its national report to the UN Human Rights Council that it would review all offences carrying the death penalty (United Nations Human Rights Council, 2009). Again, in 2012, the Malaysian Law Minister stated the country would reconsider replacing mandatory death sentences with prison terms (The Malaysian Insider, 2012). These actions stirred heated debates with the majority still seemingly favouring the death penalty. No further action has since been taken.

4 The Philippines: Roman Catholicism

Spain arrived in the islands of the Philippines in the 16th century and controlled the archipelago until 1898 when it ceded the territory to the USA (Human Rights Resource Center, 2015, p. 364). And it was under Spanish rule that the Roman Catholic Church was successfully introduced, becoming one of Spain's enduring legacies. Today, the Philippines is the only nation in Southeast Asia where the majority practices Christianity. In fact, it is the world's third largest Roman Catholic country. Over 80% of the 108 million Filipinos profess to the faith while only 5% are Muslims, mostly in the southern part of the country (pp. 366–367). But many other Christian denominations reside there too.

Under Spanish rule, the Philippines followed the doctrine of the union of church and State (Human Rights Resource Center, 2015, p. 364). However, its present legal system was influenced by American jurisprudence which advocates the separation of church and State. Likewise, its constitution follows American constitutional doctrine and prohibits endorsement of any religion while guaranteeing free exercise thereof.[17] As such, religious representatives are not entitled to reserved seats in the legislature.[18] Neither shall public money or property be used for religious purposes.[19]

In reality, though, the Philippines remains a religious nation. The idea of a union between faith and nation is strong. Further, official separation has not diminished the

[17] Constitution of the Republic of the Philippines 1987, Art. II, sec. 5 & 6.

[18] Constitution of the Republic of the Philippines 1987, Art. VI, sec. 5(2).

[19] Constitution of the Republic of the Philippines 1987, Art. VI, sec. 29(2).

influence of religion in public debate. Although canon law holds an official policy of non-interference, prohibiting its clergy from involvement in politics unless to protect the rights of the church or to promote the common good (Dionisio, 2014, pp. 13–14), politicians often try to court clergymen for approval in the hopes of winning more votes. Likewise, some clergy ignore the official policy and publicly endorse candidates whose social policies match their ideologies.[20] One example demonstrating the important role of the Roman Catholic Church to Filipinos can be witnessed in its calls for a popular uprising in 1986, a movement that eventually toppled the Marcos dictatorship (Buenaobra, 2016).

The Philippines has abolished the death penalty several times, for example, in the 1987 Constitution. Article III, section 19, stated that "Neither shall the penalty be imposed, unless, for compelling reasons involving heinous crimes, the Congress hereafter provides for it."[21] Any pending death sentences were therefore commuted to life imprisonment. But as the text suggests, it could be reinstated for compelling reasons (involving heinous crimes) by Congress. In 1993, Congress did indeed reintroduce the death penalty before President Gloria Macapagal Arroyo once again re-abolished it in 2006 (Official Gazette of the Republic of the Philippines, 2006). At present, President Rodrigo Duterte is pushing for yet another reinstatement. While the Catholic Church opposes the idea, Duterte's popularity means this is likely to turn into another clash between religious dogma and local sentiment.

4.1 God of Mercy

The death penalty issue has haunted the Christian community for thousands of years. Numerous debates support both views but ultimately, the stance of each Christian depends on his or her view of God. Is God a god of mercy or a god of justice?

The order not to kill (thou shalt not kill) is an important imperative of the Ten Commandments.[22] However, while Buddhism's first *sila* forbids the taking of life in any circumstance, this commandment is less prohibitive. Killing here seems only to refer to murder or unlawful killing as the Old Testament (like the Torah) accepts justified killings (Douglas, 2000, pp. 142–143). In biblical times, many offences were punishable by death, including murder. For example, the Book of Genesis states that "whoever sheds the blood of man, by man shall his blood be shed; for God made man in his own image" (which also demonstrates the importance of man as distinct from other animals).[23] However, the death penalty can only be imposed under stringent procedural safeguards and such vengeance cannot be senseless or disproportionate (UN OHCHR 2014, p. 179).

---

[20] See in general, Dionisio (2014).

[21] 1987 Constitution of the Philippines, Art. III, sec. 19.

[22] Exodus 20:2–17.

[23] Genesis 9:6.

Notwithstanding, another biblical reference inspired the idea of forgiveness. Thus, God did not execute Cain when he murdered his brother, Abel, and even marked his forehead to protect him from further physical vengeance. Instead, Cain's life was spared and he was sentenced to restless wandering.[24]

With the arrival of Jesus who taught love and mercy, the New Testament sets a different tone. Leading by example, Jesus demonstrated forgiveness in many circumstances, even intervening in the execution of a woman convicted of adultery. According to the law of Moses, she should have been stoned to death but Jesus interceded by asking for a person without sin to cast the first stone.[25] He also taught his disciples not to respond to violence, instructing them to turn the other cheek.[26] Further, Christians are told to not only love their neighbours but also their enemies, as illustrated by the fable of the Good Samaritan.[27]

In sum, life is inviolable. Humans shall avoid playing god by taking the lives of others. In earlier eras, Christians appreciated teachings of non-violence as they were often at the receiving end of State brutality. When faced with the dilemma of whether to be loyal to God or the Roman emperor, they refused to serve in the Roman army or to honour the emperor as divine so were frequently subject to execution (UN OHCHR 2014, p. 178). But Christianity's view on the death penalty and violence would soon change when it became the official religion of Rome. Then, as the majority, Christians supported the use of the death penalty to convert or suppress pagans and heretics, and this practice continued until the end of the Middle Ages. Hence, the death penalty, as well as war, helped advance the cause of Christianity across Europe (Douglas, 2000, pp. 146–153).

4.2 God of Justice

As aforementioned, Christian acceptance of the death penalty has biblical roots although Jesus himself never tried to be a political leader. Instead, he showed respect to the Roman authorities condemning him to death. In addition to Old Testament dictates, while the apostle Paul advised Christians to respect civil authorities, as a servant of God, he knew he could also be called upon to execute his wrath on wrongdoers (Douglas, 2000, p. 145).[28] Hence, the idea arose of divine endorsement to exact violence upon criminals.

Another rationalisation developed in the Middle Ages (around the 11th century) and became known as the "just war" theory (Beach, 2000). At that time, Christianity called for armed men to fight a holy war (known as the Crusades), in effect legitimising violence in the service of the church. However, such violence must be

[24] Genesis 4:15–16.

[25] John 8:2-11.

[26] Matthew 5:38–40.

[27] Luke 10:25–37.

[28] Romans 13:4.

governed by a set of rules or procedures and be justifiable. Further, war should only be considered as a last resort and the violence inflicted should be proportional, avoiding any collateral damage.

Mainstream views on the death penalty began to change with the Enlightenment of the 18th century when humans began to be viewed as redeemable. Thus, people were capable of self-improvement and should be allowed a second chance (Douglas, 2000, pp. 156–158).

In more recent times, the Roman Catholic Church has tended to show disapproval of the death penalty. Following the 1965 Vatican II Council, which confirmed the compatibility of human rights and Catholicism, priests expressed repudiation of the punishment to protect human dignity (Megivern, 1997, p. 339). Accordingly, leaders of the Roman Catholic Church led by example. For example, Pope John Paul II expressed scepticism in the effectiveness of the death penalty and stressed the significance of life, not only regarding the death penalty but also other issues such as abortion and euthanasia (Bromberg, 2007). Moreover, the Pope argued that Old Testament references to the death penalty should not be followed literally but read through the lens of the New Testament (Douglas, 2000, p. 166). This culminated in His Holiness eliminating the death penalty from the Vatican's Penal Code in 2001 (UN OHCHR 2014, p. 179). He also publicly called for a ban on the death penalty. For example, during a visit to St. Louis, Missouri, the Pope pled for clemency for Darell J. Mease, a convicted murderer; as a result, the Governor of Missouri commuted his sentence (Niebuhr, 1999).

Similarly, in 2018, Pope Francis ordered a change in the Roman Catholic Catechism to pronounce the death penalty an attack on the inviolability and dignity of the person declaring it inadmissible in any case (O'Connell, 2018). Finally, in 2020, His Holiness issued an encyclical (the most authoritative of Catholic documents), Fratelli Tutti, declaring the death penalty inadmissible and instructing Catholics to seek its abolition (The Holy See, 2000). In doing so, he cited mercy as a reason and also referred to the right to life of every human, even murderers, and emphasised the negative effect of revenge. Finally, he insisted peace could only be reached by placing reason uppermost. This issuance seems to settle the debate.

4.3 The Battle over the Death Penalty in the Philippines

It was not a coincidence that President Arroyo signed a bill abolishing the death penalty a day prior to visiting Pope Benedict XVI in 2006 (Javellana-Santos, 2006). In her speech, the President thanked the church for being a beacon of grace and discernment and said her country had so acted to promote peace and harmony (Official Gazette of the Republic of the Philippines, 2006). Following, she refused to sign any execution orders and commuted death sentences into life imprisonment (International Commission Against Death Penalty n.d.). In Arroyo's case, it can therefore be seen the move to abolish capital punishment was religiously motivated.

However, in 2022, it seems Roman Catholic opposition to the death penalty may no longer align with local sentiment. Although avowedly religious, Filipinos appear to prefer tougher sanctions against crime. Indeed, abolition of the death penalty was protested by victims of crime and their relatives and the tension has grown more acute with the ascension of President Duterte who openly proposes reintroducing the death penalty.

Duterte sees the death penalty as part of his notorious war on drugs which to date has claimed at least 7,000 lives (innocent victims as well as drug suspects) (Jha, 2020). Arguing the death penalty is an effective tool to deter and punish, he is clearly at odds with the Church which has criticised his disregard for human life (Catholic News Agency, 2019; Seiff, 2020). Notwithstanding, the idea remains popular among his supporters as evidenced by his overwhelming majority in Congress.

One major proponent of the reintroduction of the death penalty can be found in Manny Paquio, a famous boxer who himself is a born-again Christian. In 2016, the newly elected Senator Paquio delivered his first speech to Congress, confirming his view that the death penalty was permissible, both constitutionally and biblically. In particular, he relied on an Old Testament dictate that anyone shedding the blood of another man shall have his own blood shed (Elemia 2006a; 2006b). Further, God was a god of justice who therefore supports the death penalty to discipline and punish wrongdoers. As such, Paquio supported reintroduction of capital punishment. However, his use of the biblical quote drew criticism from liberal Christian senators and observers who echoed the stance of the contemporary Roman Catholic Church that God is a god of mercy (Cornelio, 2018).

Despite opposition, at the time of writing, it looks set that the death penalty will return to the Philippines not least because 23 bills to reinstate it for various crimes have been introduced since Duterte became president in 2016 (Jha, 2020).

5 Conclusion

The three case studies above demonstrate three different models showcasing the ways religion and law interact as regards the death penalty. In all three countries, however, the outcomes are far from straightforward. As can be seen, political leaders do not simply adopt religious canon regardless. On the other hand, religion can and often does, argue for and against the death penalty, through the canon, later commentaries, and contemporary understandings. This uncertainty allows politicians to cherry-pick a stance.

Buddhism follows a practical deferral model. Buddhist canon rejects the death penalty outright. All forms of life are deemed precious. However, because of its binary worldview which divides the monastic from the mundane, Buddhism finds a compromise, accepting State-sanctioned violence as an inevitable evil. This can be seen in the stance of the Thai Sangha which often remains silent deeming such violence necessary for the greater good of protecting Buddhism and the monarchy.

This deferral, or even complicity, allows political leaders to uphold the death penalty without criticism from Thai Buddhism.

Islam is very specific. Qur'an explicitly embraces the death penalty, but only for certain offences and under a stringent standard. Qur'an also urges repentance or forgiveness. However, the text is clear so it allows little room to argue for abolishing the death penalty. Perhaps that explains the correlation between Islamic countries and the high rate of executions. Interestingly, Malaysia's death penalty still causes friction with religious leaders because its criminal justice is too secular. Shariah is permitted only in a few topics. With mounting religious nationalistic sentiment, Malaysia has been witnessing more signs of political tinkering with the introduction of Islamic execution. It remains to be seen how long Malaysia could resist such call.

The original spirit of Christianity in the New Testament is about love and mercy, in contrast with vengeance and strict punishment of the Old Testament. It was later that Christian thinkers began to advocate for violence for a Christian cause. So emerged the narrative of the God of law and justice. However, the Roman Catholic Church, in order to appeal to a broader audience in the 20th Century, plays along with the narrative of human rights. The Church gradually, but surely, move toward an abolition of the death penalty, returning to the God of mercy narrative. Unfortunately, the Philippines show that such a move actually misaligns with the local sentiment. The country has made a few attempts to ban the punishment. But politicians, wishing to capture the populace's support, are working to reintroduce the death penalty once more.

In conclusion, all religions forbid an act of killing, but to differing degrees. Buddhist and Christian canons are explicit about not killing, in Buddhism's case, a life of any transient and, in the Bible, a human. For Buddhism, this precept is absolute. No justification is given. However, subsequent interpretations of both religions allow state violence, including the death penalty, for certain causes. Islam, on the other hand, accepts the death penalty, supposedly in order to protect its essential values. Nonetheless, different sects may interpret conditions for the death penalty in different ways as some may be more forgiving than others. The difference among the three religions may explain how followers of each faith perceive or accept the policy on the death penalty.

The idea of authority determines the level of tension between religious and political authorities when the worldly law conflicts with the faith. Buddhism offers an escape through its binary worldview, sparing monks from confronting the government on policies and laws. Islam and Christianity face great tension, for very different reasons. Muslim leaders inevitably clash with the government when the secular provision on the death penalty fails to conform with shariah while the Catholic Church's god of mercy is rejected by the popular preference for the god of justice. This misalignment raises the question of how exactly religion influences the government's death penalty policy in Southeast Asia.

Southeast Asia is religious but not theocratic. Accordingly, religious teaching alone does not dictate State policies on the death penalty. This chapter demonstrates how political authorities, juggling many concerns, utilise certain aspects of religion to support life and death decisions.

References

Adil, M. (2007). Law of apostasy and freedom of religion in Malaysia. *Asian Journal of Comparative Law, 2*, 1–36. https://doi.org/10.1017/S2194607800000065

Aljunied, K. (2019). *Islam in Malaysia: An entwined history*. Oxford University Press.

Amnesty International. (2021). *Amnesty International global report: Death sentences and executions 2020*. https://www.amnesty.org/en/documents/act50/3760/2021/en/. Accessed 1 August 2021.

Asif, N. (2021). *An introduction to Syriah law and the death penalty*. Faculty of Law, Oxford University. https://www.law.ox.ac.uk/research-and-subject-groups/death-penalty-research-unit/blog/2021/01/introduction-Syriah-law-and. Accessed 1 August 2021

Assavavirulhakarn, P. (2010). *The ascendancy of Theravada Buddhism in Southeast Asia*. Silkworm Books.

Aziz, S. A. (2015) The continuing debate on the death penalty: An exposition of international instrument, Malaysian and the Shari'ah perspectives. *IIUM Law Journal, 23*(1), 61–84. https://doi.org/10.31436/iiumlj.v23i1.156

Baker, C., & Phongpaichit, P. (2019). *From the fifty Jātaka: Selections from the Thai Paññāsa Jātaka*. Silkworm Books.

Beach, H. (2000). Interventions and just wars: The case of Kosovo. *Studies in Christian Ethics, 13*(2), 15–31. https://doi.org/10.1177/095394680001300202

Boonchalermvipas, S. (2016). *Prawattisāt kotmāi Thai [The Thai Legal History]* (15th ed.). Winyuchon.

Buenaobra, M. I. T. (2016). The politics of religion in the Philippines. The Asia Foundation. https://asiafoundation.org/2016/02/24/the-politics-of-religion-in-the-philippines/. Accessed 1 August 2021.

Catholic News Agency (2019, July 26). *Church in Philippines rejects president's call to revive death penalty*. https://www.catholicnewsagency.com/news/41892/church-in-philippines-rejects-presidents-call-to-revive-death-penalty. Accessed 1 August 2021.

Chang, W., Thio L., Tan, K., & Yeh, J. (2014). *Constitutionalism in Asia: Cases and materials* Oxford: Hart Publishing.

Chotisthayangura, P. (2010). *Khambanyai kotmai khana song [Lecture on laws of Sangha]* (2nd ed.). Mahachulalongkornrajwittayalai University.

Criminal Procedure Code [Thailand].

Collins, C. (2020, August 14). Church in the Philippines condemns efforts to resurrect capital punishment. *Crux*. https://cruxnow.com/church-in-asia/2020/08/church-in-the-philippines-condemns-efforts-to-resurrect-capital-punishment/. Accessed 1 August 2021

Constitution of the Kingdom of Cambodia 1993 (rev. 2008), art 43.

Constitution of the Republic of the Union of Myanmar 2008, art 361.

Constitution of the Kingdom of Thailand 2017, art 67 para 2.

Cornelio, J. (2018, August 10) [OPINION] Pacquiao's Christianity and death penalty. Rappler. https://www.rappler.com/voices/thought-leaders/manny-pacquiao-christianity-death-penalty. Accessed 1 August 2021

Dionisio, E. R. (2014). Catholic partisanship in the 2013 elections: 'Churchifying' democracy or democratizing the church? *Philippine Sociological Review*, 62, 11–40. https://www.jstor.org/stable/43486491.

Douglas, D. M. (2000). God and the executioner: The influence of Western religion on the use of the death penalty. *William & Mary Bill of Rights Journal, 9*(1), 137–170.

Elemia, C. (2016a, July 5) Pacquiao favors death penalty by hanging. *Rappler*. https://www.rappler.com/nation/manny-pacquiao-death-penalty-hanging. Accessed 1 August 2021.

Elemia, C. (2016b, August 8). Pacquiao's 1st privilege speech: God is for death penalty. *Rappler*. https://www.rappler.com/nation/senator-manny-pacquiao-first-privilege-speech-death-penalty. Accessed 1 August 2021.

Federal Constitution of Malaysia 1957 (rev 2007)

Gethin, R. (1998). *The foundations of Buddhism*. Oxford University Press.

Obeyesekere, G., Reynolds, F. E., & Smith, B. L. (Eds.). (1972). *The two wheels of Dhamma: Essays on the Theravada tradition in India and Ceylon*. Chambersburg. American Academy of Religion.

Harvey, P. (2000). *An introduction to Buddhist ethics: Foundations, values, and issues*. Cambridge University Press.

Howard, B. (2007). Pope John Paul II, Vatican II, and capital punishment. *Ave Maria Law Review, 6*(1), 109–154. https://repository.law.umich.edu/articles/949. Accessed 1 August 2021.

Human Rights Resource Center. (2015). Keeping the faith: A study of freedom of thought, conscience, and religion in ASEAN. http://hrrca.org/wp-content/uploads/2015/11/Book-of-Keeping-the-Faith_web.pdf. Accessed 1 August 2021.

Hung, H. T. M. (2016). *The politics of Hudud law implementation in Malaysia*. ISEAS Working Paper 2006 No.4. https://www.iseas.edu.sg/images/pdf/ISEASWorkingPaper4.pdf. Accessed 1 August 2021.

Huxley, A. (2002) Buddhist law. In H. M. Kritzer (Ed.), *Legal systems of the world: A political, social, and cultural encyclopedia* (pp. 205–208). Santababara. ABC-CLIO.

International Commission Against the Death Penalty. (n.d.). Commissioner: Gloria Macapagal-Arroyo. https://icomdp.org/comission/gloria-macapagal-arroyo-2/. Accessed 1 August 2021

Ishii, Y. (1986). *Sangha, state, and society: Thai Buddhism in history*. University of Hawaii Press.

Jackson, P. A. (2003). *Buddhadasa: Theravada Buddhism and modernist reform in Thailand*. Silkworm Books.

Javellana-Santos, J. (2006, June 25). Arroyo signs law abolishing death penalty in the Philippines. *Arab News*. https://www.arabnews.com/node/286797. Accessed 1 August 2021.

Jerryson, M. (2016). The Buddhist state of exception. In H. Kawanami (Ed.), *Buddhism and the political process* (pp. 145–166). Palgrave Macmillan.

Jha, P. (2020, August 16). Philippines death penalty: A fight to stop the return of capital punishment. *BBC News*. https://www.bbc.com/news/world-asia-53762570. Accessed 1 August 2021.

Kamali, M. H. (1998). Punishment in Islamic law: A critique of the Hudud Bill of Kelantan. *Malaysia. Arab Law Quarterly, 13*(3), 203–234.

Kamali, M. H. (2019). *Crime and punishment in Islamic law: A fresh interpretation*. Oxford University Press.

Keyes, C. F. (1978). Political crisis and militant Buddhism in contemporary Thailand. In B. Smith (Ed.), *Religion and legitimation of power in Thailand, Burma and Laos*. Chambersburg. Anima Books.

Keyes, C. F. (2016). Theravada Buddhism and Buddhist nationalism: Sri Lanka, Myanmar, Cambodia, and Thailand. *The Review of Faith & International Affairs, 14*(4), 41–52. https://doi.org/10.1080/15570274.2016.1248497

Kiefer-Pulz, P. (2014). What the Vinayas can tell us about law. In R. R. French & M. A. Nathan (Eds.), *Buddhism and law: An introduction* (pp. 46–62). Cambridge University Press.

King, S. B. (2011). Buddhism and human rights. In J. Witte & M. C. Green (Eds.), *Religion and human rights: An Introduction* (pp. 103–118). Oxford University Press.

Laothong, K. (2018, June 19). Killer put to death. *Bangkok Post*. https://www.bangkokpost.com/thailand/general/1487818/killer-put-to-death. Accessed 1 August 2021.

Lapidus, I. M. (1996). State and religion in Islamic societies. *Past & Present, 151*(1), 3–27. https://doi.org/10.1093/past/151.1.3

Leelasophit, S. (2010). Phūphiphāksā sang prahān chīwit pen bāp rư mai [Did a judge commit a sin when ordering execution?]. *Journal of Court of Justice Review, 4*(2), 46–61.

Ling, T. (1979). *Buddhism, imperialism, and war: Burma and Thailand in modern history*. George Allen & Unwin.

Liow, J. C. (2021). Malaysia's creeping islamization—and dimming prospects for covenantal pluralism. *The Review of Faith & International Affairs, 19*(2), 1–13. https://doi.org/10.1080/15570274.2021.1917127

Malay Mail (2020). *Federal Court: Parliament empowered to enact laws on offences, punishments including death penalty.* https://www.malaymail.com/news/malaysia/2020/08/13/federal-court-parliament-empowered-to-enact-laws-on-offences-punishments-in/1893651. Accessed 1 August 2021.

Megivern, J. J. (1997). *The death penalty: An historical and theological survey.* Paulist Press.

Moustafa, T. (2018). *Constituting religion: Islam, liberal rights, and the Malaysian state.* Cambridge University Press.

Na-rangsi, S. (2002). Administration of the Thai Sangha: Past, present and future. *The Chulalongkorn Journal of Buddhist Studies, 1*(2), 1–28. https://so06.tci-thaijo.org/index.php/cjbs/article/view/244823. Accessed 1 August 2021.

Niebuhr, G. (1999, January 29). Governor grants Pope's plea for life of a Missouri inmate. *The New York Times.* https://www.nytimes.com/1999/01/29/us/governor-grants-pope-s-plea-for-life-of-a-missouri-inmate.html. Accessed 1 August 2021.

O'Connell, G. (2018, August 2). Pope Francis revises Catechism, teaches that death penalty is 'inadmissible'. *America The Jesuit Review.* https://www.americamagazine.org/faith/2018/08/02/pope-francis-revises-catechism-teaches-death-penalty-inadmissible. Accessed 1 August 2021.

Office of International Religious Freedom. (2021b). *Thailand 2020 report on international religious freedom.* U.S. Department of State. https://www.state.gov/reports/2020-report-on-international-religious-freedom/thailand/. Accessed 1 August 2021b.

Office of International Religious Freedom. (2021a). *Brunei 2020 international religious freedom report.* U.S. Department of State. https://www.state.gov/reports/2020-report-on-international-religious-freedom/brunei/. Accessed 1 August 2021a.

Official Gazette of the Republic of the Philippines. (2006). *Speech of President Arroyo on the signing of the abolition of death penalty.* https://www.officialgazette.gov.ph/2006/06/24/speech-of-president-arroyo-on-the-signing-of-the-abolition-of-death-penalty/. Accessed 1 August 2021.

Che Omar bin Che Soh v. Public Prosecutor Supreme Court of Malaysia, (1986).

Pew Research Center (2020, November 10). I*n 2018, government restrictions on religion reach highest level globally in more than a decade.* Pew Research Center. https://www.pewforum.org/2020/11/10/in-2018-government-restrictions-on-religion-reach-highest-level-globally-in-more-than-a-decade/. Accessed 1 August 2021.

Reuters staff. (2017, February 21). Thousands rally in Malaysia to back Islamic penal code bill. *Reuters.* https://www.reuters.com/article/malaysia-politics-hudud-idUSKBN15X0D5. Accessed 21 Feb 2017.

William A. Schabas (2000) Islam and the death penalty. *William & Mary Bill of Rights Journal, 9*(1), 223-236. https://scholarship.law.wm.edu/wmborj/vol9/iss1/13. Accessed 1 August 2021.

Seiff, A. (2020). *Philippine President and politicians push for return of death penalty amid war on drugs.* International Bar Association. https://www.ibanet.org/article/B041B93E-63C5-4361-8997-3D83C10E22FB. Accessed 1 August 2021

Sharif, M. F. M. (2006). Baghy in Islamic law and the thinking of Ibn Taymiyya. *Arab Law Quarterly, 20*(3), 289–305. http://www.jstor.org/stable/27650553.

Shuaib, F. S. (2012). The Islamic legal system in Malaysia. *Washington International Law Journal, 21*(1), 85–113. https://digitalcommons.law.uw.edu/wilj/vol21/iss1/8. Accessed 1 August 2021

Somboon, V. (2008). *Rattatham nai adīt [Ancient Dhammic States].* Open Books.

Swearer, D. K. (2010). *The Buddhist world of Southeast Asia* (2nd ed.). State University of New York Press.

Tambiah, S. J. (1976). *World conqueror and world renouncer: A study of Buddhism and polity in Thailand against a historical background.* Cambridge University Press.

Tellenbach, S. (2014). Islamic criminal law. In M. D. Dubber & T. Hornle (Eds.), *Oxford handbook of criminal law* (pp. 248–268). Oxford University Press.

Temperman, J. (2010). *State-religion relationships and human rights law.* Martinus Nijhoff.

The 1962 Sangha Act [Thailand].

The 1987 Constitution of the Philippines

The Holy See. (2000). *Encyclical letter Fratelli Tutti of the Holy Father Francis on fraternity and social friendship.* https://www.vatican.va/content/francesco/en/encyclicals/documents/papa-francesco_20201003_enciclica-fratelli-tutti.html. Accessed 1 August 2021.

The Malaysian Insider. (2012). *Possible moratorium on death penalty pending govt's final decision.* http://www.themalaysianinsider.com/malaysia/article/possible-moratorium-on-death-sentences-pendinggovts-final-decision-nazri. Accessed 1 August 2021.

The Penal Code [Thailand]

Tonsakulrungruang, K. (2018). *Thailand's constitution capitulates to Buddhist domineering.* East Asia Forum. https://www.eastasiaforum.org/2018/01/24/thailands-constitution-capitulates-to-buddhist-domineering/. Accessed 1 August 2021.

Tonsakulrungruang, K. (2021). Buddhist influence on the ancient Siamese legal system, from Ayutthaya to the twenty-first century. In A. Harding & M. Pongsapan (Eds.), *Thai legal history: From tradition to modern law* (pp. 60–76). Cambridge University Press.

U.S. Department of State. (2017). *Malaysia 2017 Report on International Religious Freedom: Malaysia.* https://www.state.gov/reports/2017-report-on-international-religious-freedom/malaysia/. Accessed 11 Nov 2021.

United Nations Human Rights Council. (2009). *Universal Periodic Review, Report of the Working Group on the Universal Periodic Review: Malaysia (Addendum).* http://www2.ohchr.org/english/bodies/hrcouncil/docs/11session/A.HRC.11.30.Add.1.pdf. Accessed 1 August 2021.

United Nations Office of the High Commissioner for Human Rights [UN OHCHR]. (2014). *Moving away from the death penalty: Arguments, trends and perspectives.* https://www.ohchr.org/Lists/MeetingsNY/Attachments/52/Moving-Away-from-the-Death-Penalty.pdf. Accessed 1 August 2021.

Visalo, P. (2009). *Phutsātsanā Thai nai anākhot nǣonōm lǣ thang ō̧k chāk wikrit [Thai Buddhism in the future: Trend and solution to crisis]* (2nd ed.). Komol-Keemthong Foundation.

Waldau, P. (2000). Buddhism and animal rights. In D. Keown (Ed.), *Contemporary Buddhist ethics* (pp. 82–111). Routledge.

Khemthong Tonsakulrungruang, PhD, lectures constitutional law and jurisprudence at the Faculty of Political Sci-ence, Chulalongkorn University, in Bangkok, Thailand. He earned his LL.B. from Chulalongkorn University before completing his LL.M. at Yale Law School, USA. His PhD at the University of Bristol School of Law is about Buddhist constitu-tionalism, the influence of Theravada Buddhism on Thailand's constitutional structure and culture. His recent works focus on the topics of the politics of the Constitutional Court, constitutional amendments, and Buddhism and Thai law.

De Jure Abolition of the Death Penalty: Cambodia and the Philippines

Ma. Ngina Teresa V. Chan-Gonzaga

Abstract While there appears to be a movement decidedly towards the universal abolition of capital punishment, ASEAN seems to be bucking the trend with only two of its Member-States currently abolitionists *de jure*. This paper examines anew the Cambodian and Philippine experiences of abolition, both the historical contexts as well as the domestic and international factors influencing them. In addition, this chapter discusses the challenges still faced by the two countries given that even while classified as abolitionist, the situations in both Cambodia and the Philippines are not unreservedly ideal—Cambodia has not ratified the Second Optional Protocol and the Philippine government's recent authoritarian turn has seen an intensified campaign to reimpose capital punishment through legislation. The chapter concludes by conceding that while neither can be considered model abolitionist States and despite the persistence of imperfect situations, lessons can still be learned from their experiences such as the superiority of constitutional proscriptions. Hopefully, the notion that capital punishment is deeply entrenched, intractable, and necessary in the legal systems of ASEAN Member-States can soon be dispelled as fallacy.

1 The Death Penalty in the ASEAN Region

Despite an undeniable global trend towards the eradication of capital punishment, it is disturbing that the situation and conditions in Southeast Asia do not appear to reflect a similar trajectory (ECPM, 2020; Algar, 2020; Schabas, 2002, 2014, pp. 363–365 & 377).

Such resolute resistance is manifested by Brunei and Singapore in their consistent votes against the death penalty moratorium resolution of the United Nations General Assembly (UNGA, 2007; UNGA, 2008a, pp. 372–373; UNGA, 2008b; UNGA, 2009, p. 383; UNGA, 2010; UNGA, 2011, pp. 445–446; UNGA, 2012; UNGA, 2013, pp. 645–646; UNGA, 2014; UNGA, 2015, pp. 722–723; UNGA, 2016a; UNGA, 2017, pp. 778–780; UNGA, 2018; UNGA, 2019, pp. 911–913; UNGA,

Ma. N. T. V. Chan-Gonzaga (✉)
School of Law, Ateneo de Manila University, Makati City, Philippines
e-mail: mcgonzaga@ateneo.edu

S. Petcharamesree et al. (eds.), *Unpacking the Death Penalty in ASEAN*,
https://doi.org/10.1007/978-981-19-8840-0_7

2020a; UNGA, 2021a, pp. 880–882) and six of the 10 ASEAN Member-States (AMS) are also arguably retentionist (ECPM, 2020; Joseph, 2021)[1] with executions taking place in five of these States in the last five years (ECPM, 2020).[2] The situation in Myanmar is also distressing where a moratorium on executions has been lifted with 65 people being sentenced to death since the military *coup d'état* in February 2021 (Human Rights Watch, 2021). Moreover, overtures in the Philippines (one of the two abolitionist States) to re-impose capital punishment since the authoritarian regime of President Rodrigo Duterte took power have also raised alarm bells in the last few years (Buan, 2020).

Observers could very well question why the state of abolition has remained constant, if not actually worsened, in the region. Has there been actual progress in retentionist States towards absolute abolition? Is being abolitionist *de facto* an intermediary step for retentionist States to transition to abolition *de jure* status? What issues, both past and present, pose (or continue to pose) challenges to States that are abolitionist *de jure*? Does a State's attainment of the status, abolitionist *de jure*, ensure it shall permanently remain as such, or is regression a continuing threat?

These are some of the questions that guided development of this chapter which is divided into five parts. It begins with a brief overview of the status quo in the ASEAN region, including a general categorisation based on their death penalty positions followed by a discussion of current abolition prospects in selected AMS. The next part outlines the processes taken by the abolitionists *de jure* (Cambodia and the Philippines) in putting an end to capital punishment and questions the extent to which each State has actually rejected it. Following is a discussion of the challenges experienced in said countries to maintain the status, resist attempts to reintroduce the death penalty, and improve the type and condition of the proscription. This chapter concludes by examining, first, the role of international law and relations, then the complications caused by domestic factors (including municipal law and legislative processes) before offering an outline of what could be considered a stable "model abolitionist State."

1.1 Categorisation of States Based on Their Death Penalty Positions

Labels and classifications of the groupings to which a State is consigned depend on practice as well as statutory pronouncements and may differ across organisations but are still, for the most part, recognisably analogous. The UN Economic and Social Council (ECOSOC) uses the following categorisation:

[1] Brunei, Indonesia, Malaysia, Singapore, Thailand, and Vietnam (ECPM, 2020).

[2] Indonesia, Malaysia, Singapore, Thailand, and Vietnam (ECPM 2020).

> (a) Abolitionist for all crimes, whether in time of peace or war;
>
> (b) Abolitionist for ordinary crimes, meaning that the death penalty has been abolished for all ordinary offences committed in peacetime, such as those contained in the criminal code or those recognized in common law (for example, murder, rape[,] and robbery with violence), and that the death penalty is retained only for exceptional circumstances, such as military offences in wartime, or crimes against the State, such as treason, terrorism[,] or armed insurrection;
>
> (c) Abolitionist *de facto*, that is, States and territories in which the death penalty remains lawful and death sentences may still be pronounced but executions have not taken place for 10 years. States and territories that carried out executions within the previous 10 years but have made an international commitment through the establishment of an official moratorium are also designated as *de facto* abolitionist;
>
> (d) Retentionist in practice, that is, States in which the death penalty remains lawful and that have conducted executions during the previous 10 years. (ECOSOC, 2020, p. 5)

Amnesty International (AI) also has a similar categorisation although it uses the term "abolitionist in practice" for the third group (Amnesty International, 2021a). Ensemble contre la peine de mort (ECPM), on the other hand, uses "with a moratorium on executions" for the third group and defines it as "[S]tates or territories where the death penalty is implemented but no executions have been carried out for at least 10 years and which did not oppose the latest UN resolution for a universal moratorium on executions and/or having ratified [the Second Optional Protocol to the International Covenant on Civil and Political Rights, aiming at the abolition of the death penalty (Second Optional Protocol)]" (ECPM, 2020).

While most countries fall into the same grouping across organisational classifications, some variations due to nuances in groups' operational definitions may occur. For instance, under ECOSOC or AI reports, Brunei is classified as being abolitionist *de facto* as it has not carried out an execution in over 10 years but it is categorised as retentionist by ECMP because it has consistently voted against the UNGA resolutions for a universal moratorium.

So, while it is evident that there are currently two abolitionist *de jure* AMS, i.e., where abolition is constitutionally or statutorily mandated (Cambodia and the Philippines), two or three are *de facto* abolitionists (Lao PDR and Myanmar, with Brunei as the possible third). Likewise, five or six are retentionists, again depending on Brunei's categorisation.

1.2 Retentionists and De Facto Abolitionists in ASEAN: Prospects of Abolition

If we simply take the term "*de facto*" as a "state of affairs that is true in fact, but that is not officially sanctioned" (Washington University in St. Louis School of Law, 2012), it is argued that Brunei should be considered retentionist, cessation of executions in the last decade notwithstanding. It has consistently voted against the UNGA resolutions on the moratorium for the death penalty, the latest one being Resolution 75/183 adopted in December 2020 (UNGA, 2020a). While official information may be scarce on the number of recent convictions as well as the number of prisoners currently on death row, it is observed that legislative "reforms" have led to changes in the country's Penal Code which would, if implemented, impose the death penalty on additional offences. Described as draconian, the revisions raised alarm bells in 2019 with the UN High Commissioner for Human Rights and other UN agencies expressing deep concern (UNOHCHR, 2019; UN News, 2019).

While it is true that *de facto* abolitionist States are theoretically closer to a possible shift to a *de jure* acceptance of abolition, this is not necessarily an intermediary step for current retentionist States. The Philippines, for instance, reportedly executed seven people under Republic Act No. 7659, otherwise known as the Death Penalty Law (Philippine Republic Act No. 7659; Porcalla, 2000; Balay Rehabilitation Center), less than 10 years prior to it being repealed by Republic Act No. 9346 (Philippine Republic Act No. 9346).

In fact, a survey of the current situation in AMS shows that a legislative and policy shift is more conceivable in retentionist States like Indonesia and Malaysia than in any of the two (or three) *de facto* abolitionist States (Brunei, Lao PDR, and Myanmar).

In 2017, the populist president of Indonesia, Joko Widodo, publicly linked capital punishment to "the will of the people", stating that he would consider a moratorium or abolition if it had popular backing—he insists it does not—as it would be arduous to gain parliamentary support without (The Straits Times, 2017). But more recent research undertaken in Indonesia by Oxford University's Death Penalty Research Unit (DPRU), in coordination with The Death Penalty Project, contests the notion that Indonesians believe, for instance, that their safety and security require the execution of drug offenders (parenthetically, it is claimed that two-thirds of all death sentences were meted out for drug-related offences) and posits that "opinions among the public and those who guide and inform them present no barrier to … the final step of abolishing the death penalty altogether…." (Hoyle & Jabbar, 2021; Hoyle, 2021a, b).

In Malaysia, the government announced a move to abolish capital punishment in 2018, later tempering its position to changing the mandatory nature of the penalty for some offences due to the "voice of the people" (Kamarudin, 2018). Later in 2019, a Special Committee was appointed to study alternative sentences in lieu of a mandatory death penalty, and the resulting recommendations reportedly include statutory revisions to substitute mandatory death sentences with more appropriate penalties at the courts' discretion (Anti-Death Penalty Asia Network et al., 2021, p. 2). However, even this calibrated development was tempered as Malaysia went through a political crisis and change of government in 2020 (Lee, 2020; Medina, 2021). It appears that government policies and the progress of legislative amendments on the issue of capital punishment have, for the moment, been put on hold. Still, the

Anti-Death Penalty Asia Network (ADPAN) et al.,[3] in an August 2021 midterm report submitted for Malaysia's Universal Periodic Review, remarked that while the government's present stance on capital punishment is unclear, the moratorium—previously imposed in 2018 when it optimistically announced the move towards abolition—"appears likely to be maintained" (Anti-Death Penalty Asia Network et al., 2021, p. 4). The fact that, notwithstanding the political changes, Malaysia still voted in favour of the 2020 UNGA Resolution 75/183 on the universal moratorium on executions, lends hope that reforms can be deliberated on and fulfilled.[4]

While admittedly the situation is less than encouraging, these two jurisdictions—albeit currently classified as retentionist—are arguably still in a better position to table and tackle significant changes in policy and law with a view to abolition than Brunei (with its recent penal law amendments), Lao PDR (whose "restrictive [S]tate practice" has resulted in a dearth of information regarding the use of capital punishment) (Amnesty International, 2021b, pp. 6, 24, & 58), or Myanmar (where the 2021 coup has brought the country to the brink of civil war) (Nichols, 2021).

Advocacy for abolition is still predominantly country-specific and local, although there have been significant regional and international initiatives. Likewise, the United Nations, with its biennial resolution on the universal moratorium on executions, has continued to shine a light on the issue and one cannot deny the global trend towards abolition.

On the regional level, however, it is doubtful that ASEAN, with its current treatment of human rights and its "ASEAN Way" of dealing with issues, will reach consensus on any semblance of a regional policy or even declaration against capital punishment as a bloc. After all, the "sovereignty amendment" inserted in the UN moratorium resolutions since 2016 was at the instigation of Singapore (UNGA, 2016b, pp. 9–11; UNGA, 2016c, pp. 8–12; Pascoe & Bae, 2021). The 2020 iteration—which reads, "*Reaffirms* the sovereign right of all countries to develop their own legal systems, including determining appropriate legal penalties, in accordance with their international law obligations []" (UNGA, 2020b, c, paras. 42–53 & para. 89, Draft Resolution IX)—was also co-sponsored by four other AMS, namely, Brunei, Indonesia, Lao PDR, and Vietnam. While the sovereignty statement by itself cannot be considered radical—it is in fact still doctrine—it is true that, when inserted in a resolution calling for a unified global action on an issue, it "reinforces a reductionist view of the death penalty as being a criminal justice issue and erodes the human-rights aspects of the resolution" as Navi Pillay and Ruth Dreifuss point out (Pillay & Dreifuss, 2020).

---

[3] ADPAN, in collaboration with the Advocates for Human Rights (TAHR), Capital Punishment Justice Project (CPJP), Ensemble Contre La Peine De Mort (ECPM), Harm Reduction International (HRI), World Coalition against the Death Penalty (WCADP), Eleos Justice, Monash University, and Malaysian against Death Penalty & Torture (MADPET) (Anti-Death Penalty Asia Network et al., 2021, p. 2).

[4] In June 2022, the Malaysian government announced a shift in policy in that it will abolish capital punishment in the country by substituting mandatory death penalty in relation to a substantial number of crimes with alternative non-lethal sentences (UNOHCHR, 2022). This is a positive development that hopefully will lead to the Malaysian Parliament passing legislation institutionalising the same.

Still, the progressively increasing number of votes in favour of the moratorium resolutions, with the latest one garnering a positive 123 votes (with 38 votes against, 24 abstentions, and 8 absences) (UNGA, 2021a, p. 880; Pascoe & Bae, 2021) adds weight to the assertion that the global inclination is really to move away from capital punishment. Of course, as gauges of inclination go, (non-binding) resolutions are well and good, but a related indicator, i.e., an actual rise in the number of abolitionist States, is to be preferred.

2 Experience of *De Jure* Abolitionists

In determining how a shift from a retentionist to an abolitionist State can perhaps be achieved in the ASEAN region, there is value in taking a closer look at the Cambodian and Philippine experiences, seeing as they are the only AMS which are actually *de jure* abolitionists.

It can be claimed that the landmark events that ushered in what would arguably be the configuration of the current Cambodian and the Philippine States occurred approximately around the same period. The latter half of the 1980s saw the end of the Cambodian-Vietnamese War and the start of efforts that would lead to the Paris Peace Accords in the early 1990s. In 1986, the Philippine People Power Revolution also took place, ousting dictator, Ferdinand Marcos, and heralding the birth of the new Philippine Constitution. Cambodia actually abolished capital punishment in 1989 by law before such abolition saw its way into the Cambodian Constitution a few years later, and it was in 1987 that the Philippine Constitution tentatively barred the death penalty. This period will therefore be used as the starting point for a historical discussion on their abolition experiences.

2.1 The Cambodian Experience

The 1970s and the 1980s were a dark period in Cambodia's history, first because of the genocidal regime of the Maoist-influenced Khmer Rouge guerrilla movement, and subsequently because of the Vietnamese invasion. This era reportedly saw the demise of a fourth of the population, with estimates ranging from 1.2 to 2 million deaths (Chandler n.d.; Chandler & Overton, 2021; Jørgensen, 2018, p. 11). An evocative reference to this period is contained in the preamble of the 1993 Constitution itself with a reference to the people as "[h]aving fallen into a terrifying decay for the two last decades when we have been undergoing unspeakable, demeaning sufferings and disasters of the most regrettable way" (1993 Cambodian Constitution, preamble).

After the fall of the Khmer Rouge regime, the Vietnamese invaded and the Vietnam-backed People's Republic of Kampuchea (PRK) took power (1979–1989) (Jørgensen, 2018, pp. 11–12). It was soon after this transition that the two most notorious characters of the previous regime—Pol Pot and Ieng Sary—were tried *in absentia* by the People's Revolutionary Tribunal, a tribunal established by the PRK particularly to try the Khmer Rouge leaders. These two were indicted as "instigators and planners" of genocide (which was the only charge), found guilty, and sentenced to death in 1979 (Jørgensen, 2018, p. 12; Corey-Boulet, 2009). Neither being in custody, the sentence was obviously not carried out and was thereafter overtaken by events, both political and otherwise. Pol Pot died in 1998 without being taken into government custody (Mydans, 1998), and Ieng Sary was granted a pardon by Royal Decree in 1996 for his momentous defection as well as that of the rebels over which he had an influence (Jørgensen, 2018, p. 21). Prime Minister Hun Sen would observe that "this was the price that had to be paid for the sake of the nation" since the obliteration of the remains of the Khmer Rouge and the defection of the remaining cadres were seen to be of primordial importance (Jørgensen, 2018, p. 21). Moreover, at this point in time, the Cambodian Constitution—with its pronouncement on the right to life and the prohibition of the death penalty—was also already in place.

In 1989, the People's Republic of Kampuchea amended the 1981 Constitution. 1989 has been called Cambodia's "year of [] democratic revolution" (Jørgensen, 2018, p. 13; LICADHO, 2007, pp. 1–2). The 1989 amendments were described as being influenced by domestic politics as well as a positioning to inspire international aid and assistance for the fledgling government (Jørgensen, 2018, p. 13; LICADHO, 2007, pp. 1–2).

It was at this time that Cambodia seized the opportunity to display at least a textual commitment to human rights (Jørgensen, 2018, pp. 13–14; LICADHO, 2007, pp. 1–2). Respect and protection for the right to life in particular were highlighted among the amendments and underscored by uncompromising language on the abolition of the death penalty. Scholars such as Roger Hood, David Johnson, and Franklin Zimring, as well as organisations such as Amnesty International, made similar observations about the motivation behind abolition—i.e., that it may well have been triggered to a large extent by the lessons of the tragic past and a desire to overtly dissociate the new Cambodia from the previous genocidal Khmer Rouge regime (Jørgensen, 2018, pp. 13–15; LICADHO, 2007, pp. 1–2).

The country's process of transitioning to democracy was exceptional in that the United Nations deliberately took charge of its reconstruction (Jørgensen, 2018, p. 15; LICADHO, 2007, pp. 1–2). This process commenced when negotiations were undertaken in Paris in 1989—joined by the opposing Cambodian factions, representatives of other countries like UN Security Council members, as well as UN Secretary-General Javier Perez de Cuellar—to reach a comprehensive arrangement that would assure self-determination for Cambodia (Jørgensen, 2018, p. 15; LICADHO, 2007, pp. 1–2; McFadden, 2020). A framework agreement was attained in 1990 with the Supreme National Council (SNC), composed of representatives of the contending factions, which was recognised as the head of a coalition government during the transition (Jørgensen, 2018, p. 15; Encyclopedia Britannica n.d.a; n.d.b.).

The "Agreement on a Comprehensive Political Settlement of the Cambodia Conflict" (Paris Agreement) was reached in October 1991 (UNGA & UNSC, 1991, annex; Jørgensen, 2018, p. 15; LICADHO, 2007, p. 1). The UN Security Council, whose permanent members had participated in the negotiations to some extent, endorsed it and created the UN Transitional Authority in Cambodia (UNTAC) through Resolution No. 745 (1992) (UNSC, 1992; UN Peacekeeping n.d.). UNTAC was mandated to ensure the implementation of the Paris Agreement (UN Peacekeeping n.d.; Encyclopedia Britannica n.d.b) and started work in the country in March 1992 (Encyclopedia Britannica n.d.b).

In line with international obligations under the Paris Agreement, the SNC also acceded to five key international human rights instruments in 1992, including the International Covenant on Civil and Political Rights (ICCPR) and the International Covenant on Economic Social and Cultural Rights (ICESCR) (Jørgensen, 2018, p. 16). It did not, however, accede to the Second Optional Protocol to the ICCPR, notwithstanding the latter instrument already having entered into force the year before (LICADHO, 2007, pp. 2–5).

At the domestic level, the UNTAC Law—"Provisions Relating to the Judiciary and Criminal Law and Procedure Applicable in Cambodia During the Transitional Period"—was adopted by the SNC a few months later in September 1992, with Article 67 reinforcing the earlier commitment to abolish the death penalty (Jørgensen, 2018, p. 17; SNC Cambodia Provisions).

Soon after, the 120-strong Constituent Assembly was elected and finished drafting the Constitution, paving the way for its promulgation in September 1993. The Constituent Assembly subsequently converted itself into the National Assembly, in consonance with the Paris Agreement, effectively ending UNTAC's mandate and concluding the transition period (LICADHO, 2007, pp. 1–2; Jørgensen, 2018, pp. 18–20; UN Peacekeeping n.d.).

Recognising the importance of human rights was a major consideration and a particular focus of the Paris Agreement; the 1993 Constitution, in keeping with Article 23 in connection with Annex 5 of the Paris Agreement, necessarily included a thorough register of fundamental rights (LICADHO, 2007, p. 1). Basic freedoms and human rights are now constitutionally enshrined and the second paragraph of Article 32 explicitly forbids the use of capital punishment in the same constitutional article which pronounces the Khmer citizen's right to life:

> Everyone has the right to life, liberty and security of person.
>
> In any case, there shall be no death penalty. (1993 Cambodian Constitution).

To a certain extent, the Cambodian experience is a reflection (or a precursor) of the global trend of abolition, a trend that has been hastened by factors including political and legal forces in the international community as well as those in domestic spheres. An (obvious) example of such a factor would be the determined set of conditions precedent to a desired outcome, such as a sought-after seat on an international body or a prized membership in a regional bloc, e.g., the European Union requires abolition as a precondition to membership (Nicolau, 2013, p. 281).

This is not to say that the abolition of the death penalty in Cambodia was solely due to international pressure or the Paris Agreement, only that these were also arguably significant factors.

2.2 The Philippine Experience

Unlike the 1993 Cambodian Constitution which abolished capital punishment in no uncertain terms, the 1987 Philippine Constitution only reduced all death penalties already imposed to *reclusion perpetua* and proscribed its imposition at that point in time but left the door ajar for future legislation regarding re-imposition.

"[*U*]*nless, for compelling reasons involving heinous crimes, the Congress hereafter provides for it*" (1987 Philippine Constitution, Article III, Section 19 (1)). With these words, the 1986 Philippine Constitutional Commission chose to "de-constitutionalise" the issue, making the provision on abolition one which could be abrogated by legislation instead of the more exacting constitutional amendatory process.

The original wording of the abolition provision was more categorical and read as follows:

> Excessive fines shall not be imposed, nor cruel, degrading or inhuman punishment, or the death penalty inflicted. Death penalty already imposed shall be commuted to *reclusion perpetua*. (1986 Philippine Constitutional Commission, R.C.C. No. 32 on 17 July 1986, pp. 672-673 & 676)

This was the proposed provision that was reached by consensus within the Bill of Rights Committee of the Constitutional Commission. Anecdotally, it was shared that the Committee has agreed to abolition, the question deliberated was the manner by which it was to be effected, i.e., whether constitutionally or by statute. Fr. Joaquin G. Bernas, who had to present the draft to the plenary Commission, shared that:

> [T]here was a division in the Committee not on whether the death penalty should be abolished or not, but rather on whether the abolition should be done by the Constitution—in which case it cannot be restored by the legislature—or left to the legislature. The majority voted for the constitutional abolition of the death penalty. And the reason is that capital punishment is inhuman for the convict and his family who are traumatized by the waiting, even if it is never carried out. There is no evidence that the death penalty deterred deadly criminals, hence, life should not be destroyed just in the hope that other lives might be saved. Assuming mastery over the life of another man is just too presumptuous for any man. The fact that the death penalty as an institution has been there from time immemorial should not deter us from reviewing it. Human life is more valuable than an institution intended precisely to serve human life. So, basically, this is the summary of the reasons which were presented in support of the constitutional abolition of the death penalty. (1986 Philippine Constitutional Commission, R.C.C. No. 32 on 17 July 1986, p. 676)

However, while the majority of the members of the Bill of Rights Committee agreed to a constitutional abolition, such was not the case for the Commission-at-large.

It is quite unfortunate that the provision as finalised was not absolute but allowed an amendment that permitted congressional re-imposition, with the author of the amendment stating that: "We know that this is a very difficult question. The fact that the arguments yesterday were quite impassioned and meritorious merely tells us that this is far from a well-settled issue" (1986 Philippine Constitutional Commission, R.C.C. No. 33 on 18 July 1986, pp. 742–743, cited in Bernas, 2009, p. 576).

The abolition was approved by a slim margin with an initial vote by show of hands saw a 19–18 split (1986 Philippine Constitutional Commission, R.C.C. No. 33 on 18 July 1986, p. 746). After nominal voting was required by a staunch retentionist member of the Commission, the lead increased to 22–17 (1986 Philippine Constitutional Commission, R.C.C. No. 33 on 18 July 1986, pp. 746–747, cited in Bernas, 2009, p. 576). The final version reads:

> SECTION 19. (1) Excessive fines shall not be imposed, nor cruel, degrading[,] or inhuman punishment inflicted. **Neither shall death penalty be imposed, unless, for compelling reasons involving heinous crimes, the Congress hereafter provides for it.** Any death penalty already imposed shall be reduced to *reclusion perpetua.* (1987 Philippine Constitution, article III, section 19 (1), emphasis added)

It is worth noting though that even if the Constitution leaves the matter to congressional discretion, it did not do so in the usual manner of simply appending the ubiquitous clause "unless otherwise provided by law." While the power of the Philippine Legislature is otherwise plenary (Bernas, 2009, pp. 676–677), this provision does require Congress to take into account the constraining prerequisite, i.e. that the re-imposition had to be "for compelling reasons involving heinous crimes."

In 1993, only six years after the ratification of the Philippine Constitution, Congress passed Republic Act No. 7659, also known as The Death Penalty Law (Philippine Republic Act No. 7659).

The constitutionality of this law came before the Supreme Court in a case that dealt with the conviction of Leo Echegaray who would subsequently become the first person to be executed under the law. He argued that Republic Act No. 7659 was unconstitutional per se for having been enacted without any compelling reasons therefor. The Court rejected this proposition (*People v. Echegaray*, 267 SCRA 682 (1997)). It opined that the crimes identified by the law—which included murder, kidnapping and serious illegal detention, as well as rape—sufficiently met the element of heinousness and it was "inseparable" from and "interspersed" with the element of compulsion:

> Article III, Section 19(1) of the 1987 Constitution simply states that Congress, for compelling reasons involving heinous crimes, may re-impose the death penalty. Nothing in the said provision imposes a requirement that for a death penalty bill to be valid, a positive manifestation in the form of a higher incidence of crime should first be perceived and statistically proven following the suspension of the death penalty. Neither does the said provision require that the death penalty be resorted to as a last recourse when all other criminal reforms have failed to abate criminality in society. It is immaterial and irrelevant that [Republic Act] No. 7659 cites that there has been an 'alarming upsurge of such crimes,' for the same was never intended by said law to be the yardstick to determine the existence of compelling reasons involving heinous crimes. Fittingly, thus, what [Republic Act] No. 7659 states is that 'the Congress, in the interest of justice, public order and rule of law, and the need to rationalize and harmonize the penal sanctions for heinous crimes, finds compelling reasons to impose the death penalty for said crimes' (*People v. Echegaray*, 267 SCRA 682 (1997), p. 725).

Executions were carried out in the Philippines starting in 1999 with Leo Echegaray (Easton, 1999). A temporary moratorium was imposed in 2000 by then President Joseph Estrada to mark the Great Jubilee Year of the Roman Catholic Church

(Amnesty International United Kingdom, 2002). Soon after, when Gloria Macapagal Arroyo took over the presidency in 2001, the moratorium was lifted only to be restored after a few months (Conde, 2003; Villanueva, 2003). Another period without a suspension followed before a subsequent moratorium was again imposed in 2003 (Conde, 2003; Villanueva, 2003). President Arroyo then commuted the sentences of 1,230 prisoners on death row in April 2006 (Balay Rehabilitation Center). Two months later, Republic Act No. 9346 was signed into law (Philippine Republic Act No. 9346).

So thirteen years after the death penalty law was enacted, the country repealed it again with Republic Act No. 9346 (Philippine Republic Act No. 9346). The first line of Section 1 is terse and succinct: "*The imposition of the penalty of death is hereby prohibited*" (Philippine Republic Act No. 9346, Section 1).[5]

The year after, or in 2007, the Philippines ratified the Second Optional Protocol to the ICCPR (ICCPR-OP2; ICCPR-OP2 Ratification: Philippines, p. 262).

However, unlike the Cambodian situation where re-imposition is currently a non-issue, this matter still haunts Philippine society and politics constituting an ever-present controversial debate, whether on the streets, in schools, or in the political arena.

3 Continuing Challenges of Abolitionist ASEAN Member-States

3.1 Challenges in Cambodia

As the last country to join ASEAN in 1999 (Association of Southeast Asian Nations, 2021), Cambodia is in fact the only AMS that has consistently voted in favour of all the UNGA moratorium resolutions against execution since the first one in 2007 (International Commission Against Death Penalty).

There is a certain degree of incongruity between this decidedly abolitionist stance—because of a constitutionally-pronounced reverence for the right to life—and Cambodia's human rights record since its ratification of the 1993 Constitution. Such a record has been dismal and the autocratic government of Prime Minister Hun Sen, which has been in power for more than 35 years, has been marked by repression of the opposition and restrictions on fundamental freedoms (Evans, 2019; UNGA, 2021b).

[5] "SECTION 1. The imposition of the penalty of death is hereby prohibited. Accordingly, Republic Act No. Eight Thousand One Hundred Seventy-Seven (R.A. No. 8177), otherwise known as the Act Designating Death by Lethal Injection is hereby repealed, Republic Act No. Seven Thousand Six Hundred Fifty-Nine (R.A. No. 7659), otherwise known as the Death Penalty Law, and all other laws, executive orders and decrees, insofar as they impose the death penalty are hereby repealed or amended accordingly" (Philippine Republic Act No. 9346, Sect. 1).

Even when the Prime Minister broached the possibility of a referendum to bring capital punishment back in 2019, suggesting a constitutional amendment of the prohibition to enable imposing it on those found guilty of raping children in their families (Hutt, 2019; Kyodo, 2019), an about-turn was swiftly executed just two days later. Alluding to consultations with experts, Hun Sen said the re-imposition "is not what our nation is all about" and that he thought that "there is no need to amend the constitution[;] we should instead strengthen education and morality" (Sokhean, 2019a).

Despite the subsequent turnaround, this incident is worrisome since the autocratic Prime Minister is not one to declare something publicly and retract it abruptly because of expert advice (Hutt, 2019). Odd too was his broaching of the idea of a public referendum or the reports in local media that the idea of re-imposition was received positively by social media users (Hutt, 2019). According to the government spokesperson, Phay Siphan, such incidents were initially used to paint a democratic picture of Hun Sen wanting to "give an opportunity for the public to decide their country's fate, even if it will garner criticism" (Hutt, 2019; Sokhean, 2019b). Phay Siphan added that "whether or not they will approve of the death penalty, it is up to them because their voices matter in a democratic society" (Sokhean, 2019b).

In any case, as aforementioned, the reversal came quickly on the heels of the controversial pronouncement. While it may have raised a temporary commotion, it did not appear to gain traction as a real issue.

Should there be a real clamour for it, or should the government again seriously consider it, any attempt to do so will have to go through the constitutional amendment. Article 153 (formerly Article 151) of the 1993 Constitution provides the constitution of sovereignty:

> The initiative of the revision or the amendment of the Constitution belongs to the King, to the Prime Minister[,] and to the President of the National Assembly on the proposal from one-fourth of all the National Assembly's Members.
>
> The revision or the amendment of the Constitution must be carried out by a constitutional law adopted by the National Assembly at the two-third majority of all its Members. (1993 Cambodian Constitution, article 153)

This is decidedly more stringent than statutory legislation, although amendments have been made since the original ratification in 1993 (Constitutional Council of Cambodia)—unlike the Philippine Constitution which has remained unchanged since 1987.

From most accounts at present, however, re-imposition of the death penalty is largely a non-issue in Cambodia.

Yet the fact remains that Cambodia has not ratified the Second Optional Protocol. The non-governmental organisation, Cambodian League for the Promotion and Defense of Human Rights (LICADHO), posits that its non-accession may be the result of legal concerns as well as the perceived impact on the government's political agenda; that if Cambodia became a State-Party to the Second Optional Protocol and then decided to restore the death penalty, it would be tantamount to a breach of international obligations whereas all that would be needed otherwise is the municipal action of amending the Constitution and criminal law. Acceding to the Second Optional Protocol also means regular reportorial requirements on compliance (ICCPR-OP2, article 3); acceptance of a complaint mechanism (ICCPR-OP2, articles 4 & 5); and participation in an international campaign for abolition (ICCPR-OP2, preamble). These obligations mean external scrutiny and the latter could also potentially be seen as a contradiction of the non-interference principle Cambodia cleaved to, as Article 53 of its Constitution also mandates that the Kingdom of Cambodia shall not "interfere in any other country's internal affairs, directly or indirectly" (Cambodian Constitution, article 53), and which principle appears to be a key feature of its foreign policy pronouncements even within ASEAN (LICADHO, 2007, p. 3).

LICADHO also observed that considering the state of capital punishment within ASEAN, with only the Philippines as similarly abolitionist, there is little regional pressure for Cambodia to accede to the Second Optional Protocol; and, in fact, it may disaffect other AMS—as well as other financial patrons such as China—which are staunchly retentionist (LICADHO, 2007, pp. 4–5). This last observation, if indeed correct, is ironic considering how external factors earlier bore upon Cambodia's accession to other human rights instruments as well as the degree to which its Constitution showcases basic freedoms and human rights.

3.2 Challenges in the Philippines

By contrast, re-imposition of the death penalty is definitely an issue in the Philippines.

Could the polarising debate have been avoided had the 1987 Constitution been uncompromising in its language on abolition? Unlikely, but perhaps it would not have as threatening a countenance if the constitutional language had been absolute, as constitutional amendments or revisions must pass more stringent processes than mere legislation.

A bill becomes law in the Philippines when it has been approved by both the Senate and the House of Representatives (Lower House) after it passes three readings generally on separate days (the vote being taken after the last reading) and is ordinarily signed by the President (1987 Philippine Constitution, Article VI, Sects. 26 & 27). Congress's power to legislate is plenary subject only to constitutional stipulations (Bernas, 2009, pp. 676–677). On the other hand, re-introducing the death penalty would require a constitutional amendment (as would, conversely, a move to make abolition absolute). Amendments can be put forward in three ways:

(1) If proposed by Congress upon a three-fourths vote of all its members (rather than a simple majority should there be quorum as would be the case for legislation) (1987 Philippine Constitution, article XVII, Section 1);
(2) If proposed by a constitutional convention—a convention can be so called by a two-thirds vote of Congress members or the electorate if Congress, by a simple majority vote of all its members, should submit the question to the electorate (1987 Philippine Constitution, article XVII, Sections 1 & 3); or

(3) If proposed directly by the people through an initiative whereby the petition for the amendment has the assent of at least 12% of the total number of registered voters including at least 3% of all registered voters in each legislative district (1987 Philippine Constitution, article XVII, Section 2).

Section 4 of Article XVII of the 1987 Constitution would then require ratification of the amendment by a majority of the votes cast in a plebiscite called for that purpose (1987 Philippine Constitution, Article XVII, Section 4).

Suffice it to say that since the ratification of the Philippine Constitution in February 1987, no amendments or revisions have been successful although attempts by both congressional action and initiative have been made.

The issue of capital punishment has, however, remained ever-present and controversial in the sphere of public debate. This matter has often become the subject of political expediency, with most politicians positioning themselves according to the preferences of those in power. This despite the fact that due to flaws in its criminal justice system in the 1990s when the death penalty was in effect, approximately 71.77% of death convictions had to be overturned by the Philippine appellate courts for a variety of reasons (*People v. Mateo*, 433 SCRA 640 (2004), p. 657).

But even as so-called anti-crime groups derided the repeal in 2006—accusing former President Arroyo of bowing to pressure from the Roman Catholic Church, and Congress in turn of bowing to pressure from the President in the name of political expediency at the expense of criminal deterrence—the government insisted (then) that its imposition did not serve the purpose of preventing the commission of heinous crimes. In her endorsement letter to the Senate, Arroyo advocated rehabilitation, saying that this allows "the offender to be reformed and be able to contribute to the good of society" (GMA News, 2006).

Such is not the mindset of President Rodrigo Duterte and his administration (Al Jazeera, 2016). Upon taking office in 2016, the Philippines—which had consistently voted in favour of the UN moratorium resolutions since the first one in 2007—abstained for the first time. It again abstained in 2018 but surprisingly did vote in favour again in 2020 (UNGA, 2007; UNGA, 2008a, pp. 372–373; UNGA, 2019, pp. 911–913; UNGA, 2021a, pp. 880–882; International Commission Against Death Penalty).

Re-imposition of the death penalty has always ranked high on his legislative agenda (BBC News, 2016). The first bill filed in the 17th Congress by members of the Lower House sought the return of capital punishment, having been filed by pro-administration representatives (Philippine House Bill No. 1). In the 18th Congress, a total of 13 bills—12 pending at the committee level in the Lower House and one transmitted to the Senate—seek to repeal Republic Act No. 9346 and re-impose capital punishment (Philippine House of Representatives 2021). Another 10 similar bills pertaining to various crimes are pending in the Senate (Philippine Senate, 2021).

This may be a cause for concern as Philippine constitutional law assumes a dualist view of legal systems, i.e., that domestic or municipal law is separate and distinct from the sphere of international law (Bernas, 2009, pp. 60–63). International treaties only become part of the law of the land when brought into the domestic legal system by a positive act (Bernas, 2009, pp. 60–63). For the most part, international legal obligations acceded to by the Philippines have become part of municipal law when a treaty or convention negotiated by the Executive was transformed through ratification and concurrence of at least a two-thirds majority of all members of the Senate (1987 Philippine Constitution, Article VII, Section 21). The treaty or convention then becomes valid and effective, and is placed on the same level as a statute passed by the Philippine Congress. From a municipal perspective, this means that a subsequent domestic law may repeal or rescind the earlier treaty or convention.

Moreover, the validity of the ratification of the Second Optional Protocol to the ICCPR has also been previously questioned. The normal process by which a treaty or convention is transformed into domestic law would be for a president to sign and submit it to the Senate for concurrence. As aforementioned, ratification requires a two-thirds majority of the Senate. The case of the Second Optional Protocol did not quite follow the norm. Republic Act No. 9346 which abolished the death penalty was signed into law on June 24, 2006 (Philippine Republic Act No. 9346). This law was signed by a majority of the Lower House (120 in favour, 20 against, and one abstention) (Philippine Congressional Record, pp. 158–159) and by two-thirds of all members of the Senate (16 in favour, zero against, and one abstention) (Philippine Senate Journal, p. 1308). Subsequent thereto, or on September 20, 2006, the Secretary of Foreign Affairs—as the President's alter ego—signed the Second Optional Protocol (Hood & Hoyle, 2008, p. 87). On November 20, 2007, the instrument of ratification, duly signed by the President of the Republic, was transmitted and deposited with the United Nations (ICCPR-OP2 Ratification: Philippines, p. 262; Philippine CHR 2020, p. 2). Because of the then-fresh passage of Republic Act No. 9346 (16 senators voted in favour), submission of the Second Optional Protocol to the Senate for its concurrence was deemed no longer necessary prior to its official ratification with the UN (Philippine CHR 2020, pp. 2–6).

However, at the height of the 2017 efforts of pro-administration legislators to re-impose capital punishment, then Senate Majority Leader, Vicente Sotto III (one author of a death penalty bill), insisted that the Second Optional Protocol was not validly ratified by the Senate (Diaz, 2017). However, the official position taken by the government in 2006, with no objections from the Senate, was that Republic Act No. 9346's enactment made submission of the Second Optional Protocol to the Senate redundant as two-thirds had already voted in favour of abolition (Philippine CHR 2020, pp. 1–4). As an aside, it is worth noting that former Senator Sotto has since reversed his position and is no longer in favour of capital punishment (CNN Philippines Staff, 2021).

The question of whether there ought to have been a dedicated and distinct act to submit the Second Optional Protocol to the Senate, not just a reliance on the implied ratification due to the enactment of Republic Act No. 9346, is arguably a good point to raise and review from an academic perspective since the Second Optional Protocol contains obligations beyond mere abolition of the death penalty.

That said, however, as far as the community of nations is concerned, the Philippines has validly taken on the obligations associated with the Second Optional Protocol with the required ratification having taken place in November 2007.

Even the Philippine Supreme Court, citing Gerhard von Glahn, has conceded that "[r]atification is generally held to be an executive act, undertaken by the head of the State or of the government, as the case may be, through which the formal acceptance of the treaty is proclaimed" (von Glahn, p. 486, cited in *Bayan (Bagong Alyansang Makabayan) v. Zamora*, 342 SCRA 449 (2000), p. 492). In the 2000 case of *Bayan (Bagong Alyansang Makabayan) v. Zamora*, it was observed that:

> As an integral part of the community of nations, we are responsible to assure that our government, Constitution and laws will carry out our international obligation. Hence, we cannot readily plead the Constitution as a convenient excuse for non-compliance with our obligations, duties and responsibilities under international law.
>
> xxx
>
> Equally important is Article 26 of the Convention which provides that 'Every treaty in force is binding upon the parties to it and must be performed by them in good faith.' This is known as the principle of *pacta sunt servanda* which preserves the sanctity of treaties and has been one of the most fundamental principles of positive international law, supported by the jurisprudence of international tribunals (*Bayan (Bagong Alyansang Makabayan) v. Zamora*, 342 SCRA 449 (2000), p. 493)

4 Final Points and Observations

A few points can be gleaned from the Cambodian and Philippine experiences.

Based on a comparison of the two, it is obvious that a constitutional proscription is decidedly better than a legislative repeal. In the case of Cambodia, it is encouraging to see that a State having a recent history of so much violence could turn its back on the idea of nihilistic retribution in favour of a right to life. It is just as inspiring to observe that it does not appear interested in re-imposing the death penalty, the aforementioned incident in 2019 notwithstanding. As far as the Philippines is concerned, politics seemingly trumps theory as far as the imposition/repeal issue is concerned. This can be observed from the flip-flopping voting records of long-time politicians in Congress who voted in the 1993 imposition, the 2006 repeal, and re-imposition, attempted in 2017 and subsequently thereafter (Philippine Center for Investigative Journalism, 2006). But perhaps the fact that no death penalty bill has been passed into law–notwithstanding the number of such bills being proposed in both Houses of Congress and notwithstanding the support of the sitting President – is also a phenomenon that bears closer review.

In both Cambodia and the Philippines, it is noteworthy to point out that international law and relations played, and continue to play, a significant role.

Cambodia's abolition stemmed from strong conditions imposed on the (then) future Cambodian government as regards guaranteeing the observance of human rights and adherence to international human rights treaties, including the ICCPR. The influence and pressure of the Paris Agreement, the UN, UNTAC, and other factors, on the drafting of its 1993 Constitution cannot be gainsaid. While UNTAC was far from perfect, and there were other concerns regarding human rights protection and promotion in Cambodia, the textual reassurance and affirmation of the right to life in the Constitution are significant as far as abolitionism is concerned. It is unfortunate though that advocacy attempts, both domestic and international, have not succeeded (yet) when it comes to ratification of the Second Optional Protocol.

Even in the Philippines, where abolition in 2006 was mainly due to domestic factors, the repeal of the law on capital punishment was also reportedly heavily influenced by international (religious) pressure from the Vatican. Indeed, in her speech on the signing of the abolition law, then President Macapagal-Arroyo thanked the Roman Catholic Church and said that, upon meeting the Pope in the Vatican (as she was then scheduled to do), she would tell him that "we have acted in the name of life for a world of peace and harmony" (Macapagal-Arroyo, 2006).

As regards the Philippines, to a certain degree, the fact it is a State-Party to the ICCPR has proven useful as a shield against moves for re-imposition. While it is conceded that the ICCPR does explicitly acknowledge capital punishment as a permissible limitation to the right to life, this is subject to narrow restrictions. Article 6(2) confines it only to "countries which have not abolished the death penalty" and only for "the most serious crimes". It may therefore be argued that the first restriction limits capital punishment to *retentionists*, that countries like the Philippines which have already abolished it at some past point *can no longer re-impose or re-introduce it* and that to do so would be a violation of international law.

Moreover, the Philippines has ratified, without reservation, the Second Optional Protocol (ICCPR-OP2). It is posited that once abolition has been undertaken, the obligations therein are incapable of being retracted and are perpetual.

This is not subject to the vagaries of political and administrative changes in government, as one basic attribute of international law and relations is precisely the understanding that security in the world order requires stability in the adherence to international obligations. A rules-based model is required of the community of nations for any semblance of an international system to work (Commission on Human Rights & Ward, p. 9). The Second Optional Protocol does not countenance retraction. It has indeed been observed that the text and spirit of the Protocol, as well as its travaux préparatoires, make it clear that no retreat is permitted (Commission on Human Rights & Ward, p. 10).

This position now forms part of paragraph 34 of the Human Rights Committee's General Comment No. 36 on Article 6 of the ICCPR (GC 36):

> 34. States parties to the Covenant that have abolished the death penalty, through amending their domestic laws, becoming parties to the Second Optional Protocol to the Covenant, aiming at the abolition of the death penalty, or adopting another international instrument obligating them to abolish the death penalty, are barred from reintroducing it. Like the Covenant, the Second Optional Protocol does not contain termination provisions and States parties cannot denounce it. Abolition of the death penalty is therefore legally irrevocable. ... (Human Rights Committee, paragraph 34)

The arguments made above, while somewhat useful in the Philippine context, will not be applicable to AMS which are not signatories to the ICCPR, or even to those which are signatories but have not taken capital punishment off their statute books (and therefore, concededly, are factually retentionist).

The other narrow condition provided by Article 6 of the ICCPR, i.e., that imposition only be "for the most serious crimes" also bears consideration. Paragraph 35 of GC 36 stresses that this term must be read restrictively and cannot be understood to operationally mean "[c]rimes not resulting directly and intentionally in death" even if these are to be considered serious in nature (Human Rights Committee, paragraph 35). There is also a textual reminder that State Parties are (1) obliged to make a re-evaluation of their penal laws to confirm that capital punishment is inapplicable to those which do not qualify as the most serious crimes, and (2) obliged to revoke sentences already issued for crimes which do not qualify (Human Rights Committee, paragraph 35). This tightening of the operational definition, at least for those States which have ratified the ICCPR, may be worth reiterating yet again in advocacy.

A more general but less accepted argument from an international law perspective is the proposition that there is an obligation even outside treaty law regarding protection of the right to life; that under customary international law and consistent with the views of the UN General Assembly, States are *obliged* to move towards abolition (Commission on Human Rights & Ward, p. 16). What militates against this perhaps is the view that the treatment of customary law is bound by certain orthodox rules; that there is a distinction between *de lege ferenda* and actual custom.

Thus, the sticking point is whether there actually has been uniform and consistent practice which has been accepted as *opinio juris*. Has custom actually crystallised? It cannot be denied that the resolutions of nations when it comes to abolition have, recently, become nearly overwhelming. At the UN General Assembly in December 2020, 123 of 193 Member-States—a record 64%—voted in favour of a moratorium with a view to abolition, with only 38 voting against it, and 24 abstaining (UNGA, 2020a, 2021a, pp. 880–882). Of these, 108 have abolished the penalty in law (Amnesty International, 2021c). This is indeed a far cry from 1945 when only 8 of the 51 UN Member-States were abolitionists (Amnesty International, 2018).

5 Conclusion

The right to life is valued by all AMS. That they disagree on how capital punishment should be viewed in relation to the right to life—with most insisting that it is a domestic issue and a sovereign concern—is the quandary. The keenness with which a government may consider the abolition question is influenced by factors both domestic (e.g., perceived public support, political advantage, etc.) and international (e.g., "peer pressure" within a bloc or the expectations of a global church). The shift may be sudden should there be a critical or serious disruption of the government or regime, or it could come more gradually through a consistent and relentless bid on the ground to change the mindsets of peoples across ASEAN. As discussed in this chapter, the perception of firm public support in favour of the death penalty is not as unqualified and unequivocal as it is made out to be. It will still be up to those invested in the matter to take advantage of events, whether minor or momentous, to press forward.

There can also be no complacency when it comes to Cambodia and the Philippines. If one were to imagine a stable "model abolitionist State", one may describe it as a country: (1) where the proscription against capital punishment was constitutionally provided for in absolute terms; (2) which has ratified the ICCPR as well as the Second Optional Protocol thereto; and (3) which consistently votes in favour of the UNGA moratorium resolutions. Neither of the two *de jure* abolitionist States in ASEAN fulfil all the above elements. Vigilance should therefore be maintained to counter attempts at subverting measures already in place or belittling the value of improving the status quo.

Hopefully, this chapter has been helpful in contextualising the experiences of the *de jure* abolitionists, highlighting the factors that helped to assert it as a right to life issue, and identifying points in their circumstances potentially requiring extra caution for those advocating for abolition in other AMS.

References

Books and Articles

Al Jazeera. (2016, May 16). Philippines' Rodrigo Duterte recommends death penalty. *Al Jazeera*. https://www.aljazeera.com/news/2016/5/16/philippines-rodrigo-duterte-recommends-death-penalty. Accessed 16 December 2021.

Algar, C. (2020, April 21). Op-ed: New 10-year low in global executions, but progress marred by spikes in a few countries. Amnesty International. https://www.amnesty.org/en/latest/news/2020/04/op-ed-new-10-year-low-in-global-executions-but-progress-marred-by-spikes-in-a-few-countries/. Accessed 16 December 2021.

Amnesty International United Kingdom. (2002, August 23). Press release—Philippines: First execution in two years imminent. Amnesty International United Kingdom. https://www.amnesty.org.uk/press-releases/philippines-first-execution-two-years-imminent. Accessed 16 December 2021.

Amnesty International. (2018, December 17). *Death penalty: Global abolition closer than ever as record number of countries vote to end executions*. World Coalition Against the Death Penalty. http://worldcoalition.org/2018/12/17/death-penalty-global-abolition-closer-than-ever-as-record-number-of-countries-vote-to-end-executions/. Accessed 16 December 2021.

Amnesty International. (2021a). Overview: We know that, together, we can end the death penalty everywhere. https://www.amnesty.org/en/what-we-do/death-penalty/. Accessed 16 December 2021a.

Amnesty International (2021b). Amnesty International Global Report: Death Sentences and Executions 2020. London: Amnesty International Ltd. https://www.amnestyusa.org/wp-content/uploads/2021b/04/DEATH-SENTENCES-AND-EXECUTIONS-2020.pdf. Accessed 16 December 2021.

Amnesty International. (2021c, April 21). Death penalty in 2020: Facts and figures. *Amnesty International*. https://www.amnesty.org/en/latest/news/2021b/04/death-penalty-in-2020-facts-and-figures/. Accessed 16 December 2021b.

Anti-Death Penalty Asia Network et al. (2021). Malaysia Universal Periodic Review Mid Term. https://www.ohchr.org/Documents/HRBodies/UPR/NGOsMidTermReports/ADPAN_Malaysia.pdf. Accessed 16 December 2021.

Association of Southeast Asian Nations. (2021). ASEAN member states. https://asean.org/about-asean/member-states/. Accessed 16 December 2021.

Balay Rehabilitation Center. (n.d.). Fact Sheet: Note on the death penalty and the Philippines. https://balayph.net/news-events/features-and-articles/128-fact-sheet-note-on-the-death-penalty-and-the-philippines-2. Accessed 16 December 2021.

BBC News. (2016, May 16). Philippines: Duterte vows to bring back death penalty. *BBC News*. https://www.bbc.com/news/world-asia-36297583. Accessed 16 May 2021.

Bernas, J. G., & S. J. (2009). *The 1987 Constitution of the Republic of the Philippines: A Commentary*. Rex Printing Company Inc.

Buan, L. (2020, August 6). Duterte gov't, allies push for death penalty without clear data on deterrent effect. *Rappler*. https://www.rappler.com/nation/duterte-government-allies-push-death-penalty-without-clear-data/. Accessed 16 December 2021.

Cambodian League for the Promotion and Defense of Human Rights (*Ligue cambodgienne de défense des droits de l'homme*) [LICADHO]. (2007). Abolition of death penalty: Ratification of 2nd Optional Protocol to the ICCPR & Cambodia [A LICADHO Briefing Paper, January 2007]. https://www.licadho-cambodia.org/reports/files/102LICADHOPaper2ndOptionalProtocolICCPR07.pdf. Accessed 16 December 2021.

Chandler, D. (n.d.). Cambodia: A historical overview. https://asiasociety.org/education/cambodia-historical-overview. Accessed 16 December 2021.

Chandler, D. P., & Overton, L. C. (2021, March 10). *Cambodia. Encyclopedia Britannica*. https://www.britannica.com/place/Cambodia. Accessed 16 December 2021.

CNN Philippines Staff. (2021, November 4). Lacson, Sotto: Lifetime imprisonment preferred over death penalty. *CNN Philippines*. https://www.cnnphilippines.com/news/2021/11/4/lacson-sotto-imprisonment-death-penalty.html. Accessed 16 December 2021.

Commission on Human Rights & Christopher Ward. (2017, March 7). In defense of the right to life: International law and death penalty in the Philippines. http://regnet.anu.edu.au/sites/default/files/uploads/2017-03/In-Defense-of-the-Right-to-Life-IL-and-Death-Penalty-in-the-Philippines.pdf. Accessed 16 December 2021.

Conde, C. H. (2003, December 6). Philippines reinstates death penalty. *The New York Times*. https://www.nytimes.com/2003/12/06/news/philippines-reinstates-death-penalty.html. Accessed 16 December 2021.

Constitutional Council of Cambodia (n.d.). Background. https://www.ccc.gov.kh/historyccc_en.php. Accessed 16 December 2021.

Corey-Boulet, R. (2009, August 19). The world's first genocide trial, 30 years on. *The Phnom Penh Post*. https://www.phnompenhpost.com/national/worlds-first-genocide-trial-30-years. Accessed 16 December 2021.

Diaz, J. (2017, February 18). House eyes early vote on death penalty bill. *The Philippine Star*. https://www.philstar.com/headlines/2017/02/18/1672686/house-eyes-early-vote-death-penalty-bill. Accessed 16 December 2021.

Easton, A. (1999, February 6). Rapist dies as Manila brings back execution. *The Guardian*. https://www.theguardian.com/world/1999/feb/06/philippines. Accessed 16 December 2021.

Encyclopedia Britannica (n.d.a). Supreme National Council, Cambodian government. https://www.britannica.com/topic/Supreme-National-Council. Accessed 16 December 2021.

Encyclopedia Britannica (n.d.b). Vietnamese intervention. https://www.britannica.com/place/Cambodia/Vietnamese-intervention . Accessed 16 December 2021.

Evans, G. (2019, February 21). Gareth Evans, a Pillar of the Paris Peace Accords, on "Seeking Justice in Cambodia". *Voice of America (VOA) Cambodia*. https://www.voacambodia.com/a/gareth-evans-a-pillar-of-the-paris-peace-accords-on-seeking-justice-in-cambodia/4796311.html. Accessed 16 December 2021.

GMA News. (2006, May 31). Arroyo certifies as urgent bill abolishing death penalty. *GMA News*. https://www.gmanetwork.com/news/news/nation/7407/arroyo-certifies-as-urgent-bill-abolishing-death-penalty/story/. Accessed 16 December 2021.

Hood, R. G., & Hoyle, C. (2008). *The death penalty: A worldwide perspective* (4th ed.). Oxford University Press.

Hoyle, C. & Jabbar, P. (2021, June 30). No barrier to abolition: Analysing attitudes to the death penalty in Indonesia. University of Oxford Faculty of Law: Death Penalty Research Unit Blog. https://www.law.ox.ac.uk/research-and-subject-groups/death-penalty-research-unit/blog/2021/06/no-barrier-abolition-analysing. Accessed 16 December 2021.

Hoyle, C. (2021a). *Investigating attitudes to the death penalty in Indonesia part I – Opinion formers: An appetite for change*. London: The Death Penalty Project. https://www.deathpenaltyproject.org/wp-content/uploads/2021a/06/DPP-Indonesia-Opinion-Formers-Report_Web.pdf. Accessed 16 December 2021a.

Hoyle, C. (2021b). *Investigating attitudes to the death penalty in Indonesia part II – Public opinion: No barrier to abolition*. London: The Death Penalty Project. https://www.deathpenaltyproject.org/wp-content/uploads/2021b/06/DPP-Indonesia-Public-Opinion-Report_Web.pdf. Accessed 16 December 2021b.

Human Rights Watch. (2021, July 21). Myanmar: Junta tribunals impose 65 death sentences. *Human Rights Watch*. https://www.hrw.org/news/2021/07/21/myanmar-junta-tribunals-impose-65-death-sentences. Accessed 16 December 2021.

Hutt, D. (2019, March 12). Lessons from Hun Sen's death penalty U-turn. *Asia Times*. https://asiatimes.com/2019/03/lessons-from-hun-sens-death-penalty-u-turn/. Accessed 16 December 2021.

International Commission Against Death Penalty (n.d.). UNGA Moratorium Resolution Table. https://icomdp.org/map-unga/. Accessed 16 December 2021.

Jørgensen, N. H. B. (2018). *The Elgar companion to the Extraordinary Chambers in the Courts of Cambodia*. Edward Elgar.

Joseph, B. (2021, November 12). Why is Asia clinging to the death penalty?. *UCA News*. https://www.ucanews.com/news/why-is-asia-clinging-to-the-death-penalty/94935. Accessed 16 December 2021.

Kamarudin, F. (2018, October 11). Online poll reveals majority of netizens opposed to death penalty abolition. *New Straits Times*. https://www.nst.com.my/news/nation/2018/10/420315/online-poll-reveals-majority-netizens-opposed-death-penalty-abolition. Accessed 16 December 2021.

Kyodo. (2019, March 10). 'Just a thought': Cambodia leader Hun Sen considers death sentence for rapists. *South China Morning Post*. https://www.scmp.com/news/asia/southeast-asia/article/2189430/cambodia-leader-hun-sen-considers-death-sentence-rapists. Accessed 16 December 2021.

Lee, Y. N. (2020, May 18). Malaysia's political crisis could worsen coronavirus and economic challenges. *CNBC*. https://www.cnbc.com/2020/05/18/malaysia-has-triple-crisis-of-coronavirus-economy-and-politics-analyst.html. Accessed 16 December 2021.

Macapagal-Arroyo, G. (2006, June 24). Speech of President Arroyo on the signing of the Abolition of Death Penalty [Delivered at the Rizal Hall, Malacañang, 24 June 2006]. *Official Gazette*. https://www.officialgazette.gov.ph/2006/06/24/speech-of-president-arroyo-on-the-signing-of-the-abolition-of-death-penalty/. Accessed 16 December 2021.

McFadden, R. D. (2020, March 4). Javier Pérez de Cuéllar dies at 100; U.N. chief brokered peace pacts. *The New York Times*. https://www.nytimes.com/2020/03/04/obituaries/javier-perez-de-cuellar-dead.html. Accessed 16 December 2021.

Medina, A. F. (2021, August 18). Malaysian prime minister resigns, deepening political crisis. *ASEAN Briefing*. https://www.aseanbriefing.com/news/malaysian-prime-minister-resigns-deepening-political-crisis/. Accessed 16 December 2021.

Mydans, S. (1998, April 17). Death of Pol Pot; Pol Pot, brutal dictator who forced Cambodians to killing fields, dies at 73. *The New York Times*. https://www.nytimes.com/1998/04/17/world/death-pol-pot-pol-pot-brutal-dictator-who-forced-cambodians-killing-fields-dies.html. Accessed 16 December 2021.

Nichols, M. (2021, October 22). Outgoing U.N. envoy says Myanmar has spiralled into civil war. *Reuters*. https://www.reuters.com/world/asia-pacific/outgoing-un-envoy-says-myanmar-has-spiraled-into-civil-war-2021-10-21/. Accessed 16 December 2021.

Nicolau, I. (2013). Historical evolution of the death penalty abolition as a fundamental human right. *Contemporary Readings in Law and Social Justice, 5*(2), 278–283.

Office of the United Nations High Commissioner for Human Rights [UNOHCHR]. (2022, June 20). Malaysia: UN experts welcome announcement to abolish mandatory death penalty [Press release]. https://www.ohchr.org/en/press-releases/2022/06/malaysia-un-experts-welcome-announcement-abolish-mandatory-death-penalty. Accessed 11 July 2022.

Office of the United Nations High Commissioner for Human Rights [UNOHCHR]. (2019, April 1). Bachelet urges Brunei to stop entry into force of "draconian" new penal code. *UNOHCHR*. https://www.ohchr.org/EN/NewsEvents/Pages/DisplayNews.aspx?NewsID=24432&LangID=E. Accessed 16 December 2021.

Pascoe, D. & Bae, S. (2021, May 18). Latest developments in the UNGA death penalty moratorium resolutions. *University of Oxford Faculty of Law: Death Penalty Research Unit Blog*. https://www.law.ox.ac.uk/research-and-subject-groups/death-penalty-research-unit/blog/2021/05/latest-developments-unga-death. Accessed 16 December 2021.

Philippine Center for Investigative Journalism. (2006, June 24). The politics of convenience: How legislators voted on the death penalty. Philippine Center for Investigative Journalism Blog. https://old.pcij.org/blog/2006/06/24/the-politics-of-convenience-how-legislators-voted-on-the-death-penalty. Accessed 16 December 2021.

Pillay, N. & Dreifuss, R. (2020, December 17). Many countries cheer gains to ending the death penalty globally, but foes harden their stance. *PassBlue*. https://www.passblue.com/2020/12/17/many-countries-cheer-gains-to-ending-the-death-penalty-globally-but-foes-harden-their-stance/. Accessed 16 December 2021.

Porcalla, D. (2000, March 8). 2 convicts to die before Holy Week. *The Philippine Star*. https://www.philstar.com/headlines/2000/03/08/95260/2-convicts-die-holy-week. Accessed 16 December 2021.

Republic of the Philippines, House of Representatives [Philippine House of Representatives]. (2021). House Bills and Resolutions (Search Results for "death penalty" within the 18th Congress). https://www.congress.gov.ph/legisdocs/?v=billsresults (search for "death penalty"). Accessed 16 December 2021.

Republic of the Philippines, Senate [Philippine Senate]. (2021). Senate Bills (Search Results for "death penalty" within the 18th Congress). http://legacy.senate.gov.ph/lis/leg_sys.aspx?congress=18&type=bill (search for "death penalty"). Accessed 16 December 2021.

Schabas, W. A. (2002). *The abolition of the death penalty in international law* (3rd ed.). Cambridge University Press.

Schabas, W. A. (2014). The death penalty project: Annual lecture 2014 entitled "Universal abolition: Only a decade away" by William Schabas, Professor of International Law, Middlesex University London. https://www.deathpenaltyproject.org/knowledge/the-death-penalty-project-annual-lecture-2014/ (0:6:00 to 0:38:00 of the video). Accessed 16 December 2021.

Sokhean, B. (2019a, March 12). Hun Sen shifts stance on death penalty. *Khmer Times*. https://www.khmertimeskh.com/585852/hun-sen-shifts-stance-on-death-penalty/. Accessed 16 December 2021.

Sokhean, B. (2019b, March 11). Hun Sen mulls death penalty for child rapists. *Khmer Times*. https://www.khmertimeskh.com/50585534/hun-sen-mulls-death-penalty-for-child-rapists/. Accessed 16 December 2021.

The Straits Times. (2017, March 18). Indonesia's president Joko Widodo says open to death penalty review. *The Straits Times*. https://www.straitstimes.com/asia/se-asia/indonesias-president-joko-widodo-says-open-to-death-penalty-review. Accessed 16 December 2021.

Together against the Death Penalty (*Ensemble contre la peine de mort*) [ECPM]. (2020). Our interactive map: The death penalty worldwide. https://www.ecpm.org/en/the-death-penalty-worldwide/. Accessed 16 December 2021.

UN News. (2019, April 4). UN agencies urge Brunei to repeal new 'extreme and unjustified' penal code. *UN News*. https://news.un.org/en/story/2019/04/1036121. Accessed 16 December 2021.

United Nations Peacekeeping (n.d.). Cambodia—UNTAC Background [UN Peacekeeping, Cambodia—UNTAC Background]. https://peacekeeping.un.org/sites/default/files/past/untacbackgr2.html. Accessed 16 December 2021.

Villanueva, M. (2003, November 30). Moratorium on death penalty stays. *The Philippine Star*. https://www.philstar.com/headlines/2003/11/30/229792/moratorium-death-penalty-stays. Accessed 16 December 2021.
von Glahn, G. (1981). *Law among nations: An Introduction to Public International Law* (4th ed.). MacMillian.
Washington University in St. Louis School of Law. (2012). Legal English: "De Facto/De Jure". https://onlinelaw.wustl.edu/blog/legal-english-de-factode-jure/. Accessed 16 December 2021.

Legal Sources and Materials

Bayan (Bagong Alyansang Makabayan) v. Zamora, 342 SCRA 449 (Supreme Court of the Republic of the Philippines), G.R. No. 138570 (10 October 2000).
Human Rights Committee. (2019). General Comment No. 36: Article 6: Right to Life (2019 September 3). U.N. Doc. CCPR/C/GC/36. https://undocs.org/CCPR/C/GC/36. Accessed 16 December 2021.
Kingdom of Cambodia. Constitution of the Kingdom of Cambodia (1993) [1993 Cambodian Constitution] (unofficial translated version supervised by the Constitutional Council, October 2015). https://www.ccc.gov.kh/datapublic/subdata/Constitution%20of%20the%20Kingdom%20of%20Cambodia.pdf. Accessed 16 December 2021.
People v. Echegaray, 267 SCRA 682 (Supreme Court of the Republic of the Philippines), G.R. No. 117472 (7 February 1997) (resolution of motion for reconsideration).
People v. Mateo, 433 SCRA 640 (Supreme Court of the Republic of the Philippines), G.R. Nos. 147678–87 (7 July 2004).
Republic of the Philippines, 1987 Constitution [1987 Philippine Constitution]. https://www.officialgazette.gov.ph/constitutions/1987-constitution/. Accessed 16 December 2021.
Republic of the Philippines, Commission on Human Rights [Philippine CHR]. (2017). Advisory on the Validity of the Philippines' Ratification of the Second Optional Protocol. CHR (V) A2020–017. https://chr.gov.ph/wp-content/uploads/2020/10/07082020_Advisory_on_Ratification-Death-Penalty.pdf. Accessed 16 December 2021.
Republic of the Philippines, Constitutional Commission of 1986 [1986 Philippine Constitutional Commission]. (1986). Record of the Constitutional Commission [R.C.C.]: Proceedings and Debates, Volume 1.
Republic of the Philippines, House of Representatives, Congressional Record [Philippine Congressional Record]. (2006). Congressional Record: Vol. 13, No. 67, 13th Congress, 2nd Regular Session (6 June 2006). https://hrep-website.s3.ap-southeast-1.amazonaws.com/legisdocs/congrec/13th/2nd/2RS-67.pdf. Accessed 16 December 2021.
Republic of the Philippines, House of Representatives, House Bill No. 1 [Philippine House Bill No. 1]. (2016). House Bill No. 1: An Act Imposing the Death Penalty on Certain Heinous Crimes, Repealing for the Purpose Republic Act No. 9346, Entitled "An Act Prohibiting the Imposition of Death Penalty in the Philippines" and Amending Act No. 3815, as Amended, Otherwise Known as the "Revised Penal Code", and Other Special Penal Laws, House Bill No. 1, 17th Congress, 1st Reg. Session (2016). https://hrep-website.s3.ap-southeast-1.amazonaws.com/legisdocs/basic_17/HB00001.pdf. Accessed 16 December 2021.
Republic of the Philippines, Republic Act No. 7659 [Philippine Republic Act No. 7659]. (1993). An Act to Impose the Death Penalty on Certain Heinous Crimes, Amending for That Purpose the Revised Penal Code, as Amended, Other Special Laws, and for Other Purposes. (13 December 1993).
Republic of the Philippines, Republic Act No. 9346. [Philippine Republic Act No. 9346]. (2006). An Act Prohibiting the Imposition of Death Penalty in the Philippines. (24 June 2006).

Republic of the Philippines, Senate, Journal [Philippine Senate Journal]. (2006). Senate Journal: Session No. 89, 13th Congress, 2nd Regular Session (6 June 2006). http://legacy.senate.gov.ph/lisdata/57666101!.pdf. Accessed 16 December 2021.

Second Optional Protocol to the International Covenant on Civil and Political Rights, Aiming at the Abolition of the Death Penalty [ICCPR-OP2], *adopted* 15 December 1989, 1642 U.N.T.S. 414 (entered into force on 11 July 1991). https://treaties.un.org/doc/Publication/UNTS/Volume%201642/v1642.pdf. Accessed 16 December 2021.

Second Optional Protocol to the International Covenant on Civil and Political Rights, Aiming at the Abolition of the Death Penalty, Ratification: Philippines [ICCPR-OP2 Ratification: Philippines], 2482 U.N.T.S. 262 (deposit of instrument with the Secretary-General of the United Nations: 20 November 2007; date of effect: 20 February 2008). https://treaties.un.org/doc/Publication/UNTS/Volume%202482/v2482.pdf. Accessed 16 December 2021.

Supreme National Council (SNC) of Cambodia. (1992). Provisions Relating to the Judiciary and Criminal Law and Procedure Applicable in Cambodia during the Transitional Period [SNC Cambodia Provisions]. Decision of 10 September 1992 (unofficial English translation by United National Development Fund and the Council of Jurists of the Office of the Council of Ministers of Cambodia). https://ihl-databases.icrc.org/applic/ihl/ihl-nat.nsf/xsp/.ibmmodres/domino/OpenAttachment/applic/ihl/ihl-nat.nsf/B7C708687DC5D7D8C1256A3F0055A780/TEXT/Provisions%20Judiciary%20and%20Criminal%20Law%20-%20Cambodia%20-%20EN.pdf. Accessed 16 December 2021.

United Nations General Assembly [UNGA]. (2007). United Nations General Assembly Resolution, Moratorium on the Use of the Death Penalty. U.N. Doc. A/RES/62/149 (18 December 2007). https://undocs.org/A/RES/62/149. Accessed 16 December 2021.

UNGA. (2008a). Resolutions and Decisions adopted by the General Assembly during its sixty-second session, Volume 1, Resolutions, 18 September—22 December 2007. U.N. Doc. A/62/49 (Vol. I). https://undocs.org/A/62/49(Vol.I)(SUPP). Accessed 16 December 2021.

UNGA. (2008b). United Nations General Assembly Resolution, Moratorium on the Use of the Death Penalty. U.N. Doc. A/RES/63/168 (18 December 2008). https://undocs.org/en/A/RES/63/168. Accessed 16 December 2021.

UNGA. (2009). Resolutions and Decisions adopted by the General Assembly during its sixth-third session, Volume 1, Resolutions, 16 September—24 December 2008. U.N. Doc. A/63/49 (Vol. I). https://undocs.org/A/63/49(Vol.I)(SUPP). Accessed 16 December 2021.

UNGA. (2010). United Nations General Assembly Resolution, Moratorium on the Use of the Death Penalty. U.N. Doc. A/RES/65/206 (21 December 2010). https://undocs.org/A/RES/65/206. Accessed 16 December 2021.

UNGA. (2011). Resolutions and Decisions adopted by the General Assembly during its sixty-fifth session, Volume 1, Resolutions, 14 September—24 December 2010. U.N. Doc. A/65/49 (Vol. I). https://undocs.org/A/65/49(Vol.I). Accessed 16 December 2021.

UNGA. (2012). United Nations General Assembly Resolution, Moratorium on the Use of the Death Penalty. U.N. Doc. A/RES/67/176 (20 December 2012). https://undocs.org/en/A/RES/67/176. Accessed 16 December 2021.

UNGA. (2013). Resolutions and Decisions adopted by the General Assembly during its sixty-seventh session, Volume 1, Resolutions, 18 September—24 December 2012. U.N. Doc. A/67/49 (Vol. I). https://undocs.org/A/67/49(Vol.I). Accessed 16 December 2021.

UNGA. (2014). United Nations General Assembly Resolution, Moratorium on the Use of the Death Penalty. U.N. Doc. A/RES/69/186 (18 December 2014). https://undocs.org/en/A/RES/69/186. Accessed 16 December 2021.

UNGA. (2015). Resolutions and Decisions adopted by the General Assembly during its sixth-ninth session, Volume 1, Resolutions, 16 September—29 December 2014. U.N. Doc. A/69/49 (Vol. I). https://undocs.org/en/A/69/49(Vol.I). Accessed 16 December 2021.

UNGA. (2016a). United Nations General Assembly Resolution, Moratorium on the Use of the Death Penalty. U.N. Doc. A/RES/71/187 (19 December 2016a). https://undocs.org/en/A/RES/71/187. Accessed 16 December 2021.

UNGA. (2016b). United Nations General Assembly Seventy-first session: Official Records, Third Committee, Summary record of the 50th meeting, Held at Headquarters, New York, on Thursday, 17 November 2016b, at 10 a.m. U.N. Doc. A/C.3/71/SR.50. https://undocs.org/A/C.3/71/SR.50. Accessed 16 December 2021.

UNGA. (2016c). Promotion and protection of human rights: Human rights questions, including alternative approaches for improving the effective enjoyment of human rights and fundamental freedoms: Report of the Third Committee, Rapporteur: Cécile Mballa Eyenga (Cameroon). U.N. Doc. A/71/484/Add.2. https://undocs.org/A/71/484/Add.2. Accessed 16 December 2021.

UNGA. (2017a). Resolutions and Decisions adopted by the General Assembly during its seventy-first session, Volume 1, Resolutions, 13 September—23 December 2016. U.N. Doc. A/71/49 (Vol. I). https://undocs.org/en/A/71/49(Vol.I). Accessed 16 December 2021.

UNGA. (2018). United Nations General Assembly Resolution, Moratorium on the Use of the Death Penalty. U.N. Doc. A/RES/73/175 (17 December 2018). https://undocs.org/en/A/RES/73/175. Accessed 16 December 2021.

UNGA. (2019). Resolutions and Decisions adopted by the General Assembly during its seventy-third session, Volume 1, Resolutions, 18 September—22 December 2018. U.N. Doc. A/73/49 (Vol. I). https://undocs.org/en/A/73/49(Vol.I). Accessed 16 December 2021.

UNGA. (2020a). United Nations General Assembly Resolution, Moratorium on the Use of the Death Penalty. U.N. Doc. A/RES/75/183 (16 December 2020a). https://undocs.org/A/RES/75/183. Accessed 16 December 2021.

UNGA. (2020b). United Nations General Assembly, Seventy-fifth session, Third Committee, Antigua and Barbuda, Bahrain, Bangladesh, Belize, Botswana, Brunei Darussalam, China, Democratic People's Republic of Korea, Egypt, Indonesia, Iran (Islamic Republic of), Jamaica, Jordan, Kuwait, Lao People's Democratic Republic, Libya, Nigeria, Oman, Pakistan, Papua New Guinea, Qatar, Russian Federation, Saint Kitts and Nevis, Saint Vincent and the Grenadines, Saudi Arabia, Singapore, Sudan, Syrian Arab Republic, Uganda, United Arab Emirates, Viet Nam, Yemen and Zimbabwe: Amendment to draft resolution A/C.3/75/L.41. U.N. Doc. A/C.3/75/L.54. https://undocs.org/A/C.3/75/L.54. Accessed 16 December 2021.

UNGA. (2020c). Promotion and protection of human rights: Human rights questions, including alternative approaches for improving the effective enjoyment of human rights and fundamental freedoms: Report of the Third Committee, Rapporteur: Ms. Myriam Oehri (Liechtenstein). U.N. Doc. A/75/478/Add.2. https://undocs.org/A/75/478/Add.2. Accessed 16 December 2021.

UNGA. (2021a). Resolutions and Decisions adopted by the General Assembly during its seventy-fifth session, Volume 1, Resolutions, 15 September—31 December 2020. U.N. Doc. A/75/49 (Vol. I). https://undocs.org/en/A/75/49(Vol.I). Accessed 16 December 2021a.

UNGA. (2021b). Role and achievements of the Office of the United Nations High Commissioner for Human Rights in assisting the Government and people of Cambodia in the promotion and protection of human rights: Report of the Secretary-General (15 August 2014). https://undocs.org/A/HRC/48/49. Accessed 16 December 2021b.

UNGA & United Nations Security Council [UNSC]. (1991). Letter dated 30 October 1991 from the Permanent Representative of France and Indonesia to the United Nations addressed to the Secretary-General, U.N. Doc. A-46/608-S/23177. https://undocs.org/S/23177. Accessed 16 December 2021.

United Nations Economic and Social Council [ECOSOC]. (2020). Capital punishment and implementation of the safeguards guaranteeing protection of the rights of those facing the death penalty: Report of the Secretary-General, U.N. Doc. E/2020/53 (17 April 2020). https://undocs.org/en/E/2020/53. Accessed 16 December 2021.

United Nations Peacekeeping. Cambodia—UNTAC Mandate [UN Peacekeeping, Cambodia—UNTAC Mandate]. https://peacekeeping.un.org/sites/default/files/past/untacmandate.html. Accessed 16 December 2021.

UNSC. (1992). Resolution 745 (1992) of 28 February 1992 on establishment of the UN Transitional Authority in Cambodia (UNTAC), U.N. Doc. S/RES/745 (1992) (28 February 1992). https://undocs.org/S/RES/745(1992). Accessed 16 December 2021.

Ma. Ngina Teresa V. Chan-Gonzaga is currently Professor and Associate Dean for Academic Affairs of the Ateneo de Manila University School of Law. Her areas of interest include human rights, political law, civil law, and legal ethics. Prior to joining Ateneo Law full time, she served as Commissioner of the Philippine Presidential Commission on Good Government. Previous professional commitments include engagements with Romulo Mabanta Buenaventura Sayoc & De Los Angeles Law Office and the Ateneo Human Rights Center. She was also Program Officer of the Working Group for an ASEAN Human Rights Mechanism.

She obtained her Juris Doctor degree from the Ateneo Law in 2002 and obtained her Magister Juris from Oxford University in 2008. She has been teaching at Ateneo Law since admission to the Philippine Bar in 2003 and served as the Civil Law bar examiner for the Philippine National Bar Examinations in 2018.

ASEAN and the Death Penalty: Theoretical and Legal Views and a Pathway to Abolition

Sriprapha Petcharamesree, Raine Boonlong, and Danthong Breen

Abstract This concluding chapter reviews how retentionist countries often seek to justify their use of capital punishment by relying on punishment theories that draw a distinction between the infliction of just punishment and arbitrary and unjust violence by the State. It also examines how the continuing use of capital punishment in Southeast Asian countries has been explained by some experts to reflect the distinctive Asian perception of human rights, being one that oversees the prevalence of community rights over individual rights, thus reinforcing the desideratum of the State to accentuate stringent punishment for offenders who are viewed as rebelling against the regiments of State control.

There has been an undeniable worldwide decline in retention over the last forty years. This chapter, therefore, asks why, despite this inexorable global trend and the universal recognition of human rights, do most ASEAN States cling to retentionist principles and policies? Moving beyond traditional theories on criminal justice, particularly retribution and utilitarianism, this chapter attempts to conceptually unpack the factors used to justify the retention of the death penalty in the region. It concludes that the death penalty situation in the eight ASEAN countries remains rather static and the record somehow reveals a very mixed reality, reflecting the absence of any shared policy on the death penalty among AMS other than the proviso, 'in accordance with law'. Some observations and recommendations are then made for Member States to consider possible steps towards the abolition of the death penalty.

S. Petcharamesree (✉)
Institute of Human Rights and Peace Studies, Mahidol University, Nakornpathom, Thailand
e-mail: sripraphapet@gmail.com

R. Boonlong
Freelance, Huai Khwang, Thailand

D. Breen
Union for Civil Liberty, Huai Khwang, Thailand
e-mail: danthong@laposte.net

S. Petcharamesree et al. (eds.), *Unpacking the Death Penalty in ASEAN*,
https://doi.org/10.1007/978-981-19-8840-0_8

1 Introduction

The history of capital punishment can be traced back into antiquity and has been used by societies to punish a wide variety of so-called crimes. Subjecting a person to the punishment of death has, for the most part, been perceived as a customary practice. It was only after World War II when human rights spiralled in importance as a result of the world powers seeking to hinder further atrocities that the practice of capital punishment came under heightened scrutiny. This escalating importance of human rights has led to a more compassionate attitude towards punishment and was accompanied by a move towards the abolition of the death penalty, a movement that gained particular momentum in the late 1980s (Daems, 2011). Increasingly, opponents of capital punishment commonly regard it to be a blatant violation of fundamental human rights, namely, the right to life and the right not to be subject to cruel, inhuman, or degrading treatment or punishment (Hood & Kovalev, 1999).

Capital punishment entails the deliberate deprivation of life authorised by the State and encompasses a legal process by which violators of the law are condemned and subject to sanctions prescribed by specified legal procedures. Criminal punishment requires convincing justification for two main reasons. First, it causes the infliction of harm or detriment to the offender, either through loss of liberty or harsh treatment and second, it involves the expenditure of public resources that may or may not be put to better use for other more imperative needs. Retentionist countries often seek to justify the use of capital punishment by relying on punishment theories that draw a distinction between the infliction of just punishment and arbitrary and unjust violence by the State. Popular penal policy justifications alluded to by retentionist governments cite the effectiveness of capital punishment as a tool for deterring crime, as well as the necessity of capital punishment to inflict retribution, that can best be described by the scriptural expression 'an eye for an eye, a tooth for a tooth'. Also, according to retentionist countries, capital punishment ensures the incapacitation of the offender by preventing the commission of further crimes (Hodgkinson et al., 2010, pp. 8–10). Debates on capital punishment as a measure of deterrence were unpacked in Chapter 2.

Southeast Asia maintains a stronghold on capital punishment, with eight out of ten of the ASEAN Member States (AMS) adopting a retentionist stance. Conversely, Cambodia and the Philippines, as well as Timor-Leste (whose application to ASEAN has been under review since 2011), have declared themselves abolitionists for all crimes. By contrast, Brunei, Myanmar, and Laos are de facto abolitionist. Retentionist countries employ different concepts to justify capital punishment. Essentially, the four main theories of justification for criminal punishment as proposed by several seminal works on the topic are retribution, utilitarianism, incapacitation, and rehabilitation, all of which will be discussed in later sections.

This chapter intends to review how retentionist countries often seek to justify their use of capital punishment. It also examines how the continuing presence of capital punishment in ASEAN countries has been explained by experts as reflecting a distinctive Asian perception of human rights, being one that oversees the prevalence of community rights over individual rights, thus reinforcing the desideratum of the State to accentuate stringent punishment for offenders who are viewed as rebelling against the regiments of State control.

Whilst there has been an undeniable worldwide decline in retention over the last forty years, this concluding chapter asks why most ASEAN States cling to retentionist principles and policies despite this inexorable global trend and the universal recognition of human rights. Moving beyond traditional theories of criminal justice, particularly retribution and utilitarianism, this chapter attempts to unpack the factors cited to conceptually justify the retention of the death penalty in the region. Observations and recommendations are made for Member States seeking to take steps towards its abolition.

Following this introduction, the second section attempts to unpack punishment theories while section three analyses the concepts of punishment in ASEAN and the forces shaping them. This segment also examines the reasons why, despite this inexorable global trend and the universal recognition of human rights, most ASEAN States uphold retentionist principles and policies despite the nebulous distinction between just punishment and arbitrary and unjust violence by the State. Finally, section four demonstrates current progressive practices of punishment by AMS which may pave the way for further steps towards the abolition of the death penalty before the paper concludes.

2 Unpacking Punishment Theories

The fear of acts which disrupt social equilibrium has inspired the imposition of punishment by those who have the power to establish and enforce desired standards of conduct (Mayer 1969). Punishment is defined by Meyer (1969) as

> the method which society uses to enforce the desired standards of conduct and methods of dealing with the offender after a crime has been committed. This definition includes the use of torture, imprisonment and treatment (p. 595)

Several elements determine the forces shaping the concept of punishment and the type(s) of punishments being enforced in different countries. One of the cited justification is to address and prevent any acts considered to disrupt the 'social equilibrium'. The punishment is designed and decided by those in power meaning the governments and agencies concerned. It can take many forms ranging from imprisonment (which allows rehabilitation) to torture with its most extreme form arguably being capital punishment. Although the argument that the death penalty constitutes torture is not conclusive, a growing number of regional and domestic opinions and decisions have held that the death penalty constitutes cruel, inhuman, or degrading treatment or even torture, regardless of the methods or circumstances of implementation, or the particular individuals upon whom it is imposed (Mendez, 2012). So, the punishment is mainly determined and justified by the power in place.

Although from a moral perspective criminal punishment may be a universally endorsed concept across the globe, several difficulties arise. Authors espousing the moral perspectives of criminal punishment mostly point to the morality of inflicting pain or suffering on offenders. Therefore, the need to justify punishment as a legitimate form of State practice becomes paramount. Out of this need, four main theories of justification for criminal punishment were proposed: retribution, utilitarianism, incapacitation, and rehabilitation (Boonin, 2008; Hall, 2000).

Incapacitation is a theory that seeks to prevent the lawbreaker from reoffending, whilst rehabilitation seeks to provide therapy to an offender to prevent criminal recidivism. Incapacitation and rehabilitation do not seek to justify capital punishment, because incapacitation can be equally applied to imprisonment, and rehabilitation is not possible in terms of the death sentence. Because capital punishment is mainly justified by retribution and utilitarianism, this review will concentrate on the discourse surrounding those two theories.

Retribution refers to offenders receiving his or her 'just deserts' for a crime, and demonstrates the principle of *lex talionis* (commonly understood as 'giving to each his due') to define retribution or compensation perfectly proportional to the harm caused (Van Drunen, 2008). Contrary to prevalent belief, the intention of retributive justice is not to seek revenge but to impose a penalty on the offender proportionate to the crime committed. According to Hall, retributive justice is based on the rationale that when an offender commits a crime, he or she generates an imbalance in the justice system that can only be reinstated by punishing the offender (Hall, 2000, p. 195).

The philosopher, Immanuel Kant, has been afforded a prominent status among retributivists. Authors such as Hall, Finkelstein, Hill, and Yost all refer to the works of Kant in their discussions on retribution. Kant argued that retribution can be divided into two categories: 'strict retribution' and 'proportional retribution'. The former refers to the punishment being the same kind of harm as the crime committed; in other words, punishment is identical to the actual crime itself. 'Proportional retribution' constitutes punishment not identical to the crime, but rather proportionate to it. Kant's suggestion involves the use of 'strict retribution' only when it is morally and physically possible to do so. For example, the crime of murder can be punished by killing the offender. However, 'strict retribution' is not morally permissible for the crime of rape because it involves another person raping the rapist. Thus, rape must be punished by 'proportional retribution' which in today's world generally equates to imprisonment (Yost, 2010, pp. 5–6). 'Proportional retribution', according to Kant, does not entail the State inflicting on offenders the evil they inflicted on others. Rather, Kant recognised the limits of the concept, 'an eye for an eye', realising the impossibility of subjecting offenders to similarly atrocious acts. Kant's position can be best understood as an affirmation that all guilty offenders should be punished by conforming to the *lex talionis* principle *as closely as possible,* rather than literally taking 'an eye for an eye' (Hill, 1999, p. 433). Kant viewed the destruction of life (being the most valuable of man's possessions) or murder as one of the worst possible crimes because in his view, humans use life as a means of exercising freedom. Since he perceived murder as one of the worst crimes (similar to the modern concept of 'most serious crimes' discussed in Chapter 3), he urged use of the death sentence because its effect most closely resembles the crime of murder in terms of severity (Yost, 2010, pp. 7–8).

The other theory used to justify capital punishment is utilitarianism. Unlike retribution, the application of utilitarianism concerns itself with the benefits of punishment, rather than whether offenders deserve to be punished. The utilitarian theory states that punishment, including capital punishment, is morally permissible so long as it serves the greater good to society. This greater good refers to deterrence of crime in two situations: the first entails specific deterrence when offenders are personally prevented from re-offending; and the second involves general deterrence, whereby members of society are discouraged from offending after witnessing the punishment imposed on the offender—both result in a safer society (Hall, 2000, p. 209; Haist, 2009, p. 794).

As theories justifying punishment, both retribution and utilitarianism have inherent shortcomings. The inadequacies of utilitarianism stem from three contentions. First, the statistical evidence used to prove its deterrent effect is usually inconclusive in that it fails to validate capital punishment as a more effective deterrent than life imprisonment. At the same time, the evidence also fails to negate the view that capital punishment is a stronger deterrent than life imprisonment (Brudner, 1980, pp. 338–441; see also Chapter 2). Second, because utilitarianism justifies punishment based on its presumed deterrent effect, States may condone the punishment of the innocent simply to make an example of someone to further its deterrence measures. Therefore, punishing the innocent is condoned as long as it constitutes a deterrent to others as it would lead to more benefits than costs (Weiner et al., 1997, p. 448). Third, individuals presumed to be offenders are used as examples by States. This 'use' deprives individuals of their autonomy and dignity as human beings; instead, they are perceived as mere tools by the State to further its primary goal of deterrence (Hill, 1999, p. 430). The issue of dignity on death row was discussed in Chapter 4.

Likewise, retribution as a justification also has its drawbacks. Hall argues that determining the proportionality of punishment constitutes a challenge because it is difficult to balance the punishment against the severity of the crime and the degree of guilt of the offender. Oftentimes, similar crimes are given different types of punishment, depicting a lack of consistency in determining proportionality (Hall, 2000, p. 198). Moreover, in determining proportionality, mitigating factors must also be weighed against the severity of the crime. However, when mitigating factors are based on a person's emotions, the process is deprived of rationality. Further, grounding the weight of mitigating factors on emotions may lead to unwarranted leniency or even a desire for forgiveness which would further defy the purpose of retribution, requiring as it does the infliction of punishment in response to a wrongful act (Hall, 2000, p. 204).

Arguments against these theories of punishment were advanced by Boonin in *The Problem of Punishment* in which he asserts the problematic nature of criminal or legal punishment, especially questioning why it is morally permissible for States to treat offenders in ways it would be morally reprehensible to treat non-offenders. Criticising the major theories of utilitarianism and retributivism, Boonin contends there is no acceptable solution to this problem, further concluding that State-sanctioned punishment is therefore always immoral. As an alternative to legal punishment, he offers victim restitution if five elements are satisfied. First, the punishment must include harm to the offender whereby the 'harm' either inflicts an unpleasant effect on the person or removes something good. Second, the harm must be intentional. Third, it must be retributive, meaning it must be instigated in response to an illegal act. Fourth, an element of condemnation must be present, such as an expression of official disapproval of the offender's act, and finally, the harm must be authorised by the State (Boonin, 2008). Boonin's proposal itself is a problematic one.

From a legal perspective, an ongoing debate continues as to whether the death penalty is compatible with existing international law. As discussed in Chapter 3, within the context of international law, the concept of proportionality (or proportional retribution) is embedded in Article 6 of the International Covenant on Civil and Political Rights (ICCPR) which essentially restricts the use of capital punishment. Since the ICCPR came into existence, many academics have debated which acts constitute the 'most serious crimes', giving rise to allegations that the expression embodies too vague and ambiguous a concept that is subject to different interpretations by different countries due to diverse cultural and political standpoints (Hood, 2006; Schabas, 2002).

This issue is still being debated with no clear resolution either domestically or internationally. So to ASEAN. Here, the main justifications cited for retaining the death penalty are its effectiveness in deterring serious crimes and protecting society. At the same time, pursuant to the *Lotus* principle, what is not expressly prohibited by international law falls within a State's sovereign prerogative to legislate, and ultimately, States are accountable to their own people as the sole bearers of the responsibility to protect. On the other hand, the main arguments for abolishing the death penalty are the risk of wrongful convictions, the questionability of its effectiveness as a deterrent, and the sheer inhumanity of killing. What, however, bridges the two camps is a general reluctance to advocate for the inhumane treatment of prisoners on death row.

Whether viewed from the concepts and theories underpinning punishment or from a legal aspect, its implementation shows how a State exercises authority over the lives of its people through the judiciary's systems and procedures. Although international human rights regimes are calling for the abolition of the death penalty, it is still legally permissible for States to end the lives of those found guilty of certain offences. Neither is it considered 'arbitrary' by international human rights law if due process is followed. However, evidence has also shown that despite careful adherence to the law and the promise of fair and proper proceedings, criminal justice may yet reach the wrong outcome. In addition, greater respect for the right to life is becoming more pertinent resulting in growing movements for the abolition of the death penalty around the world.

3 Concepts of Punishment in Southeast Asia

The previous section outlined two overall theoretical frameworks underlying the use of capital punishment, the first perceiving it as a response to crime and the second identifying it as an instrument of State power. However, over the past two decades, these two frameworks have been criticised as overly simplistic, considering as they do, the use of capital punishment as an automatic response to disconcerting conditions. They also fail to take into account the different responses of different countries to crime or social threats (Greenberg & West, 2008).

However, despite such criticisms, traditional theories of criminal justice, particularly retribution and utilitarianism, are still being lauded as the basis of the stance taken by AMS. In focusing on the utilitarian model of capital punishment, a study opined that AMS predominantly focus on the communal or societal aspect of the justice system instead of seeing it in light of an individualist human rights approach (Miao, 2017). This inclination becomes especially apparent in the so-called 'war on drugs' waged by a number of ASEAN governments against drug offenders. For example, Indonesia's Attorney General stated in an interview that the country wages a war against drugs because such offences threaten the nation's very survival (Hutt, 2018). For him, capital punishment was necessary to save the nation despite its unpleasantness. Malaysia expressed a similar opinion with respect to drug-related crimes, i.e. that the scourge's contribution to the commission of other crimes, such as theft or murder, constitutes a main reason why drug abuse is thus criminalised (Majinbon et al., 2017) Likewise, the Philippine President has gone on record stating that drug-related offenders must be eliminated because they pose a danger to society (Miao, 2017).

Aside from the usual allusions to 'Asian/ASEAN values' which purportedly prioritise community over individual rights, this section attempts to bring in other conceptual justifications for the death penalty by ASEAN retentionist States. For example, Johnson and Zimring (2009b) observe the connection between political democracy and economic development on the one hand, and the abolition of the death penalty on the other pointing out the higher tendency for democratic and developed States to consider abolition. However, analysing which ASEAN States are de facto and *de jure* abolitionists and which continue to execute the penalty with resolve fails to lend credence to this observation.

To address the shortcomings of classical theories of punishment and in an attempt to understand why some countries abolish capital punishment whilst others retain it, Greenberg and West (2008) argue that capital punishment is primarily premised on a country's political system, and is influenced by religious traditions and composition, levels of economic development, and educational attainment. Moreover, current research appears to point to political factors as being the strongest determinant of capital punishment. This is not to decry other factors; only that they act as less significant determinants than political influences. Such factors may be added to analyse the behaviour of retentionist States in ASEAN.

3.1 Religious and Cultural Factors

As demonstrated in Chapter 6, while religion may play an influential role in the use of capital punishment, it is unlikely to be a strong determinant. Having said this, studies have shown that the greater the representation of Roman Catholics in a country, the less chance capital punishment will be used (Greenberg & West, 2008, p.304). Another common belief is that countries holding Islam as their state religion (such as those in the Middle East and parts of Africa) are more likely to condone capital punishment than their non-Islamic counterparts because those States often conflate law and religion. Moreover, Islamic law expressly endorses capital punishment. However, this belief is refuted by Johnson and Zimring in *The Next Frontier: National Development, Political Change and the Death Penalty* in Asia who use statistics to depict how Asian countries with a Muslim majority, such as Indonesia and Malaysia, all demonstrate very low rates of executions. By contrast, countries with low Muslim concentrations, such as Singapore and Vietnam (as well as China and North Korea), boast high rates of executions. This signifies that Islam is not necessarily an obstacle to the abolition of capital punishment (Johnson & Zimring, 2009a). As regards Buddhism and Hinduism, Greenberg and West contend these religions have no significant effect on whether countries condone capital punishment (Greenberg & West, 2008, p. 309).

In the context of Asia, especially Southeast and Northeast Asia, the 'Asian values' argument has been commonly used by retentionist governments as a justification for capital punishment. However, the concept of Asian values cannot be used as a determining factor because rates of executions across retentionist countries in the region are substantially diverse. Only four countries in Asia use capital punishment aggressively, including Singapore and Vietnam, whilst the remaining retentionist countries are either abolitionist in practice or have low rates of executions (Johnson & Zimring, 2009b). In addition, although there is strong popular support for capital punishment across Asian countries, policies concerning capital punishment are not determined by the public, but solely by national governments in what Johnson refers to as 'leadership from the front'. Therefore, capital punishment policies do not reflect public sentiment on any level in the sense that reasoning and open public debates on the issues are missing in the region. Thus, 'leadership from the front' and not Asian values, accounts for the huge decline in execution rates in South Korea and Taiwan, as well as the aggressive use of capital punishment in China, Singapore, North Korea, and Vietnam (Johnson & Zimring, 2009a; Johnson, 2010, p. 340). The Chapter 5 touched upon some of these debates.

3.2 Economic Factors

It is often assumed that economic development inspires a decline in the rate of executions by fostering an environment conducive to political reform or democratisation.

This may have applied in the cases of Korea and Taiwan, where economic development nurtured technological, educational, and even moral advancements that indeed generated pressure for changes in their political structures leading to a decline in the use of capital punishment. Greenberg and West (2008) argue that the economic development of a country secures a role of greater involvement in the world economy, further exposing it to cultural differences ensuing in an increased acceptance of cultural relativism that eventually undermines the support of severe punishments. However, Johnson and Zimring demur, maintaining that economic development is not a weighty determinant of capital punishment, nor of its abolition. To illustrate, some of Asia's poorest countries (for example, Cambodia, Nepal, Bhutan, and Timor Leste) have abolished capital punishment, whereas their rich counterparts (such as the United States, Japan, and Singapore) have steadfastly retained its use (Johnson & Zimring, 2009a, p. 293).

This can be explained from another angle that seems to have occurred in ASEAN/Southeast Asia where economic development has brought about social change. Adopting Giddens' concept of ontological insecurity helps to explain the link between anxiety about social change, fear of crime, and punitive emotions, all of which threaten self-identity and endanger 'aspects of the "reality" of the world' (Giddens 1991, p.65). Giddens argues that ontological insecurity is prevalent in modern societies due to the pace and scope of change entailed by modernity. This experience leads some individuals to attempt to shore up stability by reasserting their 'values as absolutes' (Seal, 2017). As such, they may become intolerant of deviance and create scapegoats for the 'troubles of the wider society'. Consequently, they may favour excessive punishments such as long prison sentences and the death penalty. Fear of crime and associated beliefs in the need for strong punishment 'represent things above and beyond the (actuarially considered) possibility of victimisation' (Jackson, 2004, 2009). Because crime is a metaphor for other social problems, feelings of insecurity induced by the rapidity of social change and anxieties about modernity are channelled through responses to crime (Jackson, 2004).

Garland further argues that the precariousness of late modern societies—in which the welfare state has declined and neoliberal economics flourish — means that such insecurity is now widely experienced (Garland, 2014). Moreover, significant transformations in family life, the consumption of culture, and the growth of mass media accelerate the pace of social change in late modernity (Seal, 2017). In addition, rising rates of recorded crime and media reporting of serious, high-profile crimes, make crime and violence 'channels for the expression of more inchoate fears'. Thus, 'pro-death penalty views frequently emphasised the need to retain capital punishment as a deterrent in order to promote safety. They linked fears of rising crime to harmful social change' (Seal, 2017, p. 6). In other words, such attitudes lie witness to the fact that economic advancement in ASEAN countries has not necessarily contributed to lower crime rates; neither have they reduced the use of capital punishment in the region.

3.3 Political Factors and Authoritarianism

A country's political ideologies regarding crime affect its punishment practices. Such ideologies can be categorised into two; the first being the perception of crime as a consequence of an individual's rational choice or personal defect, and the second being a more liberal perception of crime as a result of social injustice. The first ideology is generally linked to the use of deterrence and incapacitation as methods of punishment, whereas the second usually resorts to rehabilitation as a means to control crime. Literature seems to suggest that undemocratic countries that view crime as a manifestation of personal choice are more likely to use capital punishment (Greenberg & West, 2008, pp. 296–297).

However, the discussions raised in the paragraph above provide little in the way of conclusive support. According to Greenberg and West (2008), countries with fewer political rights are more likely to use capital punishment because they tend to be less receptive to the well-being of their people, and may be more inclined to use force or kill to maintain order and control or to stay in office. For instance, undemocratic regimes may implement policies against the public's needs or interests, and subsequently resort to using force to coerce acquiescence with unpopular policies. Statistics depict a trend that non-democratic governments are more likely than democratic ones to use capital punishment, with the obvious exception of the United States and Japan (p. 298). Many other factors further determine the extent of political rights, such as levels of wealth and education, which are indirect determinants of capital punishment. To illustrate, a country with a higher level of wealth usually also has a higher level of investment in education leading to higher literacy rates which may result in higher public demand for political rights (p. 324). However, this illustration does not hold true for such countries as Malaysia, Singapore, Thailand, and Vietnam where the level of literacy is highest compared to the rest of the region.

Johnson and Zimring are strong advocates of the view that political factors are the most important determinants of capital punishment, especially in Southeast Asia. In proving their contention, they use Singapore and Malaysia as examples, being countries sharing a similar history and culture, to show that political differences account for the large difference in the execution rates of the two countries. In fact, Singapore is amongst the four top executing countries in Asia, the other three being China, North Korea, and Vietnam. Other retentionist countries in Asia do not execute regularly or frequently. Based on this, Johnson and Zimring argue that high execution rates in some countries can be explained by their authoritarian regimes. Notably, authoritarian regimes may be necessary for high rates of executions, but not for capital punishment in itself. This is because the United States, which does not fit the description of an authoritarian government, uses capital punishment, but not to a high extent (Johnson & Zimring, 2009a, p. 296). In addition, the two authors attribute the sharp decline in execution rates in South Korea and Taiwan to the process of democratisation, reaffirming that high execution rates are associated with authoritarian political structures (p. 297). This was also reflected in Wang Yunhai's article, *'The death penalty and society in contemporary China'*. Wang (2008) explains the extensiveness of death penalty provisions, convictions, and executions in China, by defining it as a 'state-power'-based society rooted in a socialist system. Moreover, Wang asserts that three factors are attributable to the prevalence of executions in China. First, capital punishment is a political issue of State power; second, capital punishment forms an imperative part of criminal policy within a 'state-power'-based society; and third, the question of whether to retain or abolish capital punishment is ultimately a political decision rather than a legal one. This analysis can be applied to explain the cases of Singapore, Vietnam, and a few others, including the Philippines where an elected government essentially turned authoritarian.

The classical definition of authoritarianism was advanced by Linz (1970, p. 225):

> Authoritarianism are political systems with limited, not responsible, political pluralism; without elaborate and guiding ideology (but with distinctive mentalities); without intensive nor extensive political mobilization (except some points in their developments); and in which a leader (or occasionally a small group) exercises power within formally ill-defined limits but actually quite predictable ones.

Looking at Southeast Asia currently, authoritarianism now appears to be a prevalent phenomenon. The conventional perception surrounding political discourse on Southeast Asia classifies most countries therein as authoritarian, with the exception of Indonesia and Timor-Leste (and to a certain extent, Malaysia) which are given the status of democracies. Under the modernisation theory, the concept of democracy is tied to economic development, in that an absence of democracy is associated with a lack of economic development. However, this form of modernisation theory appears problematic upon closer analysis. China stands out as an exception to the trend, because non-democracy has persisted despite the country having undergone substantial economic development since late 1970s. Several countries in ASEAN/Southeast Asia seem to have followed China's path, in that economic development has failed to result in democracy. In particular, Singapore serves as an evident example, by averting democracy in spite of extensive economic growth, thus also challenging the modernisation theory that economic development frees States from authoritarianism.

Under modernisation theories, authoritarian governments continue to be perceived as lacking in legitimacy, which such theorists view as problematic considering the global aspiration for democratic values. To increase legitimacy, governments in ASEAN/Southeast Asia opt for economic development, industrialisation, and modernisation. In SEA, authoritarian regimes are viewed as more 'benign' on the basis that they are market-driven, although they may be, oftentimes, repressive. Any challenge to the system is considered a defiance to the leader, demanding a stringent response (Sim, 2006, p. 147). This includes defiance to the security and order of society. In the context of capital punishment, it is assumed that popular perception and consent give rise to legitimated authoritarianism (which has been the case in the Philippines, Singapore, and Thailand). This is related to Gramsci's (1971) theory of hegemony, which focuses on the desire of elites to secure consensus in order for their rule to seem fair and natural. Accordingly, elites in authoritarian regimes employ social and security projects to persuade other civilians to give consensus to their rule.

The determinant factors advanced by modernisation theories seem to shape the punishment policies and behaviours of many retentionist States and this can be expanded to the Philippines where attempts to re-impose the death penalty have been made by Duterte's government since his presidency in 2016. It is evident that the level of economic development in these countries has not altered their perception; rather, in most if not all cases, it has strengthened it. Cultural and political factors, as well as authoritarianism, also reinforce the already hierarchical and State power-based society that prevails in the region. Despite this, some small steps have been taken in ASEAN.

4 Examination of Some 'Good Practices': An Indication Towards Abolition of the Death Penalty in ASEAN/Southeast Asia?

Research conducted for AICHR's thematic study on the right to life concluded in early 2021[1] revealed some positive trends applied by AMS. In particular, the reports identified some 'good practices'. These so-called 'good practices' include, but are not limited to: the reform of death penalty laws; the application of moratoriums; assessments of the mentally ill in the criminal justice system; and fewer women being condemned to death. The question is can such 'good practices' be translated into indications that the death penalty may be abolished by retentionist States in the region. This section provides an overview of such 'good practices' before concluding if an abolitionist move is, in fact, taking place in ASEAN/SEA.

4.1 Reforming Death Penalty Laws

As analysed in Chapter 3, limitation to the 'most serious crimes' is an established principle of international law in relation to the death penalty. The UN Special Rapporteur on extrajudicial, summary or arbitrary executions has further clarified that the death penalty should not be given for economic crimes, drug-related offences, victimless offences, or actions related to moral values.

Whilst some ASEAN retentionist States have retained a long litany of capital crimes, Lao PDR and Vietnam have in recent years reduced the categories liable to the death penalty (although it remains for drug trafficking in all countries). Regular governmental (and inter-governmental) reviews do take place in States concerning the effectiveness, fairness, and suitability of the death penalty regime. This does not mean change is inevitable but where valid reasons exist to consider changing the criteria for certain offences, altering the offences attracting the death penalty, or giving the courts more discretion in sentencing, they may at least be considered and

[1] See AICHR (2021).

properly debated. Sometimes these reviews take the form of public consultations or specially convened commissions. Whichever the shape of such review mechanisms, insofar as the right to life is the most important human right, there must be a perpetual desire to ensure that any death penalty meted out is neither unjust nor results in human rights violations.

Vietnam deserves special mention as since 2005 it has reduced the offences to which the death penalty is applicable from 44 to 18. Vietnam also added a non-imposition of death penalty order for children under 18 years, pregnant women, women with children aged under 36 months, and persons of 75 years or older when committing crimes or during sentencing as well as non-execution of death sentence orders to persons falling into these categories. As stated in the country report for the AICHR's thematic study, these reforms relate to an ambition to advance human rights in the country.

If legislators are making it more difficult to use the death penalty by reducing the number of capital offence crimes to 'particularly serious cases' where it is used as 'the last legal resort', this could be considered a form of good practice. Vietnam, in particular, can be viewed as a reformist and reductionist country in relation to the death penalty.

Making the death penalty non-mandatory, as is the case for certain crimes in Indonesia, Malaysia, Singapore, Thailand and Vietnam, enables life imprisonment to be an alternative sentence to execution. Allowing discretionary use of the death penalty for certain crimes recognises the different circumstances in which offences may be committed and the specific context of offenders and related mitigating factors. However, there is apprehension about replacing the death penalty with a mandatory sentence of 30 years or life imprisonment without the possibility of parole is a concern in Thailand.

Finally, clemency and pardon power is a provision for leniency of capital punishment and as such can be considered a form of good practice. Whilst all the ASEAN retentionist countries have this provision, Thailand has shown a high rate of clemency in the past as has Vietnam where foreigners may receive differential treatment through the clemency process.

4.2 Moratoriums and Progress Towards Abolition

Over the last decade, the UN General Assembly has called for a general suspension of capital punishment throughout the world. Usually every two years around the time of International Human Rights Day, a resolution on the death penalty moratorium is proposed. As already analysed in Chapter 7, there have been some changes in the voting behaviour of AMS. The latest vote at the UN General Assembly was on 16 December 2020 with 123 votes in favour, 38 against, with 24 countries abstaining and 8 being absent (Pascoe & Bae, 2021). Within the ASEAN region, Brunei and Singapore have consistently voted against the resolution while Cambodia has always voted in favour. Indonesia, Lao PDR, Myanmar, Thailand, and Vietnam generally abstain.

Since 2018, Malaysia has voted in favour while the Philippines, which abstained in the 2016–2018 resolutions, voted in favour in 2020 (International Commission Against Death Penalty, 2021).

The suspension of executions (i.e. a moratorium) in a retentionist country is considered to be a key step towards abolition of the death penalty. In particular, a 10-year halt in executions is considered a major milestone for the protection of the right to life and the eventual abolition of the death penalty. Indeed, its use is becoming increasingly restrained in some retentionist countries within ASEAN. For example, the last execution in Brunei was reported in 1957 whilst the last known executions in Lao PDR were in 1988. Other countries could be in a good position to move towards a moratorium (e.g. Indonesia) while the government elected in Malaysia in 2018 planned to abolish the death penalty for all crimes and halt 1,200 pending executions (but backtracked after another change in government).

Clearly, Cambodia and the Philippines have been at the forefront of abolishing capital punishment. Unfortunately, one ASEAN country has recently resumed its use after having previously suspended the practice for long periods of time. Thailand was in its ninth year of a de facto moratorium and nearing the goal of abolition until June 2018 when it executed 26-year-old Teerasak Longji. Furthermore, in March 2017, the Philippine Lower Chamber passed House Bill 4727 which seeks to re-impose the death penalty; President Rodrigo Duterte stated he wants the death penalty re-imposed for drug crimes. Myanmar, after decades of a moratorium, announced in June 2022 the planned execution of two political dissidents by the military junta (Diamond & Nasser, 2022).

4.3 Assessing the Mentally Ill in the Criminal Justice System

Malaysia has a commendable legal process for determining whether an accused is too mentally ill to be given a death sentence. It entails a two-prong approach of assessing whether a person was insane at the time of the offence or whether the individual's insanity renders him or her unfit to stand trial. Additionally, a series of legal tests of mental insanity requires not only medical evidence but also expects courts to decide whether an accused is too mentally ill to convict or execute. These processes support global standards of not sentencing mentally insane persons to death as it recognises that the mentally ill may not have control over their actions, lack competency to stand trial, and ultimately may not understand the exact nature of the punishment they will receive (AICHR, 2019a). Finally, Myanmar has reported a stay of execution for prisoners displaying 'extraordinary' symptoms prior to execution (AICHR, 2020).

4.4 Women Condemned to Death

The Malaysia country report for the AICHR thematic study considers the treatment and facilities of female death row inmates to be generally good. The Women's Prison is housed in a separate block, away from their male counterparts and has its own healthcare facility, specifically for women prisoners. Further, the cells housing female death row inmates are in accordance with ICRC recommended standards with adequate floor space, natural light, and ventilation. Thus, according to the Malaysia report, the State does appear to be appropriately applying international standards concerning the treatment of female death row inmates.

Interestingly, the Thailand report raises the suggestion that an important first step towards the process of abolition could be the exclusion of women all together from the death penalty. In Thailand, 426 prisoners (368 men and **58 women**) were on death row in 2016. By 3 March 2021, this number had progressively decreased to 257 (228 men and **29 women**) (FIDH & UCL 2021). Drug-related offences continue to represent a disproportionate share of the crimes for which the death sentence is imposed. According to Thailand's Department of Corrections, 58% of men and 100% of women under death sentences as of 3 March 2021 had been found guilty of drug-related offences (FIDH & UCL 2021). This despite the advice of the UN Human Rights Council that drug crimes should not be subject to capital punishment. In light of the caring responsibility of their gender and of their diminished responsibility arising from male inducement to crime, the Thailand report suggests that in a country still strongly supportive of the death penalty, abolition for women may yet find acceptance.

5 Conclusion: ASEAN/SEA and the Prospect for Abolition

At a conference in 2016, Professor William Schabas showed a slide depicting the world's progress in regards to abolition and the decline in retention of the death penalty over the last forty years (Fig. 8.1).

This image deserves to be a masthead for all discussions on the abolition movement. It is dominated to the left of centre by the crossover of the lines for full abolition and for retention, which took place in about 1990. The rise of abolition and the fall of retention, are seen to be steady and continuous, with the inevitability of such natural phenomena as the rise in global temperature or the decline of glacial masses. His interpretation of the curves is that abolition is inevitable although it may slow or accelerate in different periods; despite this, one day in the increasingly predictable future, the death penalty will inevitably end.

The curves give courage and help to prevent discouragement among those who work for its abolition. They are the result of a complex interaction of many forces and tendencies, and correct the apparent decline of progress in some areas and cultures by advances in others. They include the astonishing progress of abolition in the area

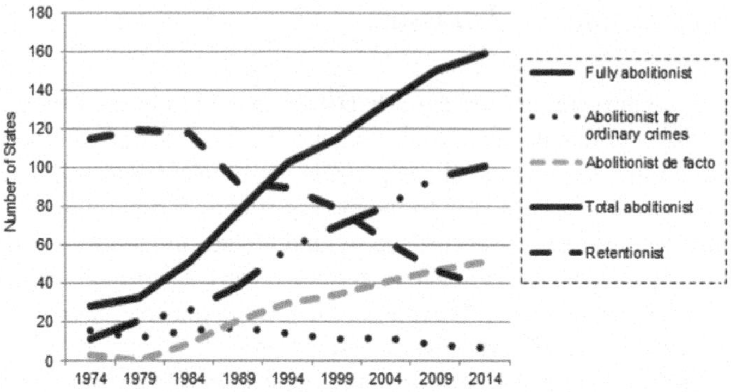

Fig. 8.1 Trend in status of capital punishment, 1974–2014 (UN Economic & Social Council, 2015)

of the 48 countries of the Council of Europe which have seen the area of abolition stretch from the Atlantic to the Pacific coastlines on the world's largest land mass. They teach us to be patient with the slow pace of change in Asia, the Middle East, and the US. They also show us the tide of history which cannot be opposed.

If one is to accept the trend presented by Professor Schabas, the course towards abolition of capital punishment in the ASEAN region is set, even if it may be slower than right to life advocates would prefer. The pace of the decrease he sees as inexorable is, after all, still impacted by factors and variables that are not so easy to define, predict, or counter. Indeed, in certain (recent) instances, backsliding of what has already been admirable progress has occurred. As previously mentioned, Thailand, for instance, which for nearly a decade prior had been an 'abolitionist de facto', saw an execution take place in June 2018 (OHCHR, 2018). Likewise, the Philippines saw a resurgence of the movement to re-impose capital punishment in 2017. It, in fact, came close, with the Lower House of the Philippine Congress voting 'yes' (217 votes to 54 'nays') for restoration.[2] This was not happenstance and the attempt was aborted due to other political factors like a lack of assured support in the Senate. But what does seem to be certain is that there will be greater efforts to re-impose it in the near future, especially if politicians close to President Rodrigo Duterte, who has made no secret of favouring re-imposition (Associated Press, 2016), wish to be seen to align with him politically. Myanmar military leaders have already reversed their practice recently.

As already presented in the introductory Chapter, the death penalty situation in the eight ASEAN countries seems to remain rather static. The record somehow reveals a very mixed reality, reflecting the absence of any shared policy on the death penalty among AMS other than the proviso, 'in accordance with law'.

The validity of exposure is provided by AMS inclusion into the UN and the obligations to which they became obliged by their accession to the human rights treaties. The extent of ASEAN commitments to these treaties is shown in their ratification

[2] The text of the bill is available at http://www.congress.gov.ph/legisdocs/?v=bills#HistoryModal.

of international human rights treaties, whereby the majority of AMS show significant attachment to the values represented therein. Furthermore, ASEAN documents proclaim and encourage the adherence of their Member States to the human rights values of these key instruments. In its opening words, the ASEAN Human Rights Declaration asserts:

> a [C]ommitment to the Universal Declaration of Human Rights, the Charter of the United Nations, the Vienna Declaration and Programme of Action, and other international human rights instruments to which ASEAN Member States are parties.

The acceptance of the 'United Nations Charter and international law, including international humanitarian law' is repeated in the ASEAN Charter. Such acceptance should include the ongoing interpretations of international law regarding abolition of the death penalty which were also the subject of UNHCHR statements. Such adherence and acceptance by AMS, hopefully, will involve them in the worldwide progress of abolition posited above.

This book serves as a stepping stone towards more in-depth studies on the right to life in ASEAN. As stated in previous chapters, the right to life was recognised by various international and regional human rights instruments. Most, if not all, countries in ASEAN enshrine the right to life in their respective constitutions. Yet, laws allowing capital punishment are still applied throughout although reform and abolition as well as de facto non-execution are the current trends in ASEAN. The concepts behind maintaining the death penalty are both utilitarianism and retentionism, as well as modernisation. Although the positive global trend is foreseeable, some AMS seem to be expanding the crimes to which the death penalty shall be applied, especially drug offences which are often considered 'most serious crimes'.

As already mentioned, currently the law and policy of ASEAN countries on the issue of the death penalty are divided. Some countries have completely abolished it. Some have suspended its execution for a period of time. Meanwhile, others have retained the death penalty with restrictions. Thus, the reinforcement of the sharing of experience and promoting ASEAN's role in the process of regional policy formulation on this issue is fundamentally important, especially in the context of Member States looking to establish an ASEAN community.

From the studies and analysis of different chapters included in this book, some observations and questions can be raised:

- It does appear, from one perspective, that the experiences of abolition in Cambodia and the Philippines were very different. Earlier chapters in this book on the right to life also show many distinctions and differences across other ASEAN States. It is important therefore to tackle the issues here more closely and critically.
- What variables are at play in executive clemency matters? What influences mandatory sentencing? What factors have led to the moratorium? These are some of the questions that can be more intensively researched regionally and domestically. It may also be useful to look into alternative criminal law theories to counter entrenched retributive and utilitarian views. A look into how rehabilitative and restorative justice can be underscored as being in step with ASEAN's communal

views and cultural norms as well as the global trend towards abolition may be warranted.

- To fill the gap between giving importance to the right to life over the imposition of capital punishment, there may be a need to undertake a more extensive assessment of the effectiveness of the death penalty in deterring crime and a pragmatic comparison of the cost-effectiveness of rehabilitations vis-à-vis the imposition of capital punishment.
- A strong stand for true criminal law reforms and a steadfast implementation of the rule of law should accompany discussions of the right to life in the region.
- There are notable common aspects of approaches to the death penalty in ASEAN. These include the exclusion of some groups of offenders from the death penalty such as pregnant women, children, and minors below 16–18, the mentally ill, as well as mothers with infants. A de facto moratorium on executions exists in a number of AMS. Despite the increasing number of death sentences, some countries do not execute prisoners on death row. It also seems there are possibilities for appeal and pardon but procedures may vary from one country to another.

As noted in Chapter 3 the issue of the death penalty has always been contentious—those against it argue, for example, that the possibility of a wrongful conviction, the lack of empirical data to show its deterrent effect, and the permanence of the punishment, are grounds for abolishing the death penalty. Conversely, retentionists maintain that its retributive effect is necessary to give closure to the victim's family and for crime control, particularly heinous crimes.

While professing commitment to the Universal Declaration of Human Rights, the ASEAN Human Rights Declaration repeats, in some ways, the provision in the ICCPR in its presentation of the right to life: 'Every person has an inherent right to life which shall be protected by law. No person shall be deprived of life save in accordance with law.' A Muslim Thai lawyer once said that although Islam allowed the death penalty, this presupposed a just legal system. Since a number of countries in ASEAN do not have a just legal system, he favoured abolition (AICHR, 2019b). Of course, the necessarily direct simplicity of the Universal Declaration of Human Rights had to be expanded in other legal treaties and was open to interpretation by UN experts. But the principle of the right to life, not the right to law, holds.

References

AICHR. (2019a). Thematic study on the right to life: Protection of the rights of personas convicted of the death penalty, Malaysia country report [Unpublished report].

AICHR. (2019b). Thematic study on the right to life: Protection of the rights of personas convicted of the death penalty, Thailand country report [Unpublished report].

AICHR. (2020). Thematic study on the right to life: Protection of the rights of personas convicted of the death penalty, Myanmar country report [Unpublished report].

Alston, P. (2007, January 29). Civil and political rights, including the questions of disappearances and summary executions: Report of the Special Rapporteur on extrajudicial, summary or arbitrary executions, Human Rights Council 5th Session, A/HRC/4/20. https://documents-dds-ny.un.org/doc/UNDOC/GEN/G07/105/00/PDF/G0710500.pdf. Accessed 24 January 2022.

Associated Press. (2016, May 16). Rodrigo Duterte, Philippines' new leader, plans to reinstate death penalty. *New York Times*. https://www.nytimes.com/2016/05/17/world/asia/rodrigo-duterte-death-penalty.html?module=inline. Accessed 12 January 2022.

Boonin, D. (2008). *The problem of punishment*. Cambridge University Press.

Brudner, A. (1980). Retributivism and the death penalty. *The University of Toronto Law Journal, 30*(4), 337–355.

Chai, C., & Chai, W. (1973). *Confucianism*. Barron's.

Daems, T. (2011). A peculiar sociology of punishment. *Oxford Journal of Legal Studies, 31*(4), 805–823.

Diamond, C., & Nasser, I. (2022, June 4). Myanmar could see first executions in decades as junta says death sentences of two activists upheld. *CNN*. https://edition.cnn.com/2022/06/04/asia/myanmar-junta-activists-death-sentences-upheld-intl/index.html Accessed 12 July 2022.

Durkheim, E. (1973). Two laws of penal evolution. *Economy & Society, 2*(3), 285–308.

Garland, D. (1986). The punitive mentality: Its socio-historic development and decline. *Contemporary Crises, 10*(3), 305–320.

Garland, D. (2014). The welfare state: A fundamental dimension of modern government. *European Journal of Sociology, 55*(3), 327–364.

Gramsci, A. (1971). *Selections from the prison notebooks of Antonio Gramsci*, (Q. Hoare & G. N. Smith, Eds. & Trans.). New York: International Publishers.

Greenberg, D. F., & West, V. (2008). Siting the death penalty internationally. *Law & Social Inquiry, 33*(2), 295–343.

Haist, M. (2009). Deterrence in a sea of "just deserts": Are utilitarian goals achievable in a world of "limiting retributivism"? *Journal of Criminal Law & Criminology, 99*(3), 789–821.

Hall, R. A. (2000). *The ethical foundations of criminal justice*. CRC Press.

Hill, T. E. (1999). Kant on wrongdoing, desert and punishment. *Law and Philosophy, 18*(4), 407–441.

Hodgkinson, P., Gyllensten, L., & Peel, D. (2010). Capital punishment briefing paper. Centre for Capital Punishment Studies, Westminster University Law School. https://studybest.com/db/files/images/pdf/1/1829_1151551.pdf. Accessed 12 January 2022.

Hood, R., & Kovalev, S. (1999). *The death penalty abolition in Europe*. Council of Europe Publishing.

Hood, R. (2006). *The enigma of the "most serious" offences*. Center for Human Rights and Global Justice, Working Paper Extrajudicial Executions Series No. 9. New York: NYU School of Law.

Hutt, D. (2018, June 21). Capital punishment far from dead in Southeast Asia. *Asia Times*. http://www.atimes.com/capital-punishment-far-from-dead-in-southeast-asia/. Accessed 24 February 2022.

Inglehart, R., & Baker, W. E. (2000). Modernization, cultural change, and the persistence of traditional values. *American Sociological Review, 65*(1), 19–51.

International Commission Against Death Penalty. (2021). *UNGA moratorium resolution table*. https://icomdp.org/map-unga/. Accessed 24 February 2022.

International Federation for Human Rights [FIDH] & Union for Civil Liberty [UCL]. (2021). *Thailand: 39th Session of the Working Group on the Universal Periodic Review submitted to UN Human Rights Council*, 25 March 2021. https://www.fidh.org/IMG/pdf/fidh_ucl_upr_thailand_march_2021.pdf. Accessed 18 January 2022.

Iyengar, R. (2016, September 15). Inside Philippine President Rodrigo Duterte's war on drugs. *Time Magazine*. http://time.com/4495896/philippine-president-rodrigo-duterte/. Accessed 24 February 2022.

Jackson, J. (2004). Experience and expression: Social and cultural significance in the fear of crime. *British Journal of Criminology, 44*(6), 946–966.

Jackson, J. (2009). A psychological perspective on vulnerability in the fear of crime. *Psychology, Crime & Law, 15*(4), 365–390.

Johnson, D. T., & Zimring, F. E. (2009a). *The next frontier: National development, political change and the death penalty in Asia.* Oxford University Press.
Johnson, D. T., & Zimring, F. E. (2009b). Death penalty lessons from Asia. *The Asia-Pacific Journal, 7*(39), No. 1. https://apjjf.org/-David-T.-Johnson/3228/article.html. Accessed 12 January 2022.
Johnson, D. T. (2010). Asia's declining death penalty. *The Journal of Asian Studies, 69*(2), 337–346.
Linz, J. (1970). An authoritarian regime: The case of Spain. In E. Allard & S. Rokkan (Eds.), *Mass politics: Studies in political sociology*. Free Press.
Majinbon, I. M., Mashor, N. A. M., Chin, Z. Y., Loh, H. Y., & Na, C. H. (2017). *Laws on drugs: Are they effective enough in eradicating drug problems in Malaysia?* Law Review 2016/2017, Asian Law Students Association. https://asianjournaloflegalstudies.files.wordpress.com/2017/06/alsa-malaysia-final-draft.pdf. Accessed 24 January 2022.
Mendez, J. E. (2012). The death penalty and the absolute prohibition of torture and cruel, inhuman, and degrading treatment or punishment. *Human Rights Brief, 20*(1), 2–6. https://digitalcommons.wcl.american.edu/hrbrief/vol20/iss1/1/. Accessed 18 February 2022.
Meyer, J. (1969). Reflections on some theories of punishment. *Journal of Criminal Law and Criminology, 59*(4), 595–598.
Miao, M. (2017). The penal construction of drug-related offenses in the context of Asian values. *International Comparative, Policy, & Ethics Law Review, 1.* https://www.academia.edu/34594611/M_Miao_The_Penal_Construction_of_Drug_related_Offenses_in_the_Context_of_Asian_Values_The_Rise_of_Punitive_Anti_drug_Campaigns_in_Asia. Accessed 24 February 2022.
OHCHR. (2018, June 19). *UN Human Rights Office expresses dismay at the resumption of death penalty in Thailand.* https://bangkok.ohchr.org/news-release-un-human-rights-office-expresses-dismay-at-the-resumption-of-death-penalty-in-thailand/. Accessed 12 February 2022.
Pascoe, D., & Bae, S. (2021, May 18). *Latest developments in the UNGA death penalty moratorium resolutions.* Faculty of Law, University of Oxford. https://www.law.ox.ac.uk/research-and-subject-groups/death-penalty-research-unit/blog/2021/05/latest-developments-unga-death. Accessed 18 January 2022.
Quinney, R. (1977). *Class, state and crime: On the theory and practice of criminal justice.* David McKay.
Rodan, G. (1993). *Political oppositions in industrializing Asia.* Routledge.
Rodan, G. (2009). Accountability and authoritarianism: Human rights in Malaysia and Singapore. *Journal of Contemporary Asia, 39*(2), 180–203.
Schabas, W. A. (2002). *The abolition of the death penalty in international law* (3rd ed.). Cambridge University Press.
Seal, L. (2017). Perceptions of safety, fear and social change in the public's pro-death penalty discourse in mid twentieth-century Britain. *Crime, History, and Societies, 21*(1), 13–34. https://doi.org/10.4000/chs.1712
Sim, S. F. (2006). Hegemonic authoritarianism and Singapore: Economics, ideology and the Asian economic crisis. *Journal of Contemporary Asia, 36*(2), 143–159.
Tan, S. H. (2010). Authoritative Master Kong (Confucius) in an authoritarian age. *Dao, 9*, 137–149. https://doi.org/10.1007/s11712-010-9157-2
UN Economic and Social Council. (2015, April 13). Capital punishment and implementation of the safeguards guaranteeing protection of the rights of those facing the death penalty: Report of the Secretary-General, E/2015/49. https://www.ohchr.org/Documents/Issues/DeathPenalty/E-2015-49.pdf. Accessed 12 February 2022.
Van Drunen, D. (2008). Natural law, the lex talionis, and the power of the sword. *Liberty University Law Review*, 2(3), 945–967. https://digitalcommons.liberty.edu/cgi/viewcontent.cgi?article=1046&context=lu_law_review. Accessed 12 February 2022.
Wang, Y. (2008). The death penalty and society in contemporary China. *Punishment & Society, 10*(2), 137–151. https://doi.org/10.1177/1462474507087196

Weiner, B., Graham, S., & Reyna, C. (1997). An attributional examination of retributive versus utilitarian philosophies of punishment. *Social Justice Research, 10*(4), 431–452.
Yost, B. (2010). Kant's justification of the death penalty reconsidered. *Kantian Review, 15*(2), 1–27.

Sriprapha Petcharamesree was a lecturer and senior advisor at the Institute of Human Rights and Peace Studies, Mahidol University in Thailand. She received her Ph.D. (Doctorat) in international politics from the University of Paris-X Nanterre, France. Sriprapha was awarded, in 2017, an Honorary Doctor by the University of Oslo, Norway for her contribution to human rights. From 2009–2012, she has served as the Representative of Thailand to the ASEAN Intergovernmental Commission on Human Rights (AICHR).

Her recent works focus, among others, on issues of citizenship, migration, refugees and asylum seekers as well as statelessness, human rights in international relations, and human rights education. She was entrusted by the AICHR (ASEAN Intergovernmental Commission on Human Rights) to synthesise the country reports on right to life focusing death penalty in ASEAN. She continues her research on the issues and advocates for the abolition of death penalty in the region.

Raine Boonlong is specialised in the subjects of Arts and Law. She received her first degree in Asian Studies as well as in Laws from Murdoch University in Australia. She earned her LL.M from the Faculty of Law, Chulalongkorn University, Thailand. She is legally trained and has been admitted as a member of the Singapore Bar as an advocate and solicitor since 2016. She spent 3 years focusing and training in the fields of Criminal Law, Family Law and Business Contract Law, and has an interest in Human Rights Law. She has several journal publications in relation to the matter of law and human rights. Raine is currently working in the business sector dealing with corporate loans.

Danthong Breen was born Irish but is now a naturalised Thai. He has been living and teaching at different Thai universities since the early 1970s. Trained as a scientist (Physics) from his first degree at the National University of Ireland, Dublin to Ph.D in Physics from the University of Oxford, UK, he became an expert in human rights advocating for civil liberty and abolition of death penalty during the past decades. He writes extensively on the issues, including the Death Penalty in Thailand and Southeast Asia. He has also written reports for FIDH.

Since 1976, he has been Chairperson and board member of the South East Asian Regional Institute of Community Education (SEARICE). Since 1988, he is a member and advisor of the Union for Civil Liberty (Thailand). He is also an advisor for advocacy on abolition of death penalty, launched by the Asian Forum for Human Rights and Development (Forum-Asia).

SPRINGER NATURE

GPSR Compliance

The European Union's (EU) General Product Safety Regulation (GPSR) is a set of rules that requires consumer products to be safe and our obligations to ensure this.

If you have any concerns about our products, you can contact us on ProductSafety@springernature.com

In case Publisher is established outside the EU, the EU authorized representative is:

Springer Nature Customer Service Center GmbH
Europaplatz 3
69115 Heidelberg, Germany

The manufacturer's authorised representative in the EU is Springer Nature Customer Service Centre GmbH, Europaplatz 3, 69115 Heidelberg, Germany. If you have any concerns regarding our products, please contact ProductSafety@springernature.com

Printed and bound by CPI Group (UK) Ltd, Croydon, CR0 4YY
01/10/2026
02225861-0009